UAE
off-road

The No.1 selling guide

Passionately Publishing...

EXPLORER   **Jeep**

UAE Off-Road Explorer
3rd Edition (Revised) 2006
First Published 2001
Second Edition 2003
Third Edition 2005
ISBN 10 976-8182-68-7
ISBN 13 978-976-8182-68-5

Explorer Publishing & Distribution
PO Box 34275, Zomorrodah Bldg, Za'abeel Rd,
Dubai , United Arab Emirates
Phone   (+971 4) 335 3520
Fax   (+971 4) 335 3529
Email   Info@Explorer-Publishing.com
Web   www.Explorer-Publishing.com

Jeep Web   www.mideast.jeep.com

Welcome

Here it is: the new and improved, fantastically funkier, third edition of the *UAE Off-Road Explorer*. To all our new readers, welcome and thanks for joining us; and to all our returning fans, thanks for making this the UAE's best-selling off-road guidebook.

This third edition has a fresh new look making it easier to use, with improved navigation and cross-referencing throughout. Sadly, some routes from our last edition have become 'industrialised', and so have dropped off the map, but we've added new routes in several sections, as well as a whole new section on the epic route down to the Liwa Oasis.

We've spent many months chasing down routes in all conditions, from digging vehicles out of the sand and driving up dead-end wadis in the heat of summer, to camping in the rain for whole weekends at a time during the wettest winter on record and battling border fences. Even freak snowstorms in Ras Al Khaimah couldn't stop us from our task in ensuring all routes are as accurate as possible.

Containing information on everything from short, easy routes to the wildest, remotest trips like Liwa or Mussandam, your weekends need never be boring again. As well as highlighting areas of historic interest, we've also pointed you in the direction of some sites of breathtaking natural beauty, such as hidden waterfalls, lush oases and untouched expanses of desert. The Activities section gives tips on enjoying outdoor pursuits like hiking, archaeology, birdwatching, off-road motorbiking and mountain biking. All of these sections have been written by experts in their field.

Now that our work is done (for now!) we ask that you go forth, Off-Road in hand, and conquer routes that you've had on that to-do list for far too long. And if you find something we've missed then we'd love to hear from you.

Just log on to www.Explorer-Publishing.com and fill in our reader response form, and you could be getting the next Off-Road book for free!

The Explorer Team

Contributing Authors and Photographers : **Adrian Gibbons, Ahmed Alshehi,** Alistair MacKenzie, Andy Whitaker, Barry Sallenbach, Carole Harris, Christian Velde, Colin Richardson, David Jupp, David Quinn, John Gregory, John Hallett, Joseph Rowland, Justin Roberts, Karen MacPherson, Louise Denly, Lulu Skidmore, Maher Khoury, Marycke Jongbloed, Michel de Martigny, Miki Binks, Mohammed Maktari, Pamela Grist, Pete Maloney, Shelley Frost, Tim Binks, Tony Kay, Tony Schroder and Victor Romero.

Special Thanks To: A big thank you to our sponsors DaimlerChrysler, Al Jallaf Trading and Trading Enterprises. Thanks also to all the members of the Explorer Collective including the experts who've provided their input and our off-road exploring companions, with a special mention to Miki the co-pilot, Peter Becker, Reem at Maps Geosystems, and Dr Matar Al Neyadi and the team at MSD.

Special thanks to our sponsor

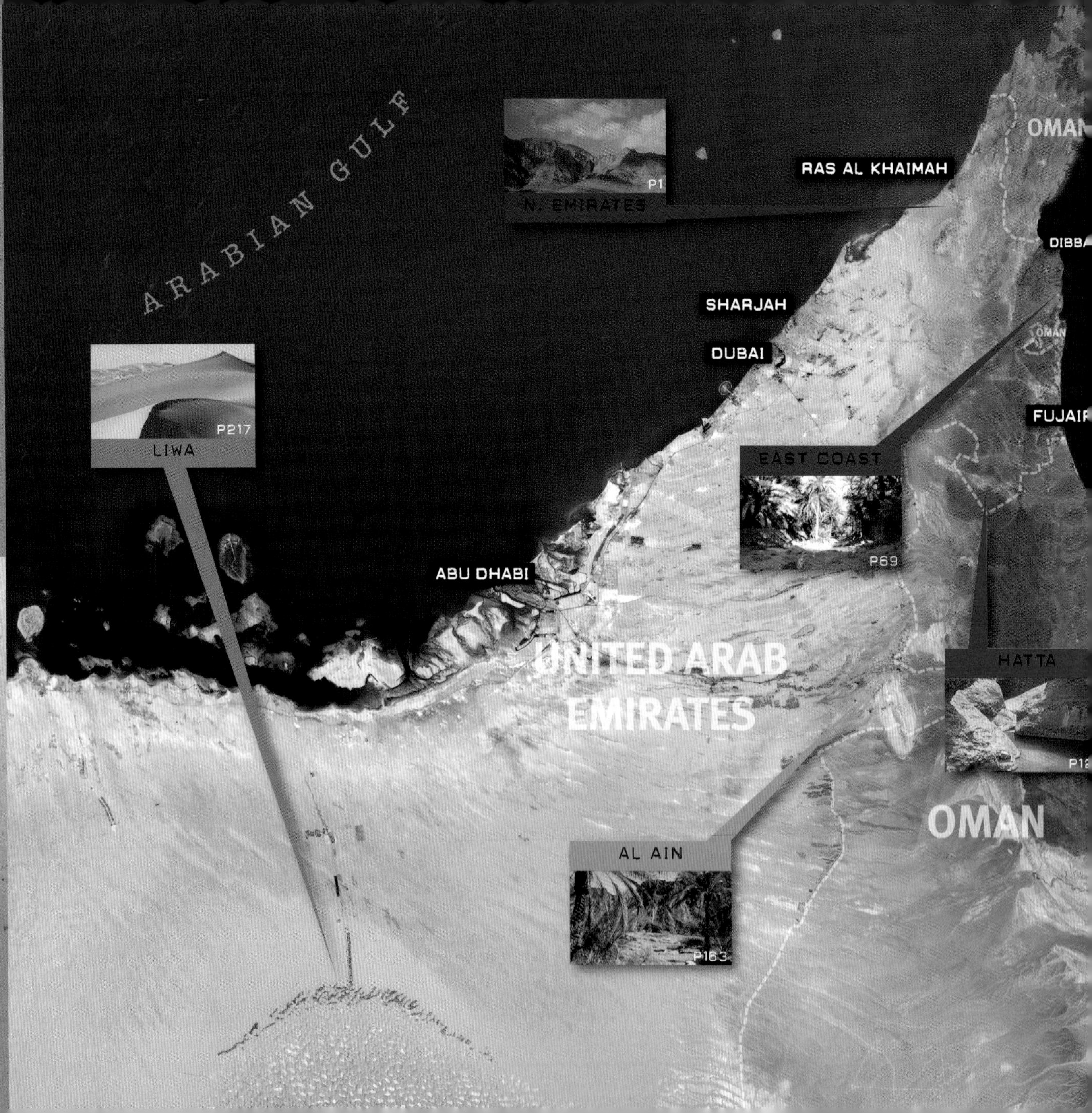

ARABIAN GULF

OMAN

N. EMIRATES   P1

RAS AL KHAIMAH

DIBBA

SHARJAH

DUBAI

OMAN

FUJAIR

LIWA   P217

EAST COAST
P69

ABU DHABI

UNITED ARAB
EMIRATES

HATTA
P1

OMAN

AL AIN
P163

ii

UAE Off-Road Explorer

Take Care

As with all advice, comments, opinions, directions etc, please use your common sense, know your limits and use the descriptions with EXTREME CAUTION.

For the hikes, we strongly recommend that you go accompanied with an experienced climber and use ropes and helmets wherever necessary. Explorer Group Ltd, Explorer Publishing and Volkswagen Middle East and their associates accept no responsibility for any accidents, injuries, loss, inconvenience, disasters or damage to persons or property that may occur while you are out and about or using this guidebook. The fact that a route is mentioned does not necessarily mean that it is always passable or safe.

Ultimately you are responsible for determining your own limitations based on the conditions you encounter.

Jeep

How to Select a Route

1) By area

The UAE country map [p.ii] shows the five areas that the routes have been divided into – Northern Emirates, East Coast, Hatta, Al Ain, and Liwa. Considering the differences between these areas is a good place to start when deciding which area to explore. Once you've selected the area you can use the tabs to locate that section. Each area begins with its own overview, with maps explaining how to get there, a table listing the routes, suggested route combinations, and detailed descriptions of the highlights you'll find. Comparing the different attributes of each of the areas will help you make your selection. Scenic highlights [p.xii] are also grouped by area allowing you to compare the general landscapes of the five areas.

2) By attributes

The route overview table [p.x] gives you an at-a-glance look at the attributes of each route. The total distance is shown, as well as the amount that will actually be driven 'off-road.' Separate columns for each terrain type help you choose between desert, mountain and wadi drives. In addition there are columns for different activities, so you can easily find a route that is good for a spot of camping, climbing, hiking, mountain biking, or swimming.

Route Overview Table

Route		Name	Page	Total Dist. (km)	Total Unpaved (km)	Terrain Mtn	Terrain Desert	Terrain Wadi	Activity Camp	Activity Climb	Activity Hike	Activity Bike	Activity Swim	Route Combinations
		Khasab Road Route	**4**	**185**	**Đ**									
1	N. Emirates	Falaj Al Moalla	16	71	28		✓		✓					4
2	N. Emirates	Mussandam	26	155	149	✓		✓	✓	✓	✓	✓		3
3	N. Emirates	Stairway to Heaven	42	22	5	✓		✓	✓		✓			3+4
4	N. Emirates	Wadi Bih	52	92	54	✓		✓	✓	✓	✓	✓	✓	1+3+8+9
		East Coast Road Route	**72**	**237**	**Đ**									
5	East Coast	Wadi Asimah	84	28	17	✓	✓	✓	✓		✓			4+8+9+11
6	East Coast	Wadi Tayyibah	90	16	6	✓		✓			✓	✓		4+5+8
7	East Coast	Wadi Hayl	96	20	Đ	✓		✓			✓			7+10
8	East Coast	Wadi Madhah & Shis	102	63	46	✓	✓	✓		✓	✓	✓	✓	6+10
9	East Coast	Wadi Wurrayah	110	25	9	✓		✓			✓		✓	6+7
10	East Coast	Wadi Sidr/Sana	116	33	25	✓		✓	✓		✓	✓		4+5+9
		Hatta Road Route	**128**	**100**	**Đ**									
11		Fossil Rock	136	40	32		✓		✓					12+13+5

3) By terrain

As well as the route overview table, the colour-coded thumbnails[p.xi] allow you to pick a route depending on the terrain and type of scenery you want to see. There is the desert, mountain and wadi drives, as well as an 'Oasis' category if you're yearning for some greenery, and a 'Water' category should you fancy a dip en route. This page also lists the six best routes we believe are absolute 'must do' trips during your time in the emirates.

Mountain Route 2	Oasis Route 15	Oasis Route 5	Desert Route 1
Mussandam Page 26	Khutwa Page 188	Wadi Asimah Page 84	Falaj Al Moalla to Ras Al Khaimah Page 16

Mountain Route 10	Oasis Route 8	Oasis Route 6	Desert Route 18
Wadi Sidr/Sana Page 116	Wadi Madhah & Wadi Shis Page 102	Wadi Tayyibah Page 90	Liwa Oasis Page 228

4) By scenic highlights

Throughout the UAE there are a number of breathtaking landscapes where your camera is a necessity. In order to give you an overview of some of the most beautiful and awe-inspiring spots we have included a scenic highlights category [p.xii]. These stunning images represent the varied terrain and dramatic landscapes that are available to off-roaders. Hopefully this page will inspire and tempt you, by giving you a sneak peak of what is in store out there. So if you're having a hard time choosing a route, just pick a picture and go!

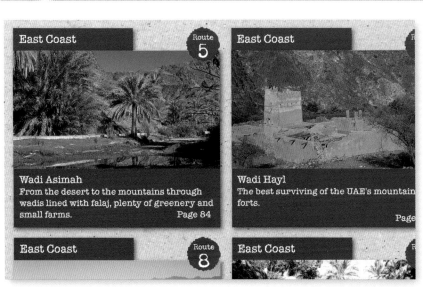

East Coast Route 5

Wadi Asimah
From the desert to the mountains through wadis lined with falaj, plenty of greenery and small farms. Page 84

East Coast

Wadi Hayl
The best surviving of the UAE's mountain forts. Page

East Coast Route 8

East Coast

The Anatomy of a Route

1) Overview

Each individual route starts with an overview page. At a glance you'll be able to see the location of the route, read a brief description of what you'll encounter along the way, and get some info about distances and the type of driving. On the left-hand map page, the coloured boxes illustrate which areas are covered in more detail on the subsequent pages. This map also shows other routes nearby, as well as highlighting attractions you may pass on your travels.

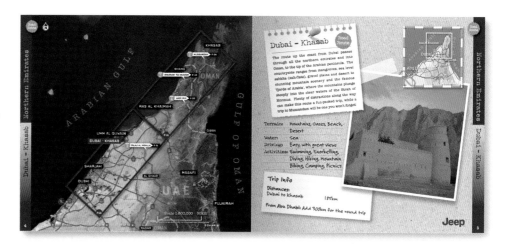

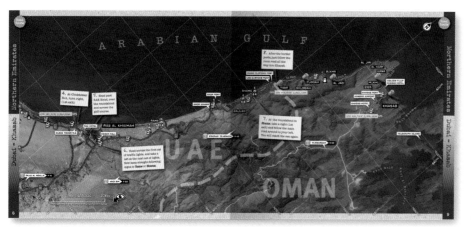

2) The maps

Following on from the overview page are the detailed route maps that utilise unique satellite imagery. Providing a bird's-eye view, the maps are superimposed with roads and tracks to make the route even clearer. Notable buildings, and town and village names, are also marked, as are GPS coordinates at important junctions. Information boxes give precise directions for following the route, and suggest some interesting diversions. The yellow 'pins' refer to highlights along the way, that are then discussed in more detail after the map pages.

3) Things to do & see

After the maps you'll find descriptions of some of the highlights and points of interest you should encounter while driving the route. Each separate entry corresponds to a lettered, yellow 'pin' on the route's map pages. These can include descriptions of villages or areas of beauty, and suggestions of where to hike, bike, or camp for the night. Sometimes there's even additional navigational or driving advice to reassure you when things get a little tricky.

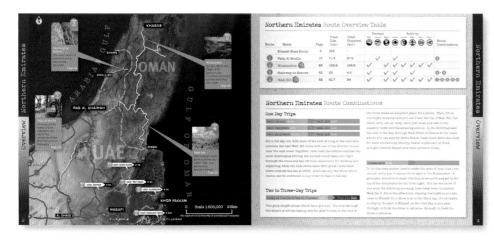

4) Other options

If you've got plenty of time on your hands and a full tank, you should consult the overview page at the beginning of each of the five areas (Northern Emirates, East Coast, Hatta, Al Ain, and Liwa). Here you'll find a table with suggested route combinations, and a short description of those we particularly recommend. There's the chance to make a full day of it with two or more short routes, or include an overnight camping stop to really make the most of your weekend.

How to Navigate a Route

In order to give all our readers the most user-friendly instructions possible for the routes we have incorporated three methods of navigation. So whether you like to be told, to calculate or to be shown our route maps simply won't let you make a wrong turn!

1) Directions

The numbered pink boxes on the map pages give you step-by-step, clear and concise instructions to be followed in numerical order.

The lettered green boxes are optional diversions that you may want to pursue along the way, such as alternative tracks and hiking or biking routes.

While each route has a start and finish point they can all be followed in reverse. This also applies to route combinations, which are displayed in the route overview table of each area.

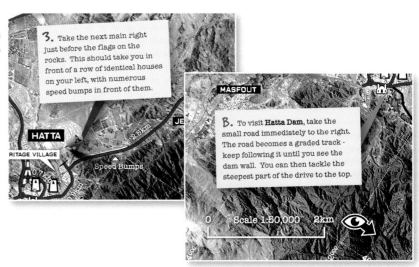

3. Take the next main right just before the flags on the rocks. This should take you in front of a row of identical houses on your left, with numerous speed bumps in front of them.

HATTA

RITAGE VILLAGE

Speed Bumps

MASFOUT

B. To visit **Hatta Dam**, take the small road immediately to the right. The road becomes a graded track - keep following it until you see the dam wall. You can then tackle the steepest part of the drive to the top.

0   Scale 1:50,000   2km

2) GPS

The maps are geo-referenced satellite images with a Universal Transverse Mercator grid, used for GPS purposes. GPS coordinates are given in UTM for the start and end of a route, and often for critical junctions in the middle of the trip.

The grid on the map follows a a UTM projection, with a WGS84 spheroid. Each digit on the grid represents one metre. The northern UAE is in UTM grid zone 40R. Liwa is zone 39Q. Example: 450,000E, 2,850,000N. In most cases we have added a 2,000 x 2,000m grid which allows you to calculate the GPS coordinates of certain points of interest by following the x and y axis and entering them into your GPS.

When reading the coordinate grids, you may find it easier to rotate the image (if necessary) so that north is pointing upwards. The vertical lines represent the Easting grid (x-axis). The horizontal lines represent the the Northing grid (y-axis).

SHUWAYAH/RAY R157

HATTA FORT HOTEL

UTM 412,454E 2,745,127N

GEO 24°48'06"N 56°08'01"E

GPS

3) The maps

The maps are displayed with the route in mind, rather than north orientated (there is a north symbol on each map), so that you can use them like a traditional line map, with important landmarks marked to aid navigation.

In addition you can keep track of your progress with the distances in kilometres between red markers that are shown on the maps.

Main roads and tracks are superimposed on the maps for clarity. Occasionally you'll see a white warning box with a red surround; this is to alert you to possible dangers or perhaps a country border. For an explanation of all other symbols see the map legend on the inside back cover flap.

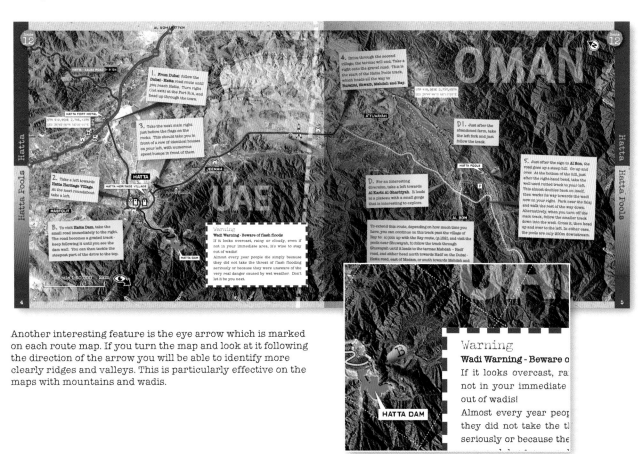

Another interesting feature is the eye arrow which is marked on each route map. If you turn the map and look at it following the direction of the arrow you will be able to identify more clearly ridges and valleys. This is particularly effective on the maps with mountains and wadis.

Route Overview Table

Route		Name	Page	Total Dist. (km)	Total Unpaved (km)	Terrain Mtn	Desert	Wadi	Activity Camp	Climb	Hike	Bike	Swim	Route Combinations
		Khasab Road Route	4	185	Đ									
1	N. Emirates	Falaj Al Moalla	16	71	28		✓		✓					4
2	N. Emirates	Mussandam	26	155	149	✓		✓	✓	✓	✓	✓	✓	
3	N. Emirates	Stairway to Heaven	42	22	5	✓		✓	✓		✓			2+4
4	N. Emirates	Wadi Bih	52	92	54	✓		✓	✓	✓	✓	✓	✓	1+3+5+8+9
		East Coast Road Route	72	237	Đ									
5	East Coast	Wadi Asimah	84	28	17	✓	✓	✓	✓		✓			4+8+9+11
6	East Coast	Wadi Tayyibah	90	16	6	✓		✓			✓	✓		4+5+8
7	East Coast	Wadi Hayl	96	20	Đ	✓		✓			✓			7+10
8	East Coast	Wadi Madhah & Shis	102	63	46	✓		✓	✓		✓	✓	✓	6+10
9	East Coast	Wadi Wurrayah	110	25	9	✓		✓			✓		✓	6+7
10	East Coast	Wadi Sidr/Sana	116	33	25	✓		✓	✓		✓	✓		4+5+9
		Hatta Road Route	128	100	Đ									
11	Hatta	Fossil Rock	136	40	32		✓		✓					12+13+5
12	Hatta	Hatta Pools	144	33	11	✓		✓	✓		✓	✓	✓	11+13+16
13	Hatta	Ray	152	81	26	✓		✓	✓		✓	✓	✓	11+12+16
		Al Ain Road Route	166	110	Đ									
14	Al Ain	Hanging Gardens	180	73	9	✓				✓	✓			15+16
15	Al Ain	Khutwa	188	40	2	✓		✓			✓			14+16
16	Al Ain	Shwaib to Mahdah	196	61	60.4	✓	✓		✓					14+15+12+13
17	Al Ain	Wadi Madbah	208	41	18.5	✓		✓	✓	✓	✓		✓	15
		Liwa Road Route	218	322	Đ									
18	Liwa	Liwa Crescent	228	150	Endless!		✓		✓					

Mountain — Route 14	Mountain — Route 4	Mountain — Route 2	Oasis — Route 15	Oasis — Route 5	Desert — Route 1	Desert — Route 11
Hanging Gardens — Page 180	Hatta Pools — Page 144	Mussandam — Page 26	Khutwa — Page 188	Wadi Asimah — Page 84	Falaj Al Moalla to Ras Al Khaimah — Page 16	Fossil Rock — Page 136
Mountain — Route 3	Mountain — Route 4	Mountain — Route 10	Oasis — Route 8	Oasis — Route 6	Desert — Route 18	Desert — Route 16
Stairway to Heaven — Page 42	Wadi Bih — Page 52	Wadi Sidr/Sana — Page 116	Wadi Madhah & Wadi Shis — Page 102	Wadi Tayyibah — Page 90	Liwa Oasis — Page 228	Shwaib to Mahdah — Page 196
Wadi — Route 12	Wadi — Route 13	Wadi — Route 5	Wadi — Route 4	Wadi — Route 7	Must Do! — Route 12	Must Do! — Route 15
Hatta Pools — Page 144	Ray — Page 152	Wadi Asimah — Page 84	Wadi Bih — Page 52	Wadi Hayl — Page 96	Hatta Pools — Page 144	Khutwa — Page 188
Wadi — Route 17	Wadi — Route 8	Wadi — Route 10	Wadi — Route 6	Wadi — Route 9	Must Do! — Route 18	Must Do! — Route 2
Wadi Madbah — Page 208	Wadi Madhah & Wadi Shis — Page 102	Wadi Sidr/Sana — Page 116	Wadi Tayyibah — Page 90	Wurrayah — Page 110	Liwa Oasis — Page 228	Mussandam — Page 28
Water — Route 12	Water — Route 13	Water — Route 17	Water — Route 8	Water — Route 9	Must Do! — Route 4	Must Do! — Route 11
Hatta Pools — Page 144	Ray — Page 152	Wadi Madbah — Page 208	Wadi Madhah & Wadi Shis — Page 102	Wurrayah — Page 110	Wadi Bih — Page 52	Fossil Rock — Page 136

Introduction

Routes by Terrain

Northern Emirates
Route ١

Falaj Al Moalla
An easy, gentle desert route, ending in the suprising greenery of the Ghaf forest near Digdagga.
Page 16

Northern Emirates
Route ٢

Mussandam
An epic drive into Oman with spectacular mountain scenery and an amazing coastline.
Page 26

Liwa
Route 18

Liwa Oasis
An adventure in the epic Empty Quarter - the biggest sand desert in the world!
Page 228

Northern Emirates
Route 3

Stairway To Heaven
The most extreme and rewarding hike in the Emirates.
Page 42

Northern Emirates
Route 4

Wadi Bih
The must-do route for any off-roader in the UAE - big mountains, massive views.
Page 52

Al Ain
Route 14

Hanging Gardens
Spectacular area for hiking with amazing rock formations and stunning views.
Page 180

Al Ain
Route 15

Khutwa
A short drive into the inviting, green Khutwa oasis for walks amid the shady tranquility.
Page 188

Al Ain
Route 16

Shwaib to Mahdah
A fun and varied drive on all types of terrain and through some stunning desert.
Page 196

Al Ain
Route 17

Wadi Madbah
The biggest waterfall of the UAE with freshwater pools to swim in and explore.
Page 208

East Coast — Route 5

Wadi Asimah
From the desert to the mountains through wadis lined with falaj, plenty of greenery and small farms.
Page 84

East Coast — Route 6

Wadi Tayyibah
A historical drive on the old road through the mountains amid lush, shady plantations.
Page 90

East Coast — Route 7

Wadi Hayl
The most dramatic of the UAE's mountain forts.
Page 96

East Coast — Route 8

Wadi Madhah & Wadi Shis
The surprising beauty of the contrasting Wadi Madhah and Wadi Shis - the latter actually in Omani territory.
Page 102

East Coast — Route 9

Wadi Wurrayah
The most popular waterfall in the Emirates - year round swimming and exploring in the wadi's pools and streams.
Page 110

East Coast — Route 10

Wadi Sidr/Sana
From wadis through the mountains, a fun and varied drive to the east coast.
Page 116

Hatta — Route 11

Fossil Rock
A great desert route with appeal and interest for beginners and experts alike.
Page 136

Hatta — Route 12

Hatta Pools
The most well-known and popular of all UAE off-road drives, for the famous Hatta Pools and the majestic Hajar Mountains.
Page 144

Hatta — Route 13

Ray
An enjoyable drive in the mountains which ends at a stream with quiet pools and a great shady camping spot.
Page 152

The Newer Roads

Since the last edition of the **UAE Off-Road Explorer** the UAE has been busy constructing silky smooth slabs of tarmac all over the country. Ok, so they may have paved one or two former off-road favourites, but these super highways have shortened journey times significantly, allowing you to spend less time on the road and more time off it.

Check out these suggested shortcuts for the quickest access to your chosen off-road routes, or get a copy of the new **Off-Road Image Maps** from Explorer Publishing, which give you a bird's eye overview of the country, so you can plan your way between routes and even explore unchartered territory.

At the time of driving (autumn '06), the border fence between the UAE and Oman (allegedly to keep debt-dodgers, resident in Oman, from sneaking across the border into the UAE) had been completed between Al Ain and Hatta road - completely cutting the Shwaib to Mahdah route in two. For tips on how to get around this, see the updates in the route on p.196. As most of this route lies in Oman, there is an alternative way in from the Mahdah road (see 'Hatta Road - Mahdah' on the right), and see p.156. The northern part of the border fence above the Dubai - Hatta road has also been completed, meaning these areas can only by accessed from the Hatta road rather than from Fossil Rock and Fili as before.

Emirates Road to RAK

Avoid the slow E11 coast road and the bottleneck that is Sharjah, by sticking to the E311 'super-bypass.' Dubai to RAK in an hour...? Wadi Bih never looked more tempting!

RAS AL KHAIMAH

ARABIAN GULF

DUBAI

1

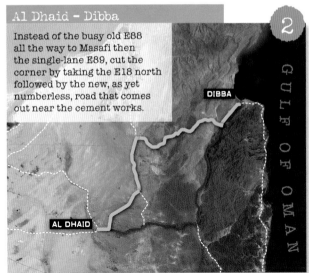

Al Dhaid - Dibba

Instead of the busy old E88 all the way to Masafi then the single-lane E89, cut the corner by taking the E18 north followed by the new, as yet numberless, road that comes out near the cement works.

DIBBA

AL DHAID

GULF OF OMAN

2

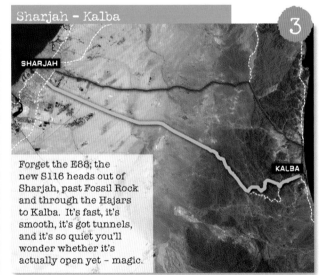

Sharjah - Kalba

SHARJAH

KALBA

Forget the E88; the new S116 heads out of Sharjah, past Fossil Rock and through the Hajars to Kalba. It's fast, it's smooth, it's got tunnels, and it's so quiet you'll wonder whether it's actually open yet - magic.

3

The E611 Sharjah Bypass

4

This road already avoids the snarl-ups around Sharjah and is useful for Dubai to East Coast trips, but it should also soon link up with the E311 Emirates Road somewhere east of Umm Al Quwain.

Dubai/Sharjah - Al Dhaid

5

Try this as an alternative to the E88 – head east through the desert on the deserted S116, then swing north onto the E55 straight into Al Dhaid.

Hatta Road - Mahdah

6

Instead of taking the E66 to Al Ain then crossing the border, head towards Hatta on the E44 and turn right after the Shell garage. A great alternative for two reasons: firstly, you'll avoid all the border hassle at Al Ain getting into Oman and then back again. Secondly, with the border fence now completed between Al Ain and Hatta road, one easy way to access the impressive dunes near Shwaib on the Shwaib – Mahdah route (p.196) is via this route (through the Sumayni Gap).

Hatta - Kalba

7

As you head east on the E44, a kilometre or so after the Hatta Fort Hotel there's a left turn. This road meets up with the new S116 at the village of Munay, from which you can easily reach Kalba.

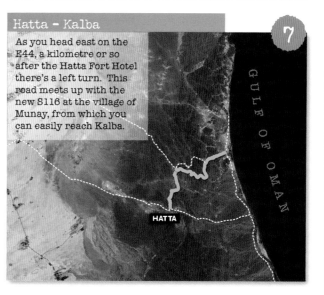

A R A B I

BURJ AL ARAB

MARSA DUBAI

JUMEIRA

UMM SUQEIM

SAFA PARK

4.2km

3.5km

4.6km

3.4km

IBN BATTUTA MALL

3.1km

5.5km

E 11

E 11

3.7km

3.0km

EMIRATES HILLS

AL QUOZ

3.2km

ABU DHABI P. 223

AL BARSHA

6.1km

4.8km

6.1km

5

4.0km

JEBEL ALI

E 44

5.5km

UTM 330,378E 2,785,923N GPS

5.0km

4.2km

3.6km

NAD AL SHEBA

GREEN COMMUNITY

DUBAI INVESTMENT PARK

2.6km

3.1km

ABU DHABI P. 223

2.6km

5.5km

5

E 57

ARABIAN RANCHES

DUBAILAND

GLOBAL VILLAGE

E 311

E 66

DUBAILAND

14.0km

4.5km

SILICON

City Overview Legend

0   Scale 1:125,000   5km

2755000   325000

2760000

4

2765000   335000

2770000

3   4

AL AIN P. 168

AL AIN P. 168

City Map

BUR DUBAI

DEIRA

MAMZAR

MAMZAR PARK

SHARJAH

AJMAN

TRADE CENTRE R/A

KHALID LAGOON

UFO R/A

CULTURE R/A

RAS AL KHAIMAH R 6

GPS UTM 327,737E 2,791,459N

2.9km

2.4km

2.6km

2.0km

3.0km

1.7km

AJMAN SOUK

ATES TOWERS

3.7km

1.0km

2.7km

3.0km

5.8km

5.4km

UTM 340,131E 2,804,974N GPS

7.0km

4.4km

AL GARHOUD BR.

DUBAI INTL AIRPORT

AL QUSAIS

RAS AL KHOR

4.4km

2.6km

2.4km

3.4km

7.7km

RASHIDIYA

2.1km

AL WARQA

2.5km

MIRDIF

AL MEEZAR

SHARJAH INTL AIRPORT

RAS AL KHAIMAH R 6

3.5km

311

18.4km

2.1km

MUSHRIF PARK

3km

DRAGON MART

14.5km

116

44

611

611

AL KHAWANEEJ

7.6km

13.5km

611

SHARJAH BYPASS

AWIR INDUSTRIAL AREA

4.8km

6.3km

3

2

HATTA R 130

KALBA / FUJAIRAH R 74

MASAFI / FUJAIRAH DIBBA R 76

345000 350000 355000 360000

2780000 2785000 2790000 2795000

2710000 350000 360000 2780000

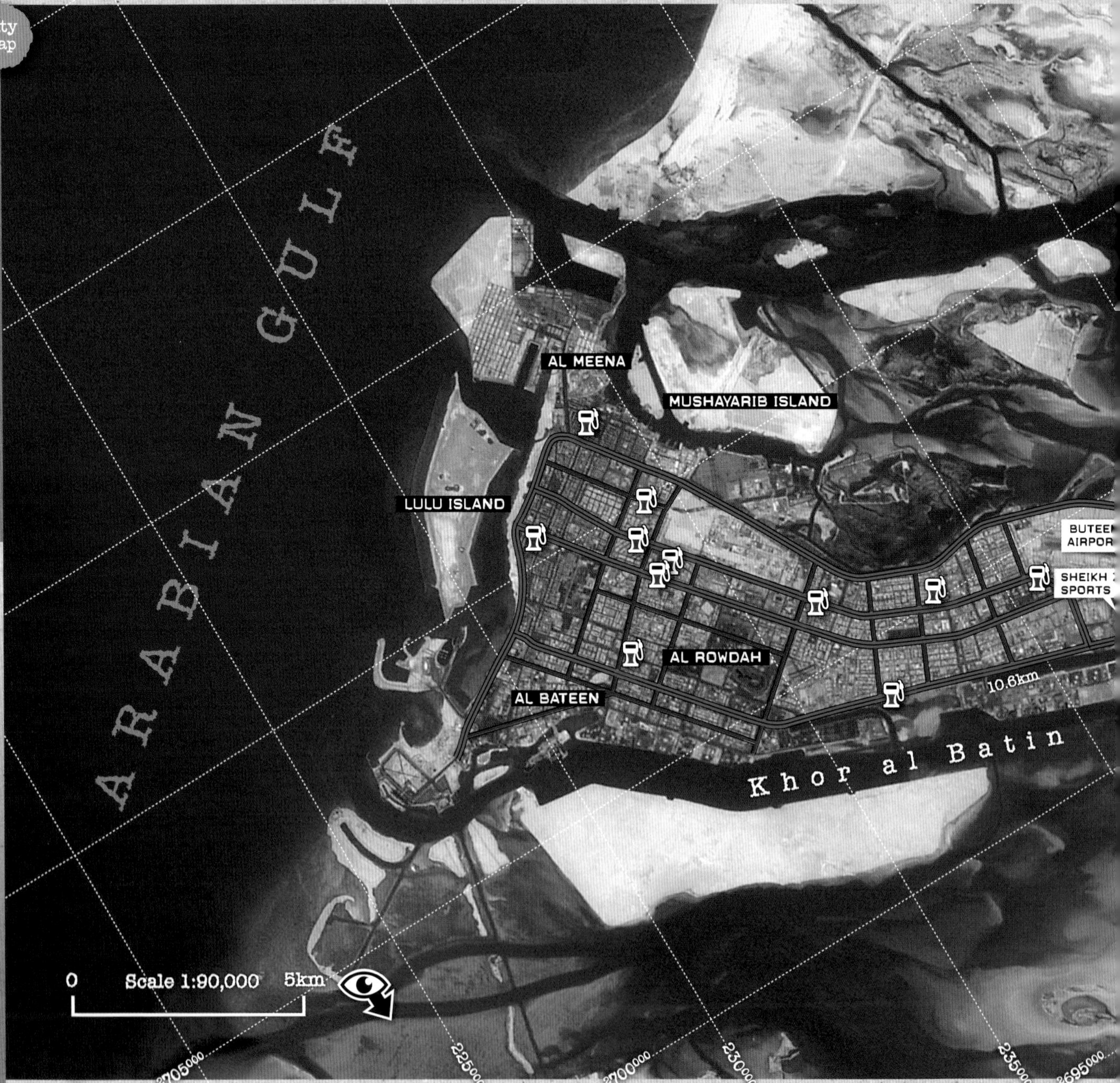

ARABIAN GULF

AL MEENA

MUSHAYARIB ISLAND

LULU ISLAND

BUTEEN AIRPORT

SHEIKH SPORTS

AL ROWDAH

AL BATEEN

10.6km

Khor al Batin

0   Scale 1:90,000   5km

2705000   225000   2700000   230000   235000   2695000

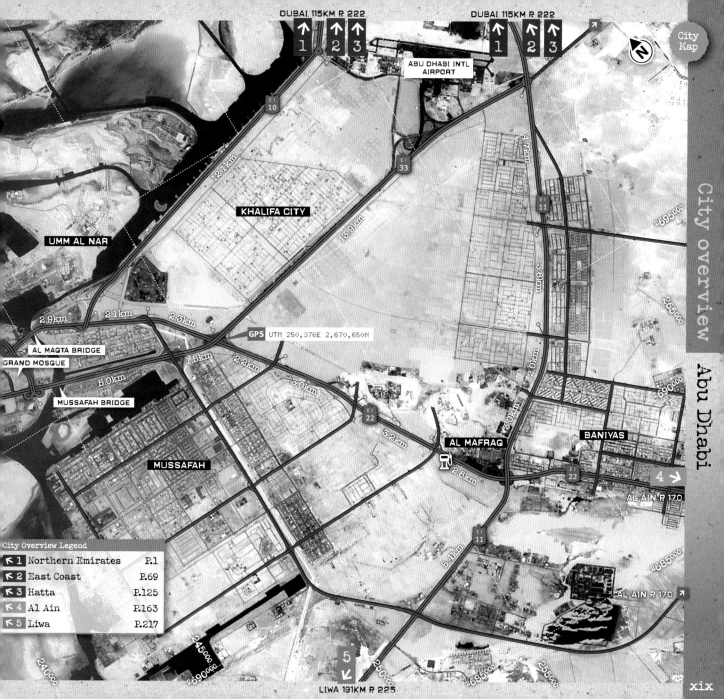

DUBAI 115KM R 222
↑1 ↑2 ↑3

DUBAI 115KM R 222
↑1 ↑2 ↑3 ↗

ABU DHABI INTL
AIRPORT

N

E1 10

E1 33

E1 11

4.2km

4.0km

KHALIFA CITY

12.1km

13.9km

5.6km

2695000

2650000

UMM AL NAR

2.9km   2.1km   2.3km

GPS UTM 250,376E 2,670,650N

AL MAQTA BRIDGE

GRAND MOSQUE

1.5km   2.2km

5.0km

2.0km

2690000

MUSSAFAH BRIDGE

5.0km

3.0km

BANIYAS

E1 22

E1 22

4 →

AL MAFRAQ

AL AIN R 170

MUSSAFAH

3.2km

2.6km

2685000

E1 11

5.4km

AL AIN R 170

240000   245000   250000   255000

2690000   2685000

5
↓
LIWA 191KM R 225

Northern Emirates

Jeep

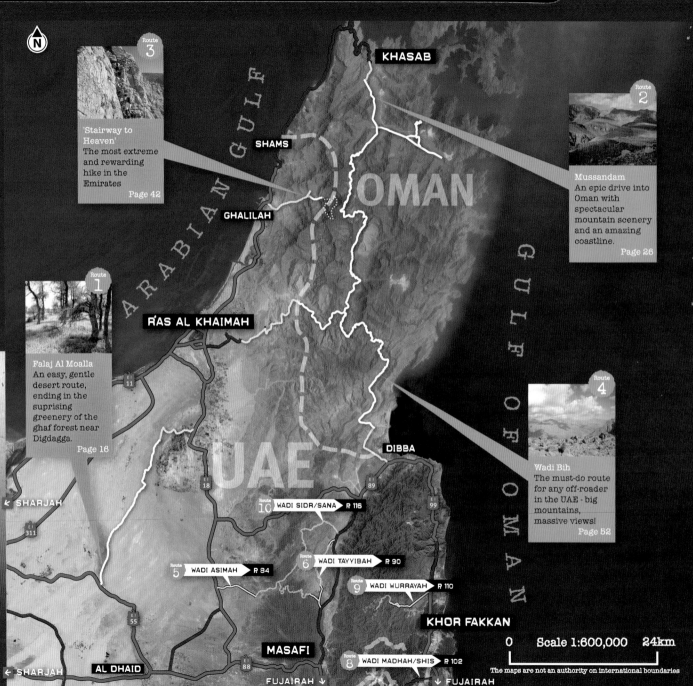

N

KHASAB

Route 3

'Stairway to Heaven'
The most extreme and rewarding hike in the Emirates

Page 42

SHAMS

OMAN

Route 2

Mussandam
An epic drive into Oman with spectacular mountain scenery and an amazing coastline.

Page 26

GHALILAH

ARABIAN GULF

Route 1

Falaj Al Moalla
An easy, gentle desert route, ending in the suprising greenery of the ghaf forest near Digdagga.

Page 16

RAS AL KHAIMAH

11

GULF OF OMAN

E 18

UAE

DIBBA

E 89

Route 4

Wadi Bih
The must-do route for any off-roader in the UAE - big mountains, massive views!

Page 52

← SHARJAH

311

E 99

Route 10 WADI SIDR/SANA ▶ R 116

Route 5 WADI ASIMAH ▶ R 84

Route 6 WADI TAYYIBAH ▶ R 90

Route 9 WADI WURRAYAH ▶ R 110

55

KHOR FAKKAN

MASAFI

0   Scale 1:600,000   24km

Route 8 WADI MADHAH/SHIS ▶ R 102

The maps are not an authority on international boundaries

← SHARJAH   AL DHAID   88   FUJAIRAH ↓   ↓ FUJAIRAH

2

Northern Emirates Route Overview Table

Route	Name	Page	Total Dist. (km)	Total Unpaved (km)	Terrain			Activity					Route Combinations
					Mtn	Desert	Wadi	Camp	Climb	Hike	Bike	Swim	
	Khasab Road Route	4	185	–									
1	Falaj Al Moalla	16	71.4	27.9		✔		✔					4
2	Mussandam	26	155.2	148.6	✔		✔	✔	✔	✔	✔	✔	
3	Stairway to Heaven	42	22	4.6	✔		✔	✔		✔			2 + 4
4	Wadi Bih	52	91.7	54	✔		✔	✔	✔	✔	✔	✔	1 + 3 + 5 + 8 + 9

Northern Emirates Route Combinations

One Day Trips

Wadi Asimah P.84	Wadi Bih P.52
Wadi Tayyibah P.90	Wadi Bih P.52
Wadi Sidr/Sana P.116	Wadi Bih P.52

For a full day out, with some of the best driving in the emirates, combine the epic Wadi Bih route with one of the shorter routes near the east coast. Tayyibah visits lush plantations and has the most challenging driving, the Asimah track takes you right through the trees and has off-route diversions for walking and exploring, while the hills above Sana offer great views back down towards the sea at Dibba. Alternatively, the three short routes can be combined in any order to make a full day.

Two to Three-Day Trips

| Falaj Al Moalla to Ras al Khaimah P.16 | ▶ | Wadi Bih P.52 |

Two good length drives which have got it all. The trip through the desert is not too taxing, and the ghaf forests at the end of the route make an excellent place for a picnic. Then, for an overnight camping spot you can't beat the top of Wadi Bih. Get there early, set up camp, then just relax and take in the massive views and the amazing silence. In the morning head the rest of the way through Wadi Khab Al Shamis to the coast where you can stop by Dibba Beach, head south down the coast for some snorkelling (Snoopy Island is popular), or head straight towards Masafi and back across to Dubai.

| Mussandam P.26 | |

To do this area justice (and to make the most of your visa), you should really aim to spend three days in the Mussandam. A good plan would be to make the long drive north and get to the top of the mountains for the first night. You can see more of this area the following morning, then head down to explore Wadi Sal A' Ala in the afternoon, staying overnight so you are close to Khasab for a dhow trip on the third day. It's advisable to stop by the port in Khasab on the first day as you pass through, to book the dhow in advance.

Road Route

N

Northern Emirates

Dubai – Khasab

ARABIAN GULF

GULF OF OMAN

KHASAB

Route 2 | MUSSANDAM | R 26

OMAN

SHAMS

Route 3 | STAIRWAY TO HEAVEN | R 42

Route 4 | WADI BIH | R 52

RAS AL KHAIMAH

DIBBA

P.14

UMM AL QUWAIN

11

DUBAI – KHASAB

Route 1 | FALAJ AL MOALLA | R 16

99

18

55

SHARJAH

88

MASAFI

AL DHAID

OMAN

89

DUBAI

311

UAE

116

11

611

55

FUJAIRAH

P.12

0   Scale 1:800,000   30km

The maps are not an authority on international boundaries

4

↙ ABU DHABI   AL AIN ↙   HATTA ↘   MADAM   OMAN   SOHAR ↓

Dubai - Khasab

Road Route

The route up the coast from Dubai passes through all the northern emirates and into Oman, to the tip of the Arabian peninsula. The countryside ranges from mangroves, sea level sabkha (salt-flats), gravel plains and desert to stunning mountain scenery and the famous 'fjords of Arabia', where the mountains plunge steeply into the clear waters of the Strait of Hormuz. Plenty of distractions along the way can make this route a fun-packed trip, while a trip to Mussandam will be one you won't forget!

Road Route

Terrain: Mountains, Oases, Beach, Desert

Water: Sea

Driving: Easy, with great views

Activities: Swimming, Snorkelling, Diving, Hiking, Mountain Biking, Camping, Picnics

Trip Info

Distances:
Dubai to Khasab   185km

From Abu Dhabi: Add 300km for the round trip

Jeep

Northern Emirates

Dubai – Khasab

Dubai/Sharjah City Overview

A R A B

DUBAI

TRADE CENTRE R/A

2.9km

UTM 327,737E 2,791,459N **GPS**

5.6km

5.4km

AL GARHOUD BR.

8.4km

2.7km 1km 2.4km

AL MULLA PLAZA

2.6km 2.1km

2.3km

2.1km

3.7km

4.4km

SHARJAH

CULTURAL PALACE SQUARE R/A

1.7km

1km

3.2km

1km

4.7km

1.4km 2.6km 2.4km 3.4km

SHARJAH INT'L AIRPORT

AJMAN

E 11

AJMAN CITY CENT

CAMEL RACETRACK

9.5km

44

2.2km

5.3km

E 311

E 66

1. Follow the **Dubai City Overview** map and the **Sharjah/Ajman Overview** map for the best way out of Dubai and through Sharjah.

2. On the outskirts of Ajman, head straight over the overpass towards **Umm Al Quwain/Ras Al Khaimah**. Keep straight, watching for speed bumps all along this route.

116

E 611

S H A R J A H   B Y P A S S

E 611

E 611

E 88

0   Scale 1:215,000   10km

2770000   350000   2780000   360000   2790000

AL AIN 89KM   HATTA 72KM   KALBA 97 KM   FUJAIRAH

N GULF

UMM AL QUWAIN

AL HAMRIYA

BARRACUDA BEACH MOTEL

UAQ FLYING CLUB

DREAMLAND WATER PARK

AL HAMRA FORT HOTEL

2.7km

SCULPTURE R/A

UAQ SHOOTING CLUB

EMIRATES MOTORPLEX

BIN MAJID RESORT

E11

E11

28.3km

P8

3. Keep straight at the roundabout on the outskirts of **Umm Al Quwain.**

3.5km

3.3km

E311

13.7km

27.5km

E311

P8

For the quickest route north towards RAK, the extension of Emirates Road (E311) opened in July 2005, and cut the time from Dubai to RAK down to 1 hour – although there's nothing to see but desert! For more to see on the drive up there, the coastal route offers more attractions, taking between 1.5 and 2 hrs (without stops).

Route 1 FALAJ AL MOALLA ▶ P 16

AL DHAID 19KM

2850000

370000

2840000

380000

390000

2830000

2820000

2810000

370000

380000

390000

7

Northern Emirates

Dubai - Khasab

ARABIAN

4. At Clocktower R/A, turn right, (1st exit)

5. Head past RAK Hotel, over the roundabout and across the golf course.

UTM 391,707E 2,850,209N **GPS**

5.5km

8.0km

E11

RAK HOTEL

CLOCK TOWER R/A

2.5km

2.0km

5.0km

RAS AL KHAIMAH

MANAR MALL

5.6km

RAMS

8km

E11

13.2km

SAQR PORT

KHOR KHWAIR

1.5k

Route 3 STAIRWAY

UAE

6. Head across the first set of traffic lights, and take a left at the next set of lights. Now keep straight following signs to **Rams** or **Shams**.

R 7

R 7

Route 1 FALAJ AL MOALLA R 16

Route 4 WADI BIH R 52

E18

DIBBA 50 KM
AL DHAID 47KM

0 Scale 1:215,000 10km

The maps are not an authority on international boundaries

400 000

2 840 000

410 000

2 850 000

2 860 000 420 000

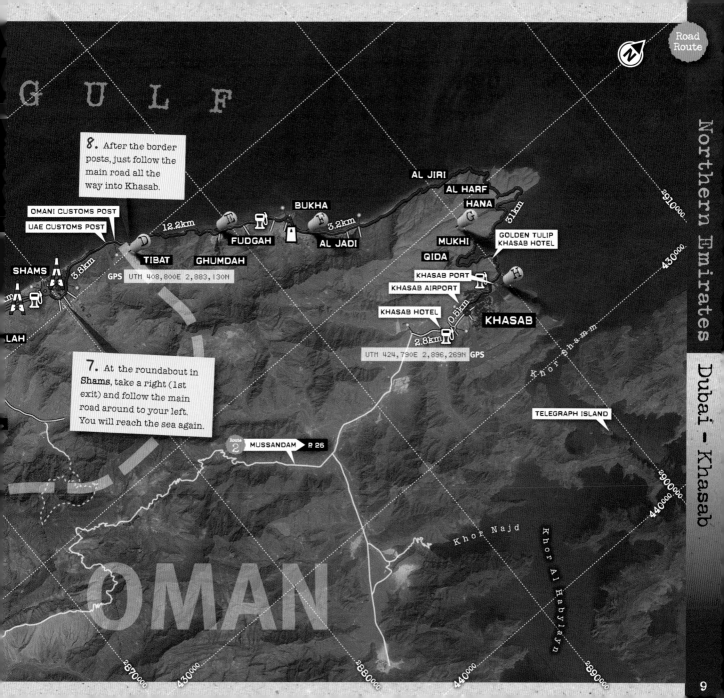

GULF

8. After the border posts, just follow the main road all the way into Khasab.

AL JIRI

AL HARF

HANA

OMANI CUSTOMS POST

UAE CUSTOMS POST

12.2km

BUKHA

31km

GOLDEN TULIP
KHASAB HOTEL

FUDGAH

3.2km

MUKHI

AL JADI

QIDA

SHAMS

3.8km

TIBAT

GHUMDAH

GPS UTM 408,800E 2,883,130N

KHASAB PORT

KHASAB AIRPORT

0.5km

LAH

KHASAB HOTEL

KHASAB

2.8km

UTM 424,790E 2,896,269N GPS

7. At the roundabout in **Shams**, take a right (1st exit) and follow the main road around to your left. You will reach the sea again.

Khor Sham m

TELEGRAPH ISLAND

Route
2 MUSSANDAM R 26

Khor Najd

Khor Al Habylayn

OMAN

2910000

430000

2900000

440000

2870000 430000 2880000 440000 2890000

Dubai to Khasab Highlights

The drive from Dubai to Ras Al Khaimah and on in to Mussandam takes you through Sharjah, Ajman and Umm Al Quwain and then into Musandam Peninsula, a stand-alone region of Oman that extends north to the Strait of Hormuz. If you have time, the coastal route has the most to see and do. At Umm Al Quwain especially, opportunities abound, with the massive lagoon and mangroves attracting water and nature lovers, while the area to the north offers fun for all at the waterpark as well as flying, shooting and motor sports. Ras Al Khaimah, the most northerly emirate before entering the Mussandam, also has a shooting club and is the starting or finishing point for the spectacular trip through the mountains via Wadi Bih to Dibba on the east coast. If you just want the quickest route north, however, the new extension of Emirates Road (E311) bypasses all the cities and gets you through the desert to Ras Al Khaimah in an hour.

An easy two-to-three hour drive from Dubai, Khasab is the northernmost of the four **wilayats** that make up the governorate of the Mussandam and is also the capital of the area. This isolated enclave of Oman is known as the 'fjords of Arabia', from the jagged cliffs that plunge into the Gulf of Oman and the Strait of Hormuz to form beautiful hidden inlets – perfect for snorkelling, picnicking and exploring. Until recently, the area was a restricted military zone (to the north is the Strait of Hormuz, through which the majority of the Gulf's oil trade passes, and Iran is only 45km across the water), but it is now open to civilian visitors.

Khasab and the Mussandam Peninsula are places of stunning beauty and hold a welcome sense of timelessness. Life here continues much as it has for centuries, with locals tending livestock, harvesting dates, citrus fruits and vegetables, and perpetuating crafts such as net weaving.

The road to Khasab is a paved highway, so we've included a few fun diversions along the way in case you want to take your time getting there. Refer to the Mussandam route (p.26) for further options once you reach Khasab.

Local Tips

- The local currency is the Omani rial (referred to as RO or OR), which is divided into 1,000 baisa (or baiza). The exchange rate is about Dhs.9.5 = OR.1. UAE dirhams are always accepted if you don't have time to buy some riyals.

- Talking on a hand-held mobile telephone while driving is illegal in Oman, as is driving a dirty car (yes, seriously!)

- Note that by car, non-GCC nationals can only enter and exit the Mussandam on the Ras Al Khaimah side of the peninsula, not via Wadi Bih.

The Sayh Plateau

- When crossing the border as a 'couple', avoid potential problems by stating if you are married if asked (even if your family names are not the same). Cases of people being turned away are not uncommon.

Visa Requirements

Visas for Mussandam are required for most nationalities, whether entering by road or by air. Different regulations apply depending on your nationality and whether you are in the UAE as a tourist or as a resident.

If you have UAE residency and are on List 1 or 2, a visa can be obtained on arrival at the border. Otherwise apply at the Oman embassy in Abu Dhabi or the consulate in Dubai (see Directory p.312). In both cases the fee is Dhs.60. Visas usually take about four days to process, although they are sometimes able to speed things up for you.

Tourists staying in the UAE wishing to enter Oman are grouped depending on their nationality, under either List 1 or 2, (see below) for which different procedures and terms apply. For those on List 1, an entry visa is issued free of charge at the border, and is valid for up to the length of time left on your UAE visa. Those on List 2 have to apply for a visa in advance and are usually required to be part of a tour group, with sponsorship from a hotel or tour operator in Oman. Check with your nearest Oman embassy or consulate for more information.

If you want to visit Oman more than once, a multiple entry visa is available at the border (for List 1) or in advance from your nearest Oman embassy or consulate (List 2). The cost in

Warning

Remember that regulations in this part of the world can change virtually overnight, so check details before you leave to avoid disappointment. Refer to the website of the Royal Oman Police, (www.rop.gov.om) to get the latest information on visitor visas.

List No.1

Europe: Andorra, Austria, Belgium, Britain, Croatia, Cyprus, Czech Rep, Denmark, Estonia, Finland, France, Germany, Greece, Hungary, Iceland, Ireland, Italy, Latvia, Liechtenstein, Lithuania, Macedonia, Malta, Moldova, Monaco, Luxembourg, Netherlands, Norway, Poland, Portugal, Rumania, San Marino, Slovakia, Slovenia, Spain, Sweden, Switzerland, Vatican

South America: Argentina, Bolivia, Brazil, Chile, Colombia, Ecuador, French Guinea, Paraguay, Peru, Suriname, Uruguay, Venezuela

Other Countries: Australia, Dar al-Salam, Canada, Hong Kong, Indonesia, Japan, Lebanon, Malaysia, Maldives, New Zealand, Seychelles, Singapore, South Africa, South Korea, Taiwan, Thailand, Tunisia, United States

List No.2

Albania, Belarus, Bosnia-Herzegovina, Bulgaria, China, Egypt, India, Iran, Jordan, Morocco, Romania, Russian Federation, Syria, Ukraine

both cases is RO 10 and the visa is valid for one year. Your passport must be valid for not less than one year at the time of applying. Holders of this visa can stay for up to three weeks at a time, but a minimum of three weeks must elapse between each visit.

Umm Al Quwain Lagoon

Umm Al Quwain has a long seafaring tradition of pearling and fishing. The lagoon, with its mangroves, is an ideal place for spotting a plethora of birdlife, and is also a popular weekend spot for boat trips, windsurfing and other watersports, since it is sheltered and free of dangerous currents.

However, this whole area is set to undergo massive change with the proposed development of the lagoon into Umm Al Quwain Marina, a 12 billion dirham project to create a waterfront town of more than 9,000 homes with a full complement of facilities all around the lagoon and on the islands. The development, starting in 2005, is planned to take seven years, but it remains to be seen what the effects of this will be on the area's natural wildlife in the shallow waters, the mangroves and on the many small islands and sand banks, including a number of rare species of bird and marine life.

Umm Al Quwain – Activities

Just to the north of the Umm Al Quwain lagoon is the 'activity centre' of this region – offering a variety of distractions to suit all tastes:

Dreamland Aqua Park combines exciting water rides with lush green shaded areas, which are pleasant places to relax or enjoy a picnic. Alternatively, away from the water rides, visit the amusement centre, or burn rubber on the 400 metre go-kart track. (Timings 10:00 - 20:00; see Directory for further details).

Covering about 100 square metres and with obstacles to dodge around and hide behind, the outdoor paintballing course at **Umm Al Quwain Shooting Club** is a great way to let off some steam. This activity is not recommended for children under ten, and reservations should be made at least two days in advance. There is also a shooting range here. (Timings 13:00 - 21:00; closed Friday lunch and Monday; see Directory for further details).

Umm Al Quwain Aeroclub is the original aviation sports club in the Middle East. The club offers flying, skydiving, paramotors and microlights, and can also arrange ten-minute air tours, either in a Cessna or a microlight, at very reasonable prices. A trip by air is the perfect way to view the beautiful lagoons and deserted beaches of Umm Al Quwain. (See Directory for further details).

The Emirates Motorplex hosts all types of motorsport events. The Emirates Motocross Championship takes place here on a specially built track. If a high-octane buzz is right up your alley, the club can be contacted on (06) 768 1166, or keep an eye on

the local press for details of upcoming events or their website www.motorplex.ae.

Ras Al Khaimah Shooting Club

Anyone interested in making a lot of noise is welcome to visit or join Ras Al Khaimah Shooting Club. A variety of guns (from 9mm pistols to shotguns and long rifles) is available. (Timings daily 15:00 - 21:00; Friday 08:00 - 11:00 & 15:00 - 21:00; Monday closed; see Directory for further details p.315)

Tibat – Border Post

The procedure for crossing into the Mussandam is normally quite straightforward; just make sure you have the correct visas, or money to pay for the visa if you qualify for one at the border (dirhams are accepted). It usually takes about 30 minutes to get through, and your bags are searched by the Oman border guard. Alcohol, if found, may be confiscated.

The road from the border post has literally been blasted out of the side of the mountain. It hugs the very edge of the water in many places giving spectacular views of the sea.

Oman's Beaches

Take a break at one of the public beaches with spectacular views of the rocky coastline. There are sunshades provided, and you'll be impressed by how spotlessly clean the municipality keep these beaches.

Bukha Fort

As you pass through Bukha, situated in its own bay surrounded by mountains, you won't miss the impressive fort right beside the main road. For many years it guarded the town and its harbour against attack from the sea. Built in the 17th century it was restored in 1990 and is certainly the town's biggest landmark. The fort is open to visitors. The ruins of another old fort, Al Qala'a Fort, also overlook the town, but there is little left to see other than the remains of one watchtower.

Rock Carvings

At the village of Tawi, you can see prehistoric rock carvings of warriors, boats and animals. Travel about 2.3km up Wadi Quida, and the carvings are on your left on two rocks at the point where the track bends sharply to the right.

Dhow/Boat Trips

Take a boat trip to experience Khasab from the sea as well as the land - travelling by dhow provides a memorable experience, incredible views of the fjords and gets you to places even the keenest off-roader can't go.

You can hire a speedboat or dhow from the harbour at Khasab (remember to negotiate the rate before you leave, but expect to pay about Dhs.100 per hour). You are almost guaranteed to see dolphins at any time. Another way to visit the 'fjords' is via Dibba on the East Coast. See Dubai - East Coast road route (Mussandam - Dhow Charters p.38).

The dhows are slower than the speedboats, but are more stable and spacious. Allow a minimum of three hours to explore the inlet closest to Khasab and back. The following are the most common options:

Telegraph Island - In a stunning location, Telegraph Island derives its name from when the British used it as a telegraph cable station from 1864 to 1869. The ruins of the original stone buildings are still there and it's possible to land and walk around this tiny island. Rumour has it that this is where the expression 'going round the bend' comes from, since you had to go around Khor Ash to reach the Shamm Island (as it's properly called), plus it was a very lonely posting for the unfortunate souls left to man the station. Take your snorkelling gear and a picnic.

Hidden Cove - Head to the back of this inlet, behind the last small island, where there is a lovely cove for swimming and relaxing.

Kumzar Village - For a longer day trip, hire a boat to Kumzar, an ancient village set in an isolated inlet on the northern-most end of the peninsula. The scenery from the boat on the way there is fantastic and the village itself has stone houses, the ruins of an old fort and an old well. The original inhabitants even spoke their own language, Kumzari, a language uniquely related to a strange mix of Persian, English, Urdu and Baluchi. There are not many visitors here, so be discreet. there are plans to renovate the fort to its previous glory - possibly to be completed sometime during 2006.

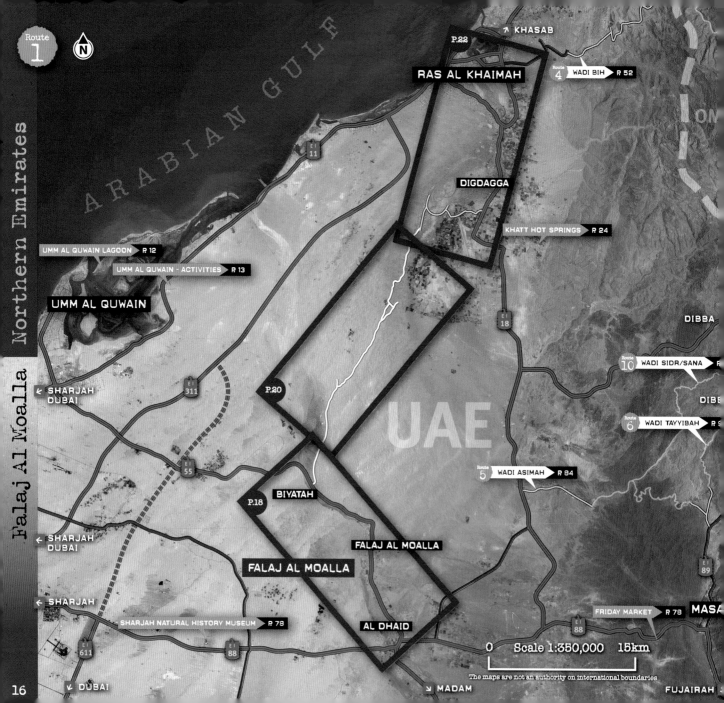

N

Northern Emirates

Falaj Al Moalla

ARABIAN GULF

ARABIAN

OM

E 11

UMM AL QUWAIN LAGOON | R 12

UMM AL QUWAIN - ACTIVITIES | R 13

UMM AL QUWAIN

↗ KHASAB

P.22

RAS AL KHAIMAH

Route 4 | WADI BIH | R 52

DIGDAGGA

KHATT HOT SPRINGS | R 24

DIBBA

E 18

Route 10 | WADI SIDR/SANA | R

DIBB

UAE

Route 6 | WADI TAYYIBAH | R 9

← SHARJAH
DUBAI

E 311

P.20

Route 5 | WADI ASIMAH | R 84

← SHARJAH
DUBAI

E 55

P.18 | **BIYATAH**

FALAJ AL MOALLA

FALAJ AL MOALLA

E 89

← SHARJAH

FRIDAY MARKET | R 78

MASA

SHARJAH NATURAL HISTORY MUSEUM | R 78

AL DHAID

E 88

E 611

E 88

0 | Scale 1:350,000 | 15km

The maps are not an authority on international boundaries

↘ DUBAI

↘ MADAM

FUJAIRAH

Falaj Al Moalla

In one of the less-driven areas of the Emirates, this is an enjoyable and tranquil sand route. After visiting the camel racetrack just outside Falaj Al Moalla you are in the desert all the way until Ras Al Khaimah. The highlight of this trip is the unexpected forest of ghaf trees just before Digdagga. If you visit during a dry period, you will it hard to believe that the ground beneath these trees becomes a carpet of green after rainfall.

Ras Al Khaimah

Dubai

Fujairah

Hatta

Abu Dhabi

Al Ain

OMAN

UAE

Arabian Gulf

Gulf of man

Terrain: Desert (tyre deflation may not be necessary)

Activities: Camping & Picnics

Trip Info

Other Names:
Falaj Al Mualla

Distances:

	Paved	Unpaved
Dubai to start of route Route	78km	–
End of route to Dubai	43.5km	27.9km
	99km	–

From Abu Dhabi: Add 300km for the round trip

Ghaf Forest

Jeep

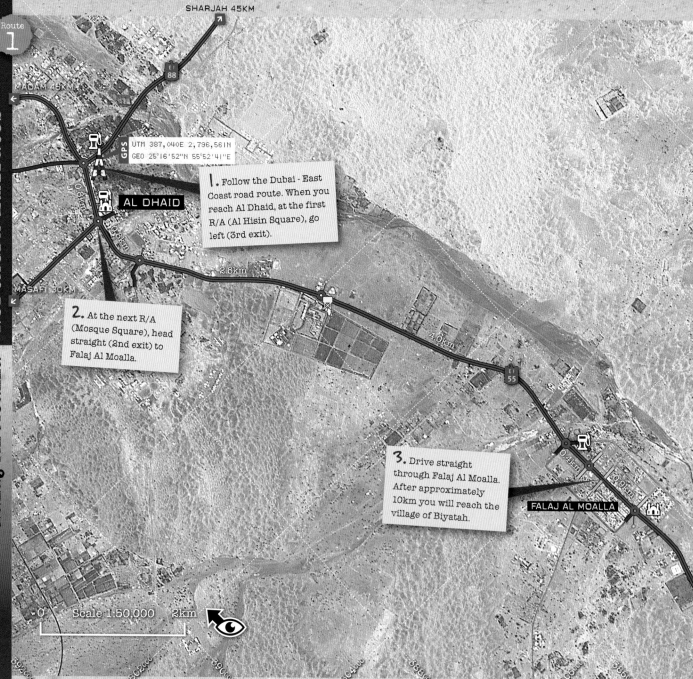

Route
1

SHARJAH 45KM

MADAM 46KM

E 88

GPS UTM 387,040E 2,796,561N
GEO 25°16'52"N 55°52'41"E

AL DHAID

MASAFI 30KM

1. Follow the Dubai - East Coast road route. When you reach Al Dhaid, at the first R/A (Al Hisin Square), go left (3rd exit).

2.6km

2. At the next R/A (Mosque Square), head straight (2nd exit) to Falaj Al Moalla.

4.0km

E 55

3. Drive straight through Falaj Al Moalla. After approximately 10km you will reach the village of Biyatah.

0.4km

0.9km

FALAJ AL MOALLA

0 Scale 1:50,000 2km

4. Almost 10km from the last roundabout in Falaj Al Moalla, turn right off the main road into the village of Biyatah. Follow the road along the front of the row of houses on your right.

5. Immediately at the end of the houses, zero your odometer and take a right. Follow the main grey track off to your left, heading for the camel racetrack.

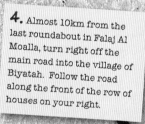

BIYATAH

UTM 378,858E 2,811,552N
GEO 25°24'57"N 55°47'43"E

GPS

9.6km

55

AL RASHIDIYA

R20

UMM AL QUWAIN 26KM

4.4km

Although this looks like the main track, it is just for access to the tower and an old farm. If you are looking for a secluded camping spot in the dunes, you could find it here.

8. At 4.6km from the end of the racetrack, take the small sand track forking off to your right and drive in a NE direction through the dunes. At the time of writing, a metal pole marked this turn, hopefully it's still there for you!

7. Smaller tracks beside the main track offer smoother driving. Just keep your eye on the main grey track and head towards the two useful landmarks; the Etisalat tower and the shed.

SH

UTM 381,074E 2,819,964N
GEO 25°29'31''N 55°49'00''E

GPS

4.6km

RED FENCE

4.4km

R/9

6. Drive alongside two parallel red fences (camel racetrack) on your left. The fence will come to an abrupt end, but keep on the gravel track. Reset your odometer at the end of the fences.

0   Scale 1:50,000   2km

12. Driving past the plantation, stay on the track heading in a northerly direction. Then, at some green fields where a track joins from the left, keep to the main track with the fields on your left.

14. At the bottom of the descent from the dunes (in sight of the red and white house), zero your odometer.

10. At the end of the 'bowl' with trees, do not take any sandy tracks off to the right or left, keep straight and level, driving parallel to the power lines on your left.

13. Follow the fence to the corner then head straight on, winding your way through the dunes. After roughly 2.5km you should see the mountains in the distance.

9. At this small fork take a right.

11. You will come to a fork in the track. Keep on the main track around to your left under the power lines.

FARM

FARM

6.4km

1.4km

1.0km

0.2km

0.5km

2.2km

7.2km

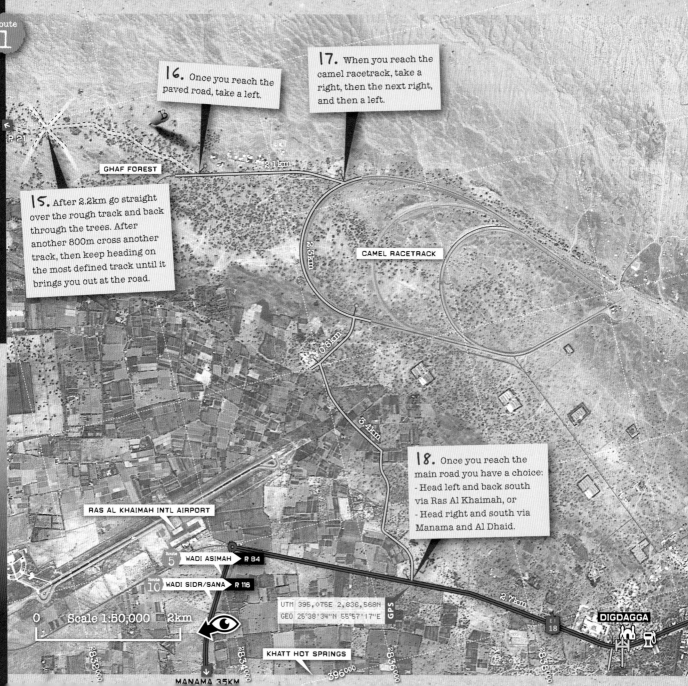

16. Once you reach the paved road, take a left.

17. When you reach the camel racetrack, take a right, then the next right, and then a left.

R 21

GHAF FOREST

2.1km

15. After 2.2km go straight over the rough track and back through the trees. After another 800m cross another track, then keep heading on the most defined track until it brings you out at the road.

2.3km

CAMEL RACETRACK

0.8km

3.4km

18. Once you reach the main road you have a choice:
- Head left and back south via Ras Al Khaimah, or
- Head right and south via Manama and Al Dhaid.

RAS AL KHAIMAH INTL AIRPORT

Route 5 WADI ASIMAH ▸ R 84

Route 10 WADI SIDR/SANA ▸ R 116

2.7km

UTM 395,075E 2,836,568N
GEO 25°38'34"N 55°57'17"E

GPS

DIGDAGGA

E 18

0   Scale 1:50,000   2km

KHATT HOT SPRINGS

MANAMA 35KM

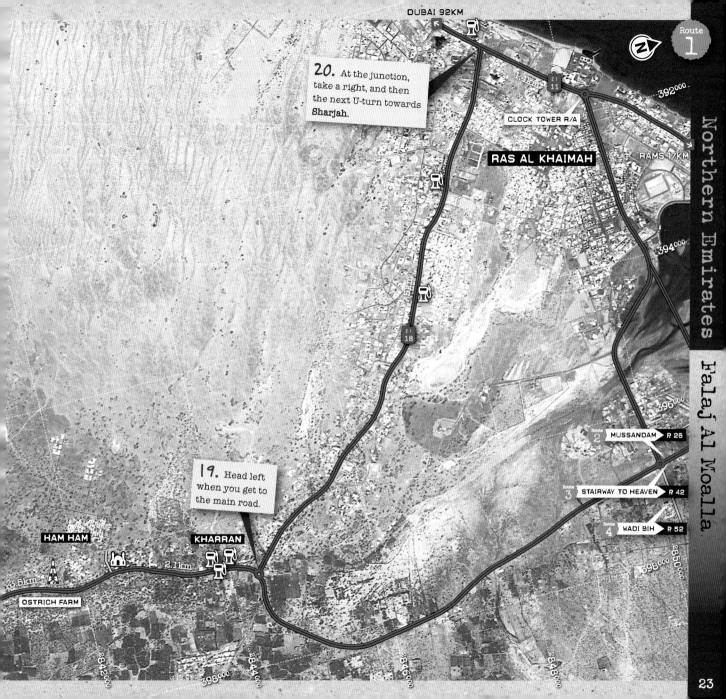

DUBAI 92KM

Route
1

Route
2 MUSSANDAM ► R 26

Route
3 STAIRWAY TO HEAVEN ► R 42

Route
4 WADI BIH ► R 52

20. At the junction, take a right, and then the next U-turn towards **Sharjah.**

CLOCK TOWER R/A

RAS AL KHAIMAH

RAMS 17KM

E I
11

E I
18

19. Head left when you get to the main road.

HAM HAM

KHARRAN

2.1km

3.5km

OSTRICH FARM

392 000

394 000

396 000

2850 000

398 000

2848 000

2842 000

398 000

2844 000

2846 000

23

Falaj Al Moalla Highlights

This is a desert route mostly on a sandy track through some dunes, although if you follow the track suggested it is straightforward and possible to go all the way without deflating your tyres. As always, it's probably best to travel out with two cars in the unlikely event that you end up getting stuck, especially if you want to do a bit of off-route exploring. If you haven't consulted the information on sand driving in the Driving section of the book, it's highly advisable to do so now! [see p.270]

In addition to wonderful desert scenery, you are also certain to encounter camels, donkeys and maybe even a glimpse of a Red Fox. Smaller various other animals and plant life are also common along this route. As you reach the outer edge of the dunes towards Ras Al Khaimah, there is an extensive forest of ghaf trees. This is a great area for a picnic or to camp, especially after rains when there's a lovely carpet of greenery under the trees.

Numerous tracks lead more or less to the same destination, so if in doubt, take the most travelled path. Basically follow your instincts, and when you see the mountains in Ras Al Khaimah, keep heading for the steepest, most northern part.

Camel Racetrack

Although used less now than in the past, you may get to see the camels going through their paces, training for their big day.

Camping - Ghaf Forest

Along the route, ghaf trees are good for picnics, camping or resting. Although not visible, there's obviously a reasonable supply of underground water to allow all these trees to survive.

Flora and Fauna

The forests of ghaf trees begin here and after good rains the area becomes incredibly green. On the right there's a large red and white house visible on top of a dune, and from here you'll find ideal places for picnics and camping. A wonderful aspect of the bare sand is the striking contrast it makes with the homes and tracks of the various desert creatures. Check carefully around your chosen site for the holes of gerbils, scorpions and ants. The plant life here is also fascinating.

Khatt Hot Springs

Soaking in the natural hot springs is the perfect way to rejuvenate, surrounded by palm trees with views of the mountains. The water in the segregated pools is around 40°C and is said to contain therapeutic minerals. A new five-star spa hotel opened here at the end of 2005. The Khatt Springs Hotel & Spa (www.khatthotel.com) offers guests more traditional and oriental treatments alongside the healing qualities of the waters, as well as massage, steam rooms and saunas.

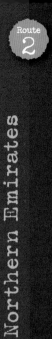

Route **2**

N

ARABIAN GULF

GULF OF OMAN

P.28

MUSSANDAM

DHOW TRIP ▸ R 14

KHASAB

OMAN'S BEACHES ▸ R 14

P.34

SHAMS

P.30

OMAN

Route **3** STAIRWAY TO HEAVEN ▸ R 42

11

RAMS

UAE

P.32

RAS AL KHAIMAH

↙ DUBAI

Route **4** WADI BIH ▸ R 52

↓ AL DHAID

↓ DIBBA

0   Scale 1:350,000   15km

The maps are not an authority on international boundaries

Mussandam

Dramatic and unspoilt with breathtaking natural scenery. This trip will take you all the way from the 'fjords' up to nearly 2,000m at the top of the pass. At sea level, the dhow trips and regular dolphin sightings are the main attractions. Once in the mountains, you can enjoy temperatures a healthy 8°C cooler than on the coast, so camping throughout the summer months is still almost pleasant. This is easily one of the most rewarding routes in the region and, surprisingly, only about 180kms away from Dubai.

Terrain: Coastal, Fjords, Mountains
Water: Sea.
Driving: 2 Wheel Drive Possible
Activities: Dhow/Boat Trip, Camping, Diving, Hiking, Snorkelling
Warnings: Not a circular route!
Oman Car Insurance,
Oman Visa

Trip Info

Other Names: Khasab, Musandam, Musandam Peninsula

Distances:

	Paved	Unpaved
Dubai to start of route	186km	–
Route (Round Trip)	6.6km	148.6km
End of route to Dubai	186km	–

From Abu Dhabi: Add 300 km for the round trip

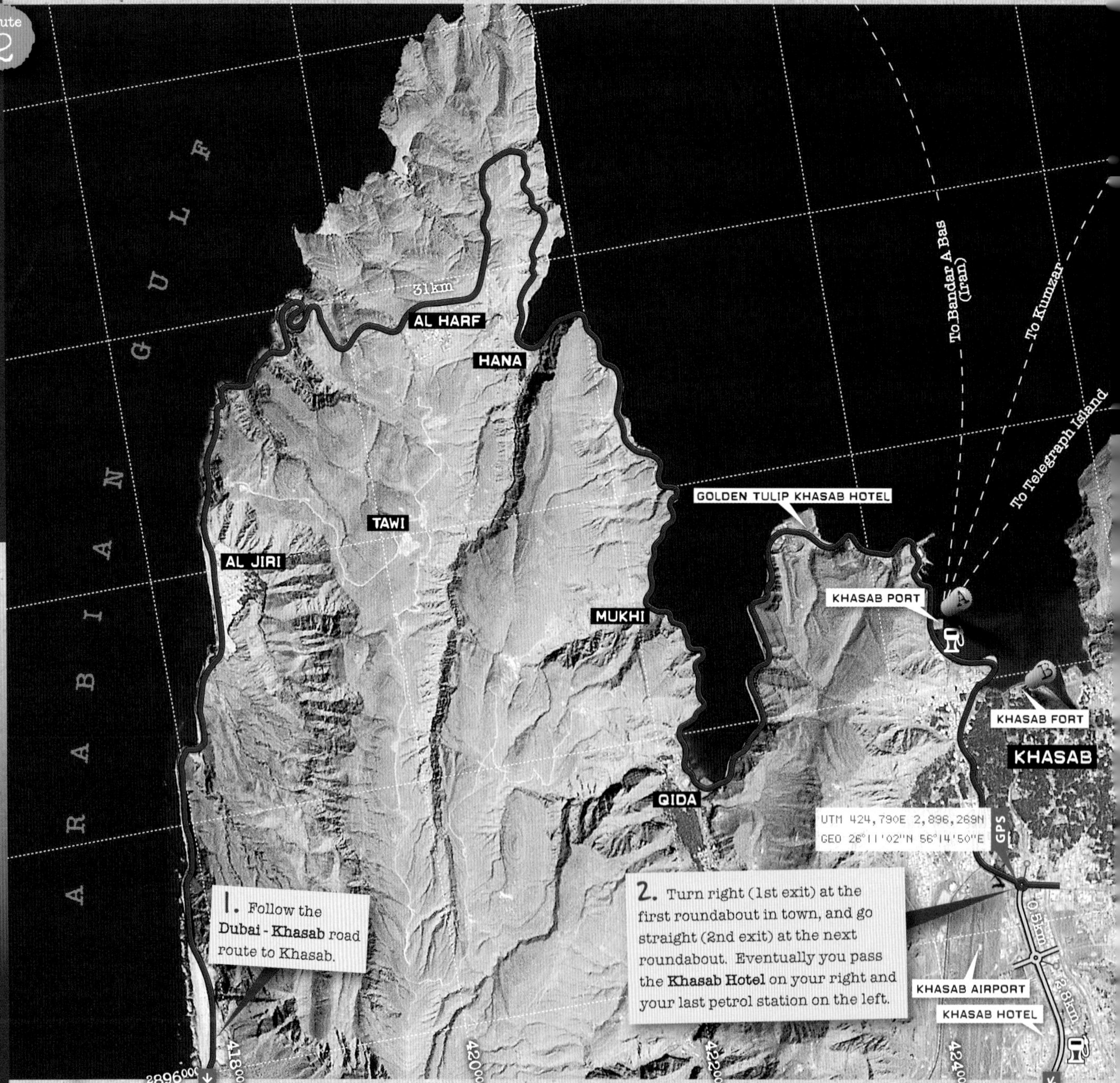

31km

AL HARF

HANA

TAWI

AL JIRI

MUKHI

QIDA

GOLDEN TULIP KHASAB HOTEL

KHASAB PORT

KHASAB FORT

KHASAB

To Bandar A Bas (Iran)

To Kumzar

To Telegraph Island

GULF

ARABIAN

UTM 424,790E 2,896,269N
GEO 26°11'02"N 56°14'50"E

GPS

KHASAB AIRPORT

KHASAB HOTEL

1. Follow the **Dubai - Khasab** road route to Khasab.

2. Turn right (1st exit) at the first roundabout in town, and go straight (2nd exit) at the next roundabout. Eventually you pass the **Khasab Hotel** on your right and your last petrol station on the left.

SHAMS/UAE BORDER 19KM - R 2

2896 000   418 000   420 000   422 000   424 000

R 30

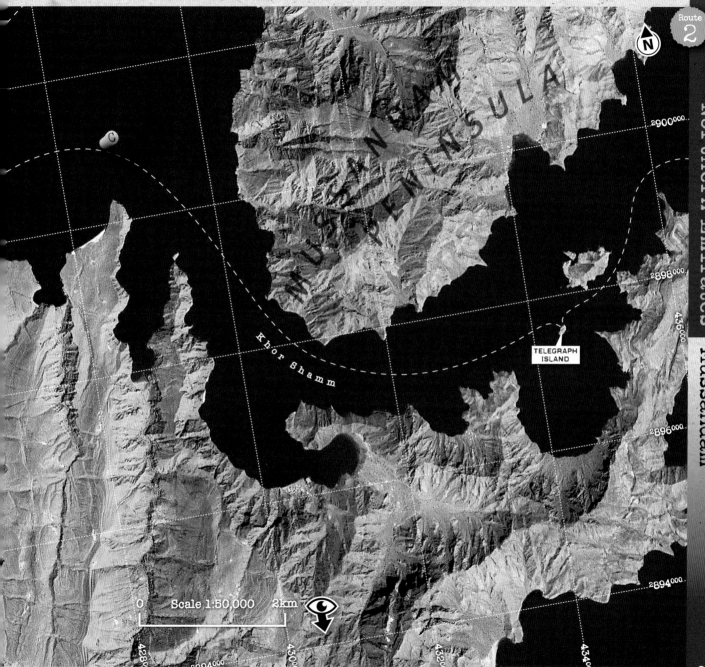

MUSANDAM

MUSSANDAM PENINSULA

C

Khor Shamm

TELEGRAPH
ISLAND

2900000

2898000

2896000

2894000

436000

434000

432000

430000

428000

2894000

N

0   Scale 1:50,000   2km

R34

K+L. For a great **diversion**, at the junction approximately 8 km from the T-junction, take the left turn signposted to **Wadi Sal Al A'la** (P.34) and drive up the wide wadi bed. You will be returning to this junction later to return to **Khasab** or to drive to the summit of Jebel As Sayh.

UTM 425,847E 2,885,634N
GEO 26°05'16"N 56°15'30"E
GPS

4.2km

Wadi Sal Al A'la

Wadi Khasab

8.4km

DAM

Wadi Khasab

R28

3. Take a left at the **T-junction** where the graded track begins and drive up **Wadi Khasab**, past the dam. Follow the signs to **Dabba** (ie. Dibba in the UAE). Now relax - **Jebel As Sayh** (the highest point in the Mussandam and the UAE), is over 30 km away!

0   Scale 1:50,000   2km

2894000

2892000

2890000

2888000

2886000

420000

15.2km

P32

4. Follow the main track which passes through the **Sayh Plateau.**

424⁰⁰⁰

422⁰⁰⁰

420⁰⁰⁰

418⁰⁰⁰

2884⁰⁰⁰

2882⁰⁰⁰

2880⁰⁰⁰

2878⁰⁰⁰

2876⁰⁰⁰

418⁰⁰⁰

BA'NEH

6. Unfortunately, you cannot drive right to the summit, but once through the small cutting, you start a scenic 17 km descent into **Wadi Bih**, **Wadi Khab Al Shamis** and the A'Rowdhah bowl.
You will probably be returning to this point (see direction 8)

2087m
MILITARY INSTALLATION

Jebel As Sayh

5. Head left at this junction and head up towards the military area. For an impressive viewpoint on the way up, just before the row of diesel generators take a sharp right up to a helipad. From here you will have spectacular vistas over Wadi Bih, Wadi Khab Al Shamis and the A'Rowdhah bowl.

2.8km

R31

SAYH

1.5km

3.4km

0.7km

GPS
UTM 420,459E 2,871,098N
GEO 25°57'23"N 56°12'19"E

E. When you see a track heading up the mountain on your right, just as the road curves around and down to the left, park your car for a quick walk up for some dramatic views over **Ras Al Khaimah** and the 'Stairway to Heaven' (p.42) hike.

OMAN

route
3
STAIRWAY TO HEAVEN   R 42

1680m

1.4km

COOL VIEW

UAE

1930m
Jebel Bil Aysh

A' ROWDHAH

424⁰⁰⁰

422⁰⁰⁰

8. At the Omani check point this is usually the end of the line where you will have to turn around and retrace your steps back via Khasab. Some people try to talk their way through, but it's unlikely as the officials have no way of processing exits from Oman back into the UAE.

Wadi Bih

8.4km

7. In the wadi bed at the bottom of the hill it's decision time. Take a sharp left (north) for **Ba'neh**, a left (east) for **A'Rowdhah**, or head straight around to your right (south) down the wadi bed towards **Wadi Bih**.

0.5km 0.6km
0.7km

DIBBA 43KM

OMANI CHECK POINT

420⁰⁰⁰

Route 4 WADI BIH ► R 52

RAS AL KHAIMAH 42KM

418⁰⁰⁰

0 Scale 1:50,000 2km

The maps are not an authority on international boundaries

2864⁰⁰⁰ 2862⁰⁰⁰ 2860⁰⁰⁰ 2858⁰⁰⁰ 2856⁰⁰⁰

K. For the only **beach** accessible by car in the fjords, take a left just past the military firing range and aim for the spectacular track carved out of the side of the mountains, running up on your left. This is sign posted **Khawr Najd** (Khor Najd, ie. creek).

Khor Najd

RIFLE RANGE

P 30

UTM 430,700E 2,884,058N
GEO 26°04'26"N 56°18'25"E

GPS

0.8km   0.8km   1.4km   0.4km

1.7km

Wadi Sal Al A'la

2.5km

1.0km

1.1km

2km

AL KHALIDIYA

L. Heading further up the wadi (4km) leads to a pleasant surprise - an **acacia forest** at the end on your right (to the south).

ACACIA FOREST

0   Scale 1:50,000   2km

428000   430000   2880000   432000   434000

34

N

L AL A'LA

GULF OF OMAN

2884000

2882000

2880000

2878000

2878000

438000

440000

442000

444000

446000

Mussandam Highlights

Many explorers familiar with this area would agree that a visit to the Mussandam Peninsula is the most rewarding trip that you can make during your time in the UAE. The mountains gain altitude here, then drop magnificently into the Strait of Hormuz. As well as enjoying some of the most breathtaking natural scenery in the region, you can visit ancient settlements (many of which are still inhabited), discover rock carvings and abandoned tombs, or snorkel with dolphins and sea turtles.

The Mussandam is carved predominantly out of limestone. Millions of years ago, this entire area was under the sea. It was forced up when the rocky plates collided, to form the Zagros Mountains in Iran and the cliffs of the Mussandam on the other side of the deepened Gulf. This happened long before the volcanic formation of the Hajar Mountains. Geological measurements have shown that the Mussandam coast is sinking at a rate of about 0.5cm a year. An unusual consequence of this is that fresh spring water that emerged on land centuries ago now bubbles up underneath the sea. There are reports that 14th century sailors would dive into the sea to bring up leather bags filled with fresh water from the seabed!

Not far from Khasab in Wadi Sal Al A'la, a road winds over to a lovely beach at Khor Najd. You can also climb the road to the plateau beneath Jebel As Sayh (Jebel Harim), the highest peak in the Mussandam at 2,087m. Both places are excellent for camping and to use as a base for further exploration.

See the Dubai – Khasab road route for details of requirements for this trip.

> ## Note
> This is not a circular route. Bear this in mind as you travel further away from Khasab. People have tried to talk their way through the border post in Wadi Bih (which would allow quick and easy access back to either Ras Al Khaimah or Dibba), but this is highly unlikely so you will have to retrace your steps to Khasab and through the border at Tibat to return to the UAE.

Khasab Port

Observing the general activity at the port can prove fascinating. With Iran only 45km across the water from Khasab, there is a regular flow of camouflaged, high-powered Iranian speedboats smuggling cigarettes to Bandar-e Abbas, the busiest port in Iran, just the other side of the Strait of Hormuz.

Khasab Fort

Unless you are a serious history buff Khasab Fort is nothing special, but its setting, dominating the coastline near the older

part of Khasab, is impressive. Best seen from the sea, its design and structure make it similar to forts in the rest of Northern Oman. You can see it clearly as you enter the bay. (Timings: roughly Sat - Wed 07:30 - 14:30; admission RO 0.500/Dhs.5)

Dhow/Boat Trips

Take a boat trip to experience Khasab from the sea as well as the land – travelling by dhow provides a memorable experience, incredible views of the fjords and gets you to places even the keenest off-roader can't go.

You can hire a speedboat or dhow from the harbour at Khasab (remember to negotiate the rate before you leave, but expect to pay about Dhs.100 per hour). You are almost guaranteed to see dolphins at any time. Another way to visit the 'fjords' is via Dibba on the East Coast. See Dubai - East Coast road route (Mussandam - Dhow Charters).

The dhows are slower than the speedboats, but are more stable and spacious. Allow a minimum of three hours to explore the inlet closest to Khasab and back. The following are the most common options:

Telegraph Island - In a stunning location, Telegraph Island derives its name from when the British used it as a telegraph cable station from 1864 to 1869. The ruins of the original stone buildings are still there and it's possible to disembark and walk around this tiny island. Rumour has it that this is where the expression 'going round the bend' comes from, since you had to go around Khor Ash to reach the Shamm Island (as it's properly called), plus it was a very lonely posting for the unfortunate souls left to man the station. Take your snorkelling gear and a picnic.

Hidden Cove - Head to the back of this inlet, behind the last small island, where there is a lovely cove for swimming and relaxing. You can also walk up and over the mountains to see the Gulf of Oman.

Kumzar Village - For a longer day trip, hire a dhow to Kumzar, (or an hour on a speedboat), an ancient village set in an isolated inlet on the northern-most end of the peninsula. The scenery from the boat on the way there is fantastic and the village itself has stone houses, the ruins of an old fort and an old well. The original inhabitants even spoke their own language, Kumzari, a language uniquely related to a strange mix of Persian, English, Urdu and Baluchi. There are not many visitors here, so be discreet. there are plans to renovate the fort to its previous glory – possibly to be completed sometime during 2006.

Sayh Plateau

After occasional rains this area is delightfully green and lush. Fences mark off various plots on this fertile plateau, and all the way along the wadi there are small settlements and houses. If you keep your eyes open, you will spot some houses built precipitously into the side of the rock. It can be difficult to distinguish where nature ends and the man-made begins!

Viewpoint towards the Arabian Gulf

Just a 40 minute walk from the main track, this is a must-see view Park at the base of this rough track (recently blocked off for vehicles) and continue up the steep hill on foot. The track bears right and then travels gently downhill before it ends. From this point, continue walking in a north-westerly direction (i.e. to the left) across the shallow wadi that lies to your left and up towards the small mound in front. After 20 minutes you will reach the most astounding view.

Unexpectedly, you will feel as though you have the rest of the world' spread out before you! Alternatively, where the track bends to your right, head up left to the summit of Jebel Bil' Aysh for views over Wadi Bih, RAK and the new 'chalets' at the top of RAK's new mountain tourism development project.

Camping at Altitude

This is a wonderful area to camp, especially during the hotter months. You are roughly 1,600m above sea level and temperatures overnight are markedly cooler than on the coast (by about 8°C) and, dare one say, comfortable! As always, be sensitive; if this flattened area looks like it is being cultivated, camp elsewhere – suitable sites are easy to find.

Then take out your barbecue and shisha, and settle in for the night. Shooting stars abound at certain times of the year, particularly during August.

Petroglyphs (Rock Carvings)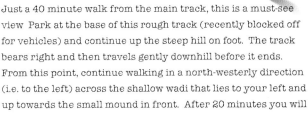

Take this last track before the fenced off area belonging to the military; it's just a short drive up to where you can park the car by the helipad. Hop out and admire the view over the expanse of mountains towards Wadi Bih – you can often see Jebel Qihwi (1,792m), looming in the distance. Look carefully where you put your feet, as there is a petroglyph on one of the flat rocks at the top. See if you can spot any others.

Northern Emirates Mussandam

Rock carvings can be found in many locations around the UAE, often on single rocks or on rocks forming cairns. They reflect a nomadic lifestyle, often depicting animals and hunting.

One of the earliest archaeological discoveries in the country was the main tomb at Hili near Al Ain, at what is now the Hili Archaeological Garden. The large tomb of the Umm An-Nar type has been beautifully restored to display petroglyphs depicting oryx, and two cheetahs feeding on a gazelle.

Military Zone

Unfortunately, you cannot access the actual summit, as it is a restricted military zone. The large globe can give quite an eerie, spaceship-like effect, especially at night.

Towards Rowdah Bowl

The superb views continue on the journey down the other side of the wadi. Deep gorges, long ridges, picturesque fields and small, old villages abound.

Wadi Bih

Just before the end of the line at the border post, there is an old graveyard that may be of interest. You can also explore the wadi bed and follow the signs to A' Rowdhah to find a good spot for a picnic before continuing your journey back to Khasab.

Khor Najd Beach

A great view awaits you as you come over the crest of the hill. This is a good spot to camp as there are shaded areas, as well as a tank of fresh water. Although the beach is a little muddy and pebbly, a swim is still very refreshing. Don't be alarmed if a turtle pops up near you to take a breath!

Acacia Forest

As you drive along, everything seems barren and dry, and you will feel like you might have to do a U-turn in a dusty, abandoned village. However, although the road does eventually peter out, it does so right at an acacia 'forest'. As it's rare to see more than two or three trees grouped together in this part of the world, make the most of this glorious place – it's perfect for camping because of the shade. Here again, there is a water tank and also a play area for kids.

Acacia Forest

Khor Najd

N

ARABIAN GULF

KHASAB

<... >

Route
2 MUSSANDAM R 26

SHAMS

P.44

GHALILAH

STAIRWAY TO HEAVEN

OMAN

RAMS

E 11

RAS AL KHAIMAH

E 11

Route
4 WADI BIH R 52

UAE

GULF OF OMAN

0   Scale 1:350,000   15km

The maps are not an authority on international boundaries

↙ DUBAI   FUJAIRAH ↓

Stairway to Heaven

Taking you from sea level up to 1,930m, this is a phenomenal 8-12 hour hike involving considerable physical challenge. The 'stairway' you will climb was built by the Shihu tribe and requires a good head for heights, especially along the exposed ledges. To tackle this hike you need perseverance, stamina & luck, and it is ESSENTIAL to do it for the first time with someone who knows the route inside out. Your reward will be great views of the entire area and a whopping sense of achievement!

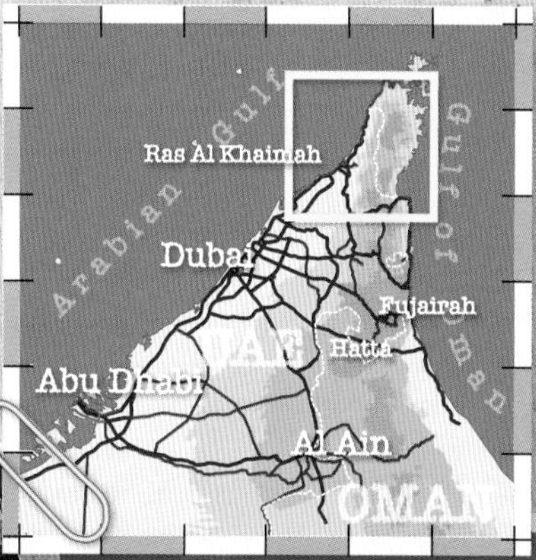

Terrain: Cliffs, Mountains, Wadis

Activities: Climbing, Hiking

Warning: Long and extremely strenuous hike, exposed in places

Trip Info

Other Names:
Wadi Ghalilah, Wadi Litibah

Distances:

	Paved	Unpaved
Dubai to start of route	134km	–
Route		
Hike	17.4km	4.6km
End of route to Dubai	11km	–
	134km	–

From Abu Dhabi: Add 300 km for the round trip

Jeep

43

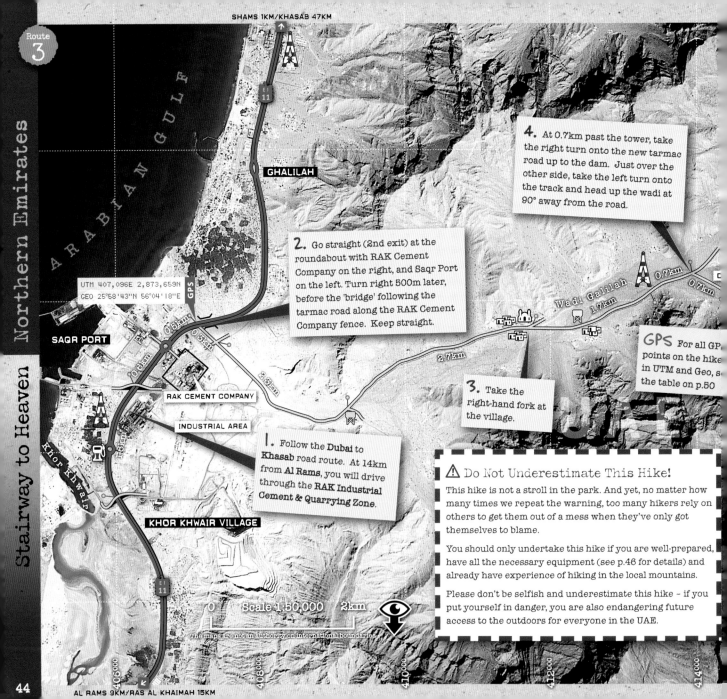

SHAMS 1KM/KHASAB 47KM

E 11

GHALILAH

UTM 407,096E 2,873,659N
GEO 25°58'43"N 56°04'18"E

GPS

SAQR PORT

Khor Khwair

RAK CEMENT COMPANY

INDUSTRIAL AREA

KHOR KHWAIR VILLAGE

Wadi Galilah   0.7km   0.7km

0.05km   0.5km   1.45km   0.6km   1.9km   2.5km   2.7km   1.7km

4. At 0.7km past the tower, take the right turn onto the new tarmac road up to the dam. Just over the other side, take the left turn onto the track and head up the wadi at 90° away from the road.

2. Go straight (2nd exit) at the roundabout with RAK Cement Company on the right, and Saqr Port on the left. Turn right 500m later, before the 'bridge' following the tarmac road along the RAK Cement Company fence. Keep straight.

GPS For all GPS points on the hike in UTM and Geo, see the table on p.50

3. Take the right-hand fork at the village.

1. Follow the **Dubai** to **Khasab** road route. At 14km from **Al Rams**, you will drive through the **RAK Industrial Cement & Quarrying Zone**.

⚠ Do Not Underestimate This Hike!

This hike is not a stroll in the park. And yet, no matter how many times we repeat the warning, too many hikers rely on others to get them out of a mess when they've only got themselves to blame.

You should only undertake this hike if you are well-prepared, have all the necessary equipment (see p.46 for details) and already have experience of hiking in the local mountains.

Please don't be selfish and underestimate this hike – if you put yourself in danger, you are also endangering future access to the outdoors for everyone in the UAE.

0   Scale 1:50,000   2km

The maps are not an authority on international boundaries

E 11

ARABIAN GULF

AL RAMS 9KM/RAS AL KHAIMAH 15KM

5. After 2.3km on the track, we recommend that you park your car on the left, well before the inhabited houses. Some of the people living here seem unhappy to see strangers, and hence it is best to keep a low profile. There have been a couple of incidents in the past, further up the wadi, of parked cars being vandalised. It's a good idea to remove all valuables from your car and to lower the radio aerial.

6. Follow the track into the wadi until you come across a two-storey stone house up on your left at the end of the track, nestled at the bottom of the cliff. This is where the hike (and the pain!) begins.

OMAN

MUSSANDAM ▶ R 26

SAYH

2876 000

19 GPS UTM 418,656E 2,874,617N

1100m

UTM 417,517E 2,874,054N GPS 10

23 GPS UTM 419,034E 2,874,024N

Wadi Litibah

UTM 416,759E 2,874,227N GPS 1

UTM 418,134E 2,873,770N GPS 13

Jebel As Sayh

2874 000

2087m

MILITARY INSTALLATION

UTM 417,289E 2,873,200N GPS 30

Vertical Drop

24 GPS UTM 418,875E 2,872,816N

1680m

UTM 416,718E 2,872,536N GPS 29

UTM 417,151E 2,872,295N GPS 26

2872 000

Line only intended as a rough reference. Use GPS table

UTM 418,300E 2,870,800N GPS 25

⚠ Although this hike comes close in places to tracks in Mussandam (Route 2 p. 26) and looks like a great escape route for those who want to quit the route proper, this will only take you into Oman with no way of getting back into the UAE (due to passport and visa problems), so it is best to stick to the route or retrace your steps.

1930m

Jebel Bil 'Aysh

2870 000

Stairway to Heaven Highlights

This is surely the most spectacular, breathtaking and awe-inspiring hike in the country! However, from the outset, it must be stressed that this is a very, very serious hike that includes sections of exposed ledges. As in any mountainous terrain, temperatures and weather conditions can vary greatly, adding to the difficulty of the trek.

The mountain areas are still extremely tribal, even retaining the old custom of requesting permission to pass through another tribe's territory in places. Ancient tribes include the Hamous, Bani Shimaili and the Shihu. On this particular route, it is the Shihu who have constructed an intricate trail up a vertical rock face. Some of the stairways are masterpieces of stonework, but the exposure is terrific. It's hard to comprehend that this used to be the normal way up to the village on the plateau from the valley.

If you decide to tackle the walk in its entirety (8 - 12 hours), you must study the directions very carefully and definitely take a GPS receiver with you. As a minimum requirement, you should be very fit and active, with plenty of stamina and a good head for heights. Take plenty of water, food and suitable equipment (including, depending on the season, waterproofs and warm clothing, since it can be very cold at the top). It is strongly recommended to do the trip in a group, and with someone who knows the route.

Warning!

It cannot be overstated how serious this hike is – increasing numbers of people have been caught out by the exposure and severity of the staircase, the potential change in weather conditions between the bottom and the top and the extreme length of the hike. Some people have had to stay overnight on the summit, due to being completely unprepared. And in extreme cases, some have required the help of the Ras Al Khaimah Police helicopter. This is a hike for the big boys (and girls!), and should not be attempted by novices.

As well as definitely being best to do it with someone who knows the route, make sure your group has at least one GPS, carry plenty of water (at least three litres per person) and enough warm clothing and food to keep you going. Strong boots are absolutely essential, and make sure everyone knows what they are undertaking! The full hike can take 12 hours in some cases, which means in winter this will be longer than a full day of daylight. Therefore you must try to stick to the timings given in the route description to ensure you finish the route in before sunset.

↙ The final staircase

Stairway to Heaven

The hike mainly follows the old Shihu trail up to an inhabited village at around 1,100m, then up to the summit at around 1,930m Part of this trail, which is still occasionally used by people living in the village, heads up a 200m rock wall. This wall involves some rock climbing and considerable exposure – definitely not for the faint-hearted! The rest of the walk is steep in places, but straightforward. People who are not interested in the entire hike may enjoy a 'stroll' up the wadi; however, even for this you will need appropriate walking boots and plenty of water.

Hiking in the UAE is completely different to what most people expect or are used to. There are hardly any established tracks, apart from either goat trails or rough paths between settlements, and there is often little shade or relief from the constant sun. Rocks and boulders are sharp and often unstable, the general terrain often heavily eroded and shattered due to the harsh climate, and so much of the time is spent watching where you are walking. In addition, no signposts, combined with a lack of distinguishable features, can make it difficult to orientate yourself. However, having said this, once you become more experienced and accustomed to the local environment, your perceptions change, and you will find it easier to recognise different rocks and trees, and simpler to navigate.

If you would like to do the hike in experienced company, Explorer Publishing organises one or two trips up to do the hike every year – depending on demand – in the winter season. For more info on these trips, get in touch with us at Hiking@Explorer-Publishing.com.

NB: For a trip that caters to all tastes, send the hikers up 'Stairway' while the others drive to Khasab and loop around, meeting up at the top for a camp with fantastic views. Visas are required for Khasab.

Into Wadi Litibah

Initially follow the path on the right-hand side of the wadi, close to the side of the cliff. Look out for the old Shihu trail, which you can recognise by the dark, polished rocks. When you reach a boulder slope on the right (opposite an obvious cleft in the left-hand cliff wall), go almost straight up the slope, heading towards the upper two trees 100m above the track. Look out for the first staircase, just above the trees, heading up to your left.

You will then reach a sort of plateau. You may lose the path, but persevere! Head diagonally up to your left, towards a pathetic lone tree. Follow the ridge path around to a bushy tree, behind which you will see a layered rock face with stone stairs. Go up to your left around the edge.

Follow the trail high above the wadi floor, then head for a distinctive gravel mound on your right beneath the cliff face. Soon you will reach the junction of gullies at the end of Wadi Litibah. (Time ~ 1½ hours.)

Wadi Junction/Scree Slope

Now you will be completely surrounded by magnificent, towering, and seemingly unscalable rock faces. The ascent is up the scree slope to your left, aiming for the base of the cliff in the distance.

Head straight across the wadi to the tree on the left, nestled near the cliff just above the wadi bed. The track starts from under the tree and proceeds up to the right. Patience and careful observation will reveal the Shihu trail. The trail first ascends diagonally to the right and then back left, up above a very large square boulder.

Don't panic if you lose the trail, just follow the line of least resistance more or less straight up the scree and boulder slope to its highest point. Now keep to your right towards the trees, and head even higher onto the finer scree slope, which is directly above the main gully you have been following for the last hour. (Time ~ 1½ hour.)

The Stairway

From the top of the scree slope, traverse left along the upper ledge for about 100--150m, until you reach a man-made stone stairway doubling back on yourself, which you will ascend. The start of the ascent is not difficult to miss as the path continues straight after the start of the staircase, so keep turning back regularly after 100m to check back and make sure you haven't missed it. When you do find it, follow the black polished marks on the rocks up to the left, eventually ascending a large slab of rock after about 100m. There is an exposed step over a gap in the ledge, and then shortly after, another stone stairway. From here the route follows a series of ledges and stairways to the right.

Actually finding the stairway and following the 'path' at this point may prove quite difficult, and you might have to walk back and forth along ledges searching for the way up. Just keep trying, the trail really is there and it's worth the effort! Looking for man-made 'stairs' of rock is not made any easier by

being so close to the rock face or by the fact that there is fallen rock everywhere. However, after finding the first staircase it does get easier.

It is recommended that you:

• Look out for the 'famous' trees, keeping close under them.
• Stay as close to the cliff face as possible.
• Look out for polished black marks on the stones.
• Look out for man-made stone staircases.
• Choose the route of least resistance.

(Time ~ 1½ hours – depending on confidence/photographs.)

Roof of the World

At the top of the rock wall is a small, inhabited settlement and a large, flat cultivated area. The views from here back down the cliff and across to the huge rock wall at the head of the valley are spectacular. This is a great place for a rest. There are also good views of the route up Bil Aysh on the other side of the valley, which is an alternative descent for the intrepid hiker.

Up or Down?

After a good rest you basically have two options:

1. Descend the way you came up – but be very careful, as going down is much trickier than going up and some sections require 'down-climbing', rather than just a simple hike down. For some people the exposure has much more effect on the way down, so take your time. (Time ~ 3 hrs).

2. Alternatively, you can continue along the full route (another 6 - 8 hours). To complete the hike, turn right at the top of the staircase, following the edge of the cliff, but moving uphill and heading for the closest peak. Follow the curve of the cliff, then branch off left until you reach a ruined stone hut on the peak of Jebel Bil 'Aysh (1930m) – an excellent point for a breather. To the south-east, Jebel As Sayh(2,087m), with its radar station perched on top, dominates the skyline.

Now head in a north-easterly direction to go back down into the wadi. Walk to the right of the deserted settlement on the edge of the cliff, down a scree slope with large boulders (the left route is very steep), heading for the two cultivated areas that you can see below. Carry on down until you reach the point where you branched off the wadi to climb the first scree slope, point B. You're now on the home stretch – just retrace your steps down the wadi to your car.

NB. If you need a quick way down from the top but can't face descending the staircase, there is an easier route if you turn left upon reaching the top. Although it involves some steep sections with down-climbing in some places, compared to the stairway it takes you down a more gradual trail back around under the cliff edge to the top of the scree slope, point B. However, finding the path can be tricky, so you're on your own!

Waypoints

ID	UTM	Geo	Alt.	Note
1	416,759E 2,874,224N	25°59'03"N 56°10'06"E	241	Start/end of route
2	416,952E 2,874,215N	25°59'03"N 56°10'13"E	256	
3	417,211E 2,874,166N	25°59'03"N 56°10'22"E	320	
4	417,238E 2,874,135N	25°59'01"N 56°10'23"E	346	
5	417,286E 2,874,083N	25°58'59"N 56°10'25"E	370	
6	417,293E 2,874,040N	25°58'58"N 56°10'25"E	387	
7	417,336E 2,874,032N	25°58'57"N 56°10'26"E	396	
8	417,379E 2,873,993N	25°58'56"N 56°10'28"E	403	Start of W.Litibah
9	417,502E 2,874,041N	25°58'58"N 56°10'32"E	422	
10	417,517E 2,874,054N	25°58'58"N 56°10'33"E	432	
11	417,844E 2,873,905N	25°58'53"N 56°10'45"E	431	
12	417,959E 2,873,797N	25°58'50"N 56°10'49"E	464	
13	418,134E 2,873,770N	25°58'49"N 56°10'55"E	490	
14	418,362E 2,874,117N	25°59'00"N 56°11'03"E	711	
15	418,432E 2,874,297N	25°59'06"N 56°11'06"E	820	
16	418,557E 2,874,288N	25°59'06"N 56°11'10"E	860	

Waypoints

ID	UTM	Geo	Alt.	Note
17	418,592E 2,874,413N	25°59'10"N 56°11'12"E	934	
18	418,593E 2,874,621N	25°59'17"N 56°11'12"E	1,079	
19	418,656E 2,874,617N	25°59'17"N 56°11'14"E	1,133	Roof of the World
20	418,717E 2,874,562N	25°59'15"N 56°11'16"E	1,134	
21	418,744E 2,874,528N	25°59'14"N 56°11'17"E	1,146	
22	418,680E 2,874,492N	25°59'13"N 56°11'15"E	1,236	
23	419,034E 2,874,024N	25°58'57"N 56°11'28"E	1,338	
24	418,875E 2,872,816N	25°58'18"N 56°11'22"E	1,680	1st Peak
25	418,300E 2,870,800N	25°57'13"N 56°11'02"E	1,930	Top of Jebel Bil 'Aysh
26	417,151E 2,872,295N	25°58'01"N 56°10'20"E	1,459	Small village
27	419,077E 2,872,836N	25°58'19"N 56°11'29"E	1,719	Small village
28	416,740E 2,872,428N	25°58'05"N 56°10'05"E	1,428	
29	416,718E 2,872,536N	25°58'09"N 56°10'05"E	1,418	Cliff edge - Down
30	417,269E 2,873,200N	25°58'30"N 56°11'16"E	989	1st Plateau
31	417,651E 2,873,205N	25°58'31"N 56°10'38"E	799	2nd Plateau
32	417,897E 2,873,378N	25°58'36"N 56°10'47"E	647	

*UTM Co-ordinates - WGS84 datum, UTM Zone 40R, Units metres, Height derived from altimeter

[After No. 32, See 13 -> 1 for the way back...]

√ Spectacular ledge descent

N

↑ KHASAB

ARABIAN GULF

OMAN

Route 3 STAIRWAY TO HEAVEN P. 42

RAMS

Route 2 MUSSANDAM P. 26

Northern Emirates

RAS AL KHAIMAH

P. 56

WADI BIH

P. 54

EI 11

P. 58

DREAMLAND P. 13

↙ DUBAI

Wadi Bih

DIGDAGGA

DIBBA BEACH P. 67

↙ DUBAI

DIBBA

KHATT HOT SPRINGS P. 24

UAE

EI 18

ROAD TO RAK P. 82

GULF OF OMAN

EI 99

Route 10 WADI SIDR/SANA P. 116

EI 89

Route 6 WADI TAYYIBAH P. 90

0   Scale 1:350,000   15km

The maps are not an authority on international boundaries.

↓ MASAFI

↓ MASAFI

FUJAIRAH ↓

Wadi Bih

Rising to a spectacular 1,000m, Wadi Bih is considered to be the 'Grand Canyon' of the UAE. This coast-to-coast route is simply one of the most dramatic drives in the country. You actually pass through two wadis, each with their own distinct feel; Wadi Bih on the West Coast and the narrower Wadi Khab Al Shamis on the East Coast. Over recent years, this trip has become easier as the route is now tarmac all the way to the emirati checkpoint. Look forward to majestic views and the outdoors at its best.

Terrain:	Coastal, Mountains, Wadis
Water:	Sea
Driving:	2 Wheel Drive Possible
Activities:	Camping, Climbing, Mountain Biking, Hiking, Snorkelling
Warnings:	Impassable after heavy rains, Oman Car Insurance, Original passports required!

Trip Info

Other Names: Wadi Beh / Byh, Wadi Khab Al Shamis

Distances:

	Paved	Unpaved
Dubai to start of route	98km	-
Route	37.7km	54km
End of route to Dubai	147km	-

From Abu Dhabi: Add 300km for the round trip

Jeep

A R A B I A N   G U L F

HILTON BEACH CLUB

NATIONAL MUSEUM

HILTON HOTEL

MANAR MALL

RAS AL KHAIMAH

2. At the R/A turn right.

3. At the **Lantern R/A** continue straight over, straight on at the **Coffee Pot R/A**, and straight over the stop junction.

GPS   UTM 391,707E 2,850,209N
GEO 25°45'57"N 55°55'12"E

RAK HOTEL

CLOCK TOWER R/A

2.0km

TOWER LINKS GOLF CLUB

.5km

COFFEE POT R/A

E 11

1. Follow the **Dubai - Khasab** route. The first roundabout you hit in RAK will be the **Clocktower R/A**. Take the first exit off to the right and head straight.

3.0km

0.5km 0.6km

2.4km

LANTERN R/A

DUBAI 82KM

394000

396000

398000

400000

402000

EAST COAST/AL AIN

RAMS 4KM

Route 3 STAIRWAY TO HEAVEN ▶ R 42

Route 2 MUSSANDAM ▶ R 26

N

Route 4

²856000

²854000

R 56

This dam forms a natural catchment area for the mountains around it. It reduces the impact to the surroundings during flooding.

10.6km

²852000

DAM

4. Just as the road bears left, keep going straight on, across a small junction and then right onto the main road from the village to Wadi Bih.

SATELLITE STATION

6. Take a right at this T-junction.

5. After the speed bumps, with an old military camp on your left, the road bears around to your left. Take the next paved right, with a sign marked **Wadi Bih**.

5.1km

DISUSED ARMY CAMP

²850000

1.5km

Speed Bumps

DAM

0   Scale 1:50,000   2km

404000   406000   408000   410000   412000

55

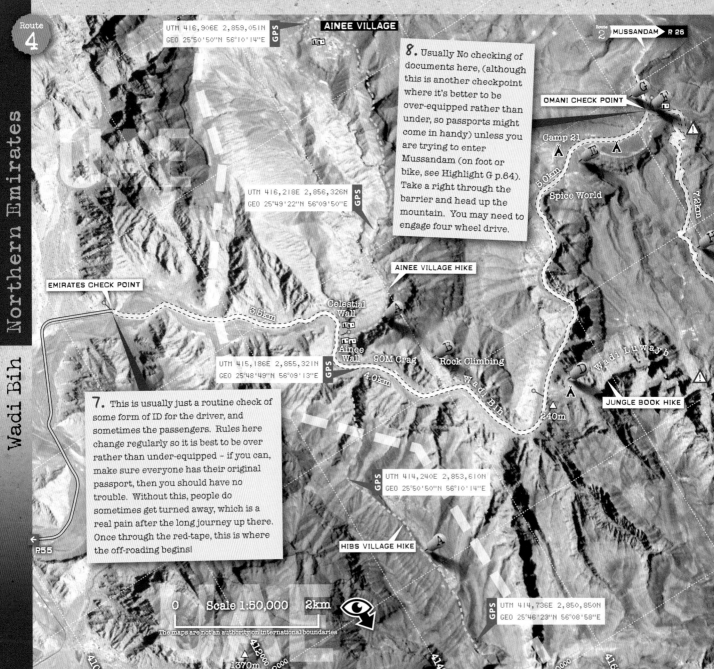

UTM 416,906E 2,859,051N
GEO 25°50'50"N 56°10'14"E

GPS

AINEE VILLAGE

OMANI CHECK POINT

Camp 21

5.0km

Spice World

7.2km

UTM 416,218E 2,856,326N
GEO 25°49'22"N 56°09'50"E

GPS

8. Usually No checking of documents here, (although this is another checkpoint where it's better to be over-equipped rather than under, so passports might come in handy) unless you are trying to enter Mussandam (on foot or bike, see Highlight G p.64). Take a right through the barrier and head up the mountain. You may need to engage four wheel drive.

AINEE VILLAGE HIKE

EMIRATES CHECK POINT

3.5km

Celestial Wall

Ainee Wall

90M Crag

Rock Climbing

4.0km

Wadi Bih

Wadi Luwayb

JUNGLE BOOK HIKE

UTM 415,186E 2,855,321N
GEO 25°48'49"N 56°09'13"E

GPS

240m

7. This is usually just a routine check of some form of ID for the driver, and sometimes the passengers. Rules here change regularly so it is best to be over rather than under-equipped – if you can, make sure everyone has their original passport, then you should have no trouble. Without this, people do sometimes get turned away, which is a real pain after the long journey up there. Once through the red-tape, this is where the off-roading begins!

UTM 414,240E 2,853,610N
GEO 25°50'50"N 56°10'14"E

GPS

HIBS VILLAGE HIKE

R55

0   Scale 1:50,000   2km

The maps are not an authority on international boundaries

UTM 414,736E 2,850,850N
GEO 25°46'23"N 56°08'58"E

GPS

410000
412000
1370m
2852000
414000
2850000
416000

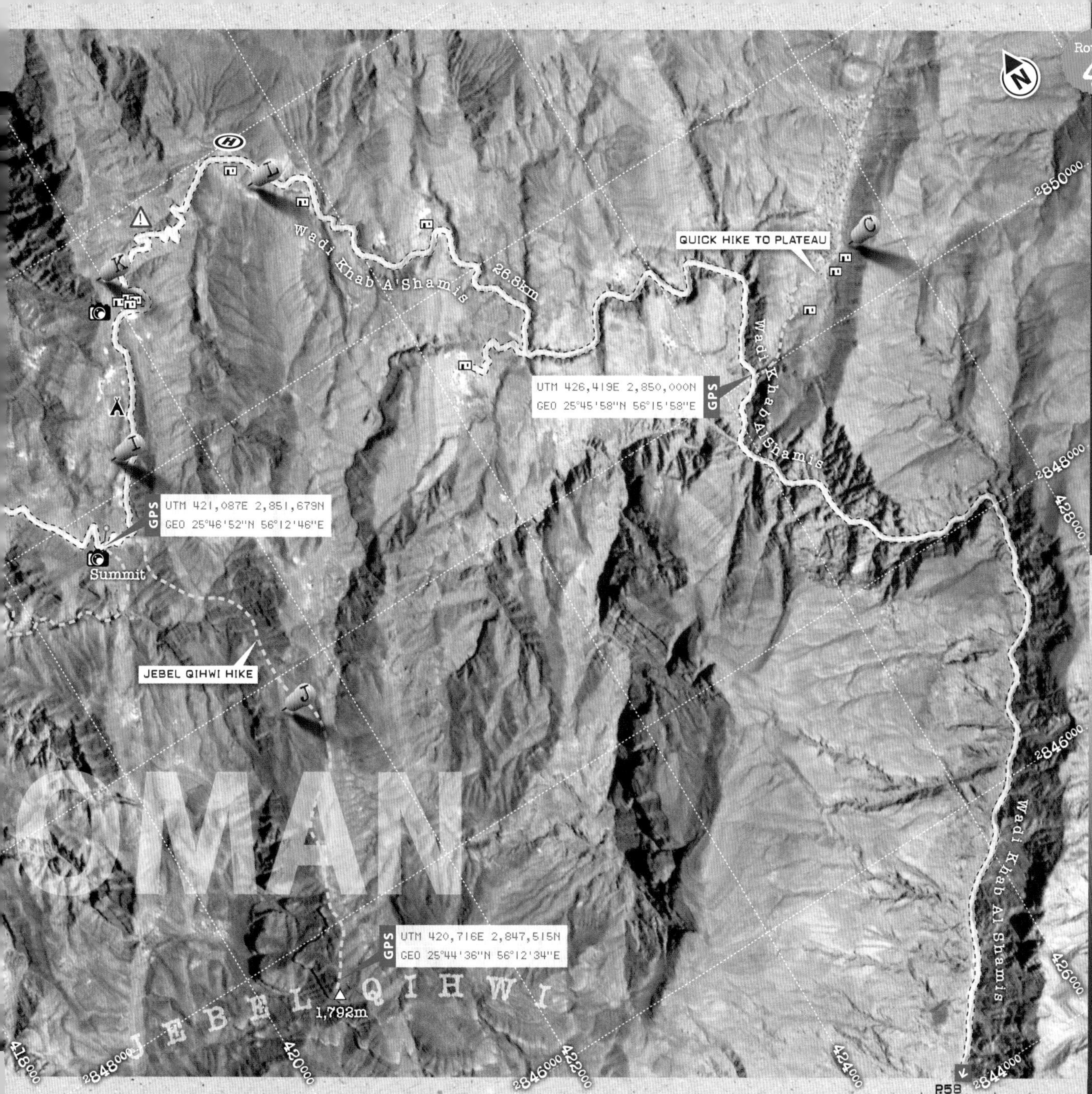

QUICK HIKE TO PLATEAU

UTM 426,419E 2,850,000N
GEO 25°45'58"N 56°15'58"E

Wadi Khab A'Shamis

26.8km

Wadi Khab A'Shamis

UTM 421,087E 2,851,679N
GEO 25°46'52"N 56°12'46"E

Summit

JEBEL QIHWI HIKE

OMAN

UTM 420,716E 2,847,515N
GEO 25°44'36"N 56°12'34"E

JEBEL QIHWI

1,792m

Wadi Khab Al Shamis

KHASAB 110KM R57

ZIGHI

EVASON HIDEAWAY & SPA (U/C)

Dhow trip to Mussendam

Wadi Khab Al Shamis

Beach

GOLDEN TULIP RESORT (U/C)

5.5km

DABA POR

10. Take a right back onto the velvet paved road, turn right at the roundabout (1st exit), and follow the sign to Daba Airport or Madha (the only Omani enclave in the vicinity).

GLOBE R/A

Speed Bumps

1.1km

QUROON A' SAYD

1.3km

0.8km

GPS UTM 425,386E 2,837,
GEO 25°38'56"N 56°15'

0.6km

0.6km

9. Take a left, and follow the sign to Daba (Dibba)

418000 2840000 2838000 420000 2836000 422000 2834000

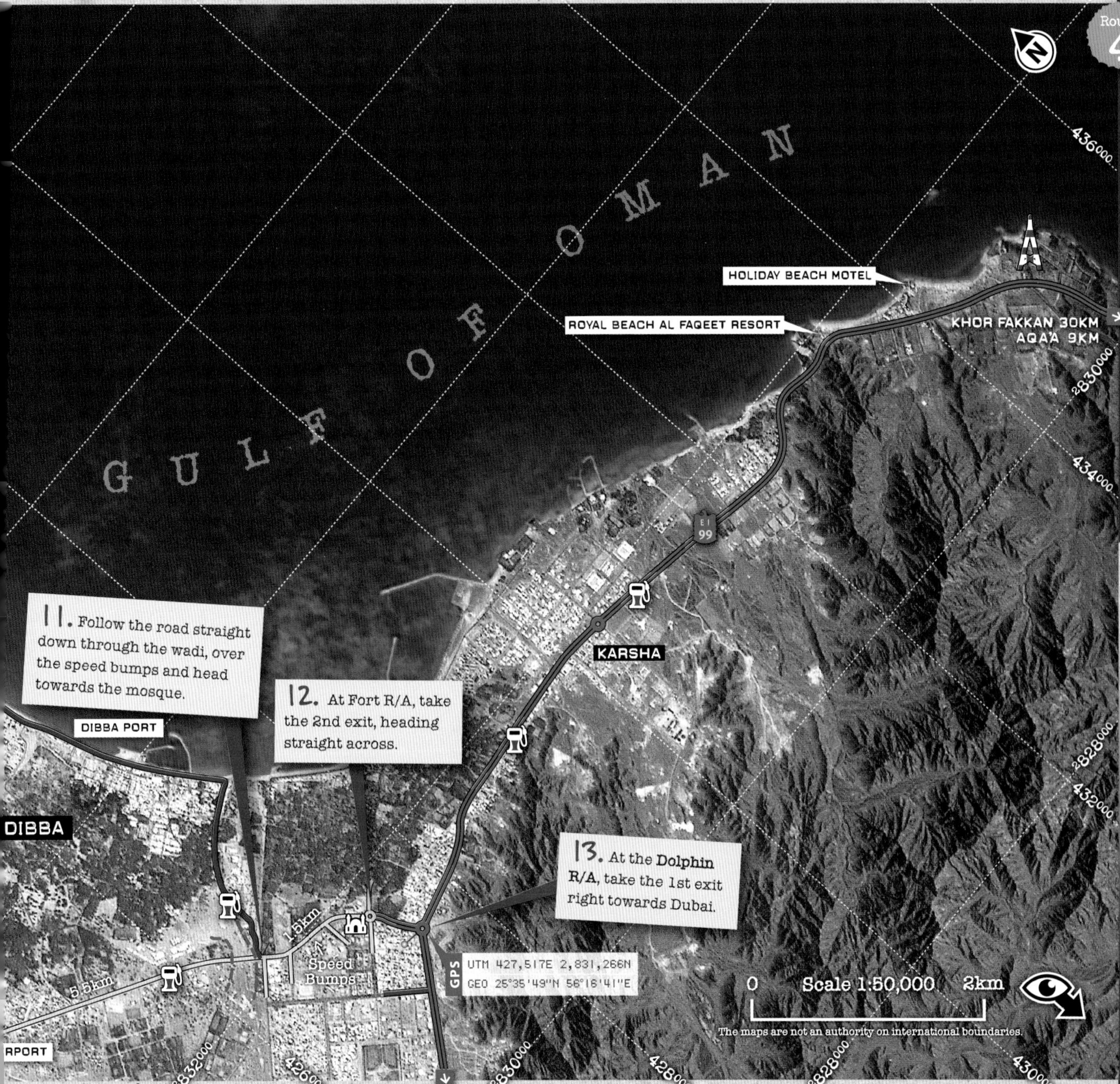

GULF OF OMAN

HOLIDAY BEACH MOTEL

ROYAL BEACH AL FAQEET RESORT

KHOR FAKKAN 30KM
AQA'A 9KM

436,000

2,830,000

434,000

E 99

432,000

KARSHA

11. Follow the road straight down through the wadi, over the speed bumps and head towards the mosque.

DIBBA PORT

12. At Fort R/A, take the 2nd exit, heading straight across.

DIBBA

13. At the **Dolphin R/A**, take the 1st exit right towards Dubai.

1.5km

Speed Bumps

GPS

UTM 427,517E 2,831,266N
GEO 25°35'49"N 56°16'41"E

5.5km

AIRPORT

0   Scale 1:50,000   2km

The maps are not an authority on international boundaries.

MASAFI 40KM R 2

2,832,000

426,000

2,830,000

428,000

2,828,000

430,000

Wadi Bih Highlights

Cutting and twisting through the mountains from Ras Al Khaimah on the West Coast to Dibba on the East, this route is one of the most dramatic yet accessible drives in the country. The track through Wadi Bih on the Ras Al Khaimah side is long and relatively wide, with enormous crags towering over the winding track. The climb out of the wadi is quite lengthy and rises steadily to almost 1,000 metres with some of the most beautiful views in the country.

Towards Dibba, the road descends very quickly, heading down through a narrow, twisting gorge called Wadi Khab Al Shamis. The carved, smooth faces of the rock provide welcome shade, accompanied by a surprising amount of greenery, which gives Wadi Khab Al Shamis a different, refreshing feel compared with the stony sparseness of Wadi Bih.

You can access Wadi Bih from both sides of the country, starting at Clock Tower Roundabout in Ras Al Khaimah or from the Dibba–Masafi highway on the east coast. Remember to carry your passport (original!) for the border checkpoint, it used to be possible to get through by just showing your driving license, but not anymore.

Ainee Village Hike & Hibs Village Hike

The Ainee Village hike is a great, relatively straightforward loop of a hike. It follows a well-established path (once out of the wadi), taking you initially along the wadi floor, then up and out of the wadi, before winding your way up to a deserted village of about 30 houses nestled at the base of the cliffs.

Start hiking along the wadi floor, keeping to the left-hand side, then gradually climb up and above the wadi bed (30 minutes). If you reach a fork in the wadi where the wadi narrows considerably, you have gone too far. You need to backtrack, climbing up above the wadi bed to your left.

The path then winds up around the hills before reaching a plateau and a single house (one hour), as well as some terraced fields and interesting orange tombstones at the far end of the plateau.

At this point, if you stand with your back to the door of the lone house, you need to hike up and behind the small hill directly in front of you (N direction). Ainee Village is behind the hill, slightly to the left. Head for the dip on your left (30 minutes). After you reach the village, you can have a look around, have lunch and relax under the trees.

To get back, either go the same way you have come, or head in a SE direction through the village and towards the slight dip in the hill on your left. You should reach a flat slab terrace. At this point keep looking to your right down a boulder slope, and the path should be easy to spot. This path takes you down past a spring (although don't hold your breath - it is more of a trickle

Ainee Village hike

and into the wadi bed you originally started from. Keep looking up and to your left, as the path stays out of the wadi for the most part until the point where you separated.

Just on the other side of Wadi Bih from the entrance to the Ainee Village hike, Hibs Village is another great hike to a deserted village high up above Wadi Bih, with a steep and quick climb up and out of the valley bottom. The beginning of the hike is hard to explain, but very clear to follow when you come down! So scramble up wherever you can, and from slightly above the plateau you can clearly see the straightforward path back.

Once up on the plateau, you will need to head in a S direction and drop down into the wadi, before climbing a short, steep section to reach the far end of the terraced plateau with the house. Many of the houses have recently been renovated and look great. You can walk up and past numerous houses, heading for the peak and a great view at the far end of the village.

↖ Ainee Village hike

Rock Climbing

Almost every weekend this whole area is crawling with climbers. There are epic multi-pitch routes and short hard climbs (on crags like Ainee Wall and 90 Metre Crag), as well as bouldering on the huge rocks in the spot known to expats as Spice World. There are several campsites popular with climbers – a good place to meet some like-minded people.

Quick Hike to Plateau

This is a good introductory hike as the majority is on flat terrain and follows a clearly marked track (thanks to the local inhabitants). Don't be dissuaded by the steep ascent at the start as this only lasts for 25 minutes. The track takes you through a sprawling village, dotted with date palm and wheat enclosures. There are plenty of trees along the way that provide welcome shade in the warmer months. The hike took nearly five hours in mid May, which allowed for numerous stops and a break for lunch. However, it could be done a lot quicker in cooler weather.

The start of the hike is from a water tank on the side of the road, often marked by local farmers' vehicles parked next to it. The large sign in Arabic asks you not to park your cars next to the tank as it blocks access for the water tankers. Please make sure you observe this request. There is a small clearing on about 100m along the road on the right-hand side (away from Dibba) where you can park.

The hike starts above the water tank heading straight up a steep slope in a NNE direction (towards the left). There is a well-worn track and it is just a matter of picking your way around some of the larger rocks near the top. After 25 minutes, you come to a large plateau (550m). A lone tree stands beside a drum, providing a good resting spot and some shade.

Still heading in a NNE direction, the track crosses the plateau and rises through a gully. After 15 minutes it opens onto a valley dotted with tress and you have your first view of the village. Continue through the village to the far end of the valley and up a small rise for an interesting view over a large basin surrounded by mountains.

If you are feeling energetic, you can head east up a steep slope for an uninterrupted view towards the Mussandam and Dibba at 740m. There is another small village in the valley below. You have the option of exploring the next village or retracing your steps back to the car.

Jungle Book/Wadi Luwayb Hike

From here you can follow Wadi Luwayb all the way to the top of the pass on a hike that has become known as Jungle Book. The complete walk takes about six hours and involves some basic climbing in three places, plus lots of scrambling up, over and around large boulders. A shorter version of about one hour is possible. If you do not feel like tackling the entire walk, just do the first kilometre or so up the wadi to the first deep water basin. The atmosphere is extraordinary.

Be properly prepared – sturdy boots or shoes, water, sunscreen, snacks and a good length of rope to help any non-climbers are all necessities for this hike.

At 7.5km from the Emirates check point, turn right into the wadi, leave your car as far up as you can and head left up the wadi. At the fork take a left, you can only really go in one direction, so taking the wrong route is not an option. At the first water basin (on the right), the wadi bends sharply left and you eventually reach a very murky pool at the foot of a wall where the rock is worn smooth by rushing water. The first climb is actually 100m before this on the left as you face the pool, and is a basic climb up several 'stairs', before turning right to walk along a ledge past a simple stone shelter built into the cliff.

At the second climb, you come to another smooth basin, where you climb straight up the back, following the course of the wadi. It's best climbed from the right-hand side (the opposite side to your approach).

About 400m after this second climb there is a scree slope up to the left; you are now faced with two options. You can either choose this scree slope route and rejoin the wadi further on just above the cultivated plateau, or alternatively, carry on for the third and definitely the scariest climb. If you continue

along the wadi, you are eventually faced with what looks like a dead end. Follow the wadi left to where the water has worn the rocks into wonderful smooth shapes and find a way up there. The **Off-Road Explorer team** has installed a sturdy rope ladder to help you over this part. If the rope ladder is not there you may want to use a rope at this stage – this is an exposed bit of climbing; proceed with caution.

The best method of attack is to climb onto the 'rim' of the washed-out oval shape in the rock. Then climb the sloping rock face on your right. It may look scary, but there are plenty of pockets in the rocks to stick your fingers and feet into.

You will eventually reach a cultivated plateau in a large bowl. Your greatest challenge lies ahead – turn left and head for the top of the bowl, taking the line of least resistance. After your exertions, this is a tough uphill slog over an area with small, loose rocks and thorny bushes.

Turn left when you hit the road at the top and follow it down to where you left your car in the wadi 11km away. If you're doing the trip with two cars, it may be best to leave one up here before the walk and run a shuttle service down.

Brandt's Hedgehog

This is prime real estate for the very cute Brandt's Hedgehog. They are nocturnal animals, so watch out for them on the roads when driving here after sundown.

Omani Checkpoint

At this point, the route deviates from Wadi Bih, and the track curves around the front of the checkpoint then climbs steeply to almost 1,000m. The track to the left is the real continuation of Wadi Bih and is also the end of the Mussandam Peninsula route. No non-local traffic seems to be allowed through the

checkpoint - it isn't a proper border post, as there's no facility for checking visas or stamping passports.

Mussandam Summit - Mountain Biking

A great biking route follows the Khasab pass into Oman. It starts at the Omani border post at the bottom of Wadi Bih (Ras Al Khaimah side). However, you will have to convince the border guards to let you in with your bikes - take your passport and be prepared to leave your vehicle and passport at the gate.

This ride is even more spectacular than the one up out of Wadi Bih, and is one of the toughest climbs you'll experience in the UAE. It's a challenge at 25km over a vertical of 1,500m, but it has to be done if you're mad about biking. The downhill? Well just make sure your brakes and tyres are in good shape because this one is fast and furious!

More Mountain Biking

Even after a couple of zigzags, there's an amazing view over the wadi surrounded by the UAE's highest mountains. This is a good physical challenge for runners and mountain bikers alike. On a bike, the hour's slog uphill is rewarded by turning around and taking the screaming downhill back to the base. The record climb (that we know of) on a bike is 45 minutes, while anyone running the hill in less than an hour is in cracking form.

Alternatively, for some spectacular scenery, bikers can carry on over the top and down the other side to Dibba. Initially, the downhill is steep with soft dirt in places, but once you're down the steep stuff, it's a gentle slope almost all the way to Dibba (about 25km) - a great reward if you climbed the other side.

As you approach the end of the wadi there's a small village, before which, off to your left, is the extremely steep, twisting road that climbs over the mountain range to Zighi Village on the beach. The route out is the same as the route in, but at least it's a short ride. You'll probably have to walk your bike in places, unless you're all muscle and steroids! The view from the top down to the coast is impressive and worth taking the time to see.

Jungle Book hike

✓ Terrace on Ainee Village hike

Camping

Once over the top, you'll find the remains of one of many old farming villages. Terraced fields frame scattered ruins of small stone dwellings - look for petroglyphs on the walls of some of these.

As a rule, the settlements are still inhabited, so please respect the owners' privacy. Many of these fields are used to grow crops to feed animals, so the farmers (and the goats) would appreciate it if you find somewhere else to camp. Try the good, flat, gravel area, left of the road, just before you reach these particular fields.

Jebel Qihwi Hike

From here you can see Jebel Qihwi, clearly visible as twin peaks in a south-westerly direction. A straightforward hike to the summit takes about three hours each way. Facing Jebel Qihwi, take the used path that runs to the left of the parking area. You will follow a donkey track across the hillside to a quaint settlement overlooking the east coast (about 45 minutes). To reach this, go along the track, and at the first fork head upwards towards the ridge (an alternative route that initially descends across the valley is also possible). Once at the settlement, pass through it, keeping to the right and maintaining your height. From here onwards the track deteriorates. Keeping roughly the same height as the settlement, follow the contours around and out of the steep hillside to an exposed area. At this point, with the summit in view, we recommend you head slightly up and to the left, keeping on the slabs of rock where possible, to the top.

The slope levels off slightly before the final, steep section leading to the northern summit (the right-hand peak). Directly in front there is an obvious chimney and this is ascended by climbing over a wedged block and then scrambling up to emerge through a hole close to the summit.

The southern summit is probably a metre or two higher than the northern, and the two are separated by a gap that's just too far to jump!

Terraced Fields

The houses and terraced fields in the mountains around Wadi Bih date from the 13th and 14th centuries and were built during the Julfar period (1200 - 1600). Julfar was a successful trading town located north of Ras Al Khaimah. To supply enough food for its growing population, a large system of fields was created for crops; at sea level, alfalfa and feed were planted, as these thrived in the very humid conditions on the coast, while wheat and barley were cultivated in the mountains.

It's interesting to be reminded that the terraced fields that you see in Wadi Bih were all built by hand; it took years of work for each field to silt up before beginning on the next terrace. Since the rains come in winter, most of the planting and ploughing would have been done then. It's unlikely that people would have lived here all year round, since they normally had to rely on water stored from the last rains. This obviously limited the

Northern Emirates   Wadi Bih

length of time they could stay here during the summer months.

Nowadays, the farms are generally run by hired labour. These people usually live on the property to tend the fields and goats. Although the dwellings were not originally used as summer houses, many of the present owners use them for this purpose.

Wadi Khab Al Shamis

Now you start the descent through the narrow and picturesque Wadi Khab Al Shamis. This is the more dramatic part of the route, and the section that can be blocked by large boulders after heavy rains (be prepared to turn back if necessary).

East Coast Hike

For a hike on the east side of the country, from the village in the bottom of Wadi Khab A' Shamis, just north of the Zighi turnoff, a trail takes you up to a plateau which is home to the locals' summer houses and some amazing views down over the east coast and Dibba. It is best to park your cars just south of the village, to the northern edge of the houses, then look for the beginning of the track on which to start your ascent up the steep, rocky hillside. The route can be difficult to find, but get into the spirit of exploring and blaze your own trail – for the first part of the hike, just gaining height is the aim. Then when you reach the top, you can take as much time as you want walking on the gently sloping plateau to the highest point, or admiring the views from the edge. Allow yourself enough daylight to make the return trip, as the descent is quite tricky.

NB. Cars have been the object of some 'curiosity' in this area, so it is best to park out of sight of the village (but in open view of the road for security). Keep everything inside tucked away under seat or locked in the boot, and make sure you lock all doors.

View from Hibs Village

Sunrise over Dibba Beach

Zighi Beach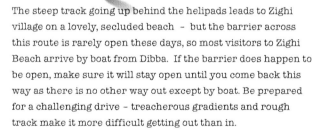

The steep track going up behind the helipads leads to Zighi village on a lovely, secluded beach – but the barrier across this route is rarely open these days, so most visitors to Zighi Beach arrive by boat from Dibba. If the barrier does happen to be open, make sure it will stay open until you come back this way as there is no other way out except by boat. Be prepared for a challenging drive – treacherous gradients and rough track make it more difficult getting out than in.

However, this bay is undergoing transformation as the location for a resort run by Six Senses Resorts & Spas of Thailand. Due to open mid 2007, the Evason Hideaway Resort (www. sixsenses.com) will provide exclusive accommodation with poolside villas, its own spa facilities and a range of dining options including a restaurant set on top the hills overlooking the bay. At the time of writing, a new access route was under construction, but as is only for the development, Zighi Beach may be off limits for a while.

Dibba Beach – Camping / Swimming

When you reach the east coast, it's well worth taking a relaxing dip in the ocean before the drive home. Even better, camp for the night on Dibba Beach and spend the next day snorkelling or exploring one or two of the east coast off-road routes. Dibba is a fishing village; it's easy to hire a dhow or speedboat to take you along the coast towards the Mussandam. You could even have lunch on your own private beach!

Oman's current tourism drive is in evidence on Dibba Beach, where construction is underway for the second resort hotel in Mussandam. The resort will be run by the Golden Tulip group (www.goldentulip.com) and is planned for opening in late 2006. The ongoing development in this area may affect public access to this popular beach in the future, but for now it's still open to anyone.

Escape. Explore. Enjoy.

AL AQAH BEACH RESORT, FUJAIRAH

Whether you're hard to please or find it tough to unwind, Le Méridien's Al Aqah Beach Resort comes as a revelation. It's not just a getaway, it's more like an ode to pleasure. Nestled between the majestic Hajar mountains and the sapphire blue waters of the Indian Ocean, this island of calm is just 50 kilometres from Fujairah city and an easy 90-minute drive from Dubai.

Here, follow your impulse, not your itinerary. Soak in the luxury of your room, surrender to bliss at the Cleopatra Spa or soothe the soul with the touch of Ayurveda. Hit the beach or UAE's largest free-form swimming pool. Go diving or deep-sea fishing.

Delve into delight served with every meal here – a candlelit dinner with the sea and stars for company, a delicious breakfast at the start of another sun-kissed day. Feel the relief wash over you once you've handed the kids over to The Penguin Club – specially designed to keep the young ones entertained.

If you mean business - meeting, conference or banquet - order anything and you'll get it on a platter.

Unexpected, unimagined, unforgettable.
That's the kind of break you can expect at Al Aqah Beach Resort.

Le MERIDIEN
AL AQAH BEACH RESORT

Toll Free: 800 4041
www.lemeridien.com
www.lemeridien-alaqah.com
Tel: +971 (9) 244 9000
e-mail: reservations@lemeridien-alaqah.com
In Partnership with Nikko Hotels International

ABU DHABI • AL KHOBAR • AMMAN • BANGALORE • BEIRUT • CHENNAI
DAMASCUS • DUBAI • JEDDAH • KUWAIT • LATTAKIA • MUMBAI • NEW DELHI

East Coast

Jeep

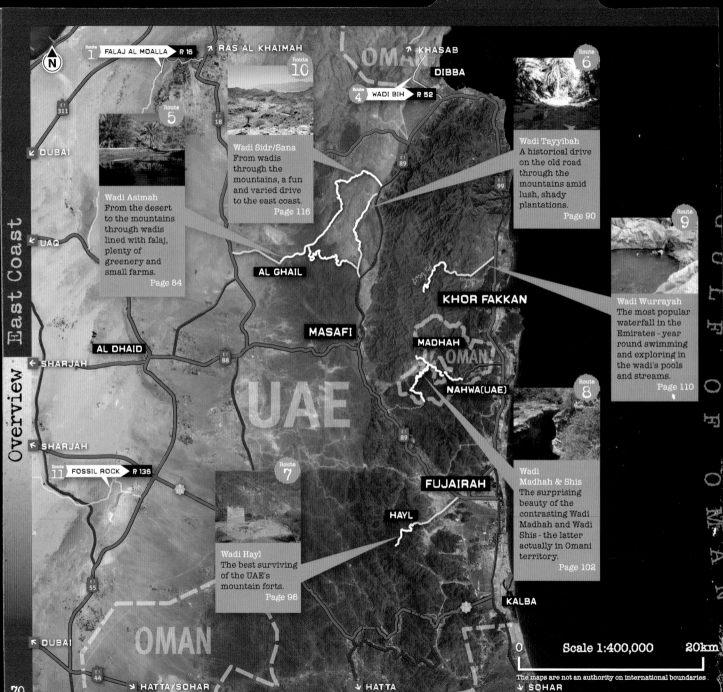

N

Route 1 FALAJ AL MOALLA ▶ R 16

↑ RAS AL KHAIMAH

↑ KHASAB

OMAN

DIBBA

Route 4 ◀ WADI BIH ▶ R 52

Route 10

Route 5

E 311

↙ DUBAI

↙ UAQ

Wadi Sidr/Sana
From wadis through the mountains, a fun and varied drive to the east coast.
Page 116

Route 6

Wadi Tayyibah
A historical drive on the old road through the mountains amid lush, shady plantations.
Page 90

Wadi Asimah
From the desert to the mountains through wadis lined with falaj, plenty of greenery and small farms.
Page 84

AL GHAIL

KHOR FAKKAN

Route 9

Wadi Wurrayah
The most popular waterfall in the Emirates - year round swimming and exploring in the wadi's pools and streams.
Page 110

MASAFI

AL DHAID

MADHAH

OMAN

NAHWA(UAE)

← SHARJAH

UAE

Route 8

← SHARJAH

89

Route 11 FOSSIL ROCK ▶ R 136

Route 7

FUJAIRAH

Wadi Madhah & Shis
The surprising beauty of the contrasting Wadi Madhah and Wadi Shis - the latter actually in Omani territory.
Page 102

HAYL

Wadi Hayl
The best surviving of the UAE's mountain forts.
Page 96

E 55

KALBA

↙ DUBAI

OMAN

0   Scale 1:400,000   20km

The maps are not an authority on international boundaries

E 44

↘ HATTA/SOHAR

↓ HATTA

↓ SOHAR

East Coast Route Overview Table

Route	Name	Page	Total Dist. (km)	Total Unpaved (km)	Terrain Mtn	Desert	Wadi	Activity Camp	Climb	Hike	Bike	Swim	Route Combinations
	East Coast Road Route	72	237km	-									
5	Wadi Asimah	84	27.7km	16.8km	✓	✓	✓	✓		✓			4 + 8 + 9 + 11
6	Wadi Tayyibah	90	15.7km	6.4km	✓		✓			✓	✓		4 + 5 + 8
7	Wadi Hayl	96	19.8km	-	✓		✓			✓			7 + 10
8	Wadi Madhah & Shis	102	63.2km	45.8km	✓		✓	✓		✓	✓	✓	6 + 10
9	Wadi Wurrayah	110	25.4km	8.8km	✓		✓			✓		✓	6 + 7
10	Wadi Sidr/Sana	116	32.8km	25.4km	✓		✓	✓		✓	✓		4 + 5 + 9

East Coast Route Combinations

One-Day Trips

Wadi Asimah P.84	➤	Wadi Bih P.52
Wadi Sidr/Sana P.116	➤	Wadi Bih P.52
Wadi Tayyibah P.90	➤	Wadi Bih P.52

Combine one of the shorter mountain routes from the heart of the country through towards the east coast, with the massive Wadi Bih trip from Dibba through the Hajar Mountains to Ras Al Khaimah. A long drive, but immensely rewarding.

| Fossil Rock P.136 | ➤ | Wadi Asimah P.84 |

The 'Fossil Rock' route offers a great all-round desert experience, and can be tackled by any level of driver (although you'll find some challenging dunes off the main track). The drive through Wadi Asimah then provides completely different scenery and driving, with mountains, farms, plantations and villages where life hasn't changed in decades.

Two-Day Trips

| Wadi Wurrayah P.110 | ➤ | Wadis Madhah & Shis P.102 |

Two great wadi routes on the east coast, both with year round pools and waterfalls - ideal for a weekend of camping among the mountains, cooling off in the pools and exploring the canyons and oases.

| Fossil Rock P.136 | ➤ | Wadi Madhah & Shis P.102 |

Combine this classic desert route with a trip into the Omani enclave just off the east coast for the two contrasting wadis of Madhah and Shis. While at the coast you should explore Kalba, either on foot or by hiring a canoe. Then head up the coast where good camping can be found in Wadi Madhah if you get there in time, or in among the foothills of the Hajar near Kalba.

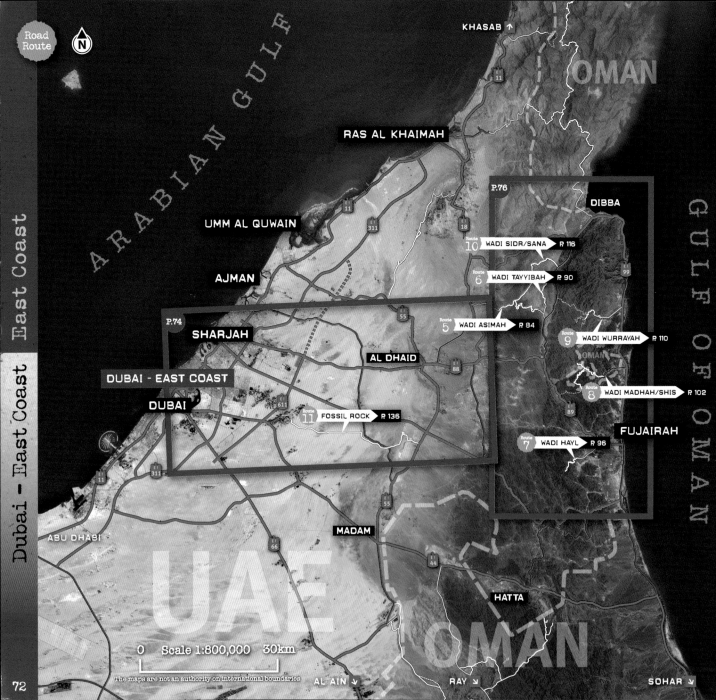

ARABIAN GULF

KHASAB ↑

OMAN

11

RAS AL KHAIMAH

GULF OF OMAN

P.76

DIBBA

UMM AL QUWAIN

311

18

Route
10 WADI SIDR/SANA ▶ R 116

E
99

AJMAN

Route
6 WADI TAYYIBAH ▶ R 90

P.74

E
55

Route
5 WADI ASIMAH ▶ R 84

SHARJAH

Route
9 WADI WURRAYAH ▶ R 110

OMAN

AL DHAID

88

DUBAI - EAST COAST

Route
8 WADI MADHAH/SHIS ▶ R 102

DUBAI

611

89

Route
11 FOSSIL ROCK ▶ R 136

FUJAIRAH

Route
7 WADI HAYL ▶ R 96

11

311

55

ABU DHABI

MADAM

E
66

44

UAE

HATTA

OMAN

0   Scale 1:800,000   30km

The maps are not an authority on international boundaries

AL AIN ↓

RAY ↓

SOHAR ↓

East Coast

From Dubai, the east coast can be reached in about 2 hours, so even if you are only in the UAE for a short time the trip is well worth the effort. The mountains and beaches are fantastic spots for camping, barbecues and weekend breaks, as well as various activities. This area is a popular diving destination, and there is some excellent snorkelling close to shore. Look out for Snoopy Island, which has an abundance of coral and diverse marine life (even small sharks make an appearance from time to time).

Terrain:	Mountain, Oasis, Wadi, Beach
Water:	Pools, Streams, Waterfalls, Creek, Sea
Driving:	Easy, with great views
Activities:	Swimming, Snorkelling, Diving, Hiking, Mountain Biking, Canoeing, Picnics

Trip Info

Distances:

Dubai to Masafi	97km
East Coast Loop	140km

From Abu Dhabi: Add 300 km for the round trip

Jeep

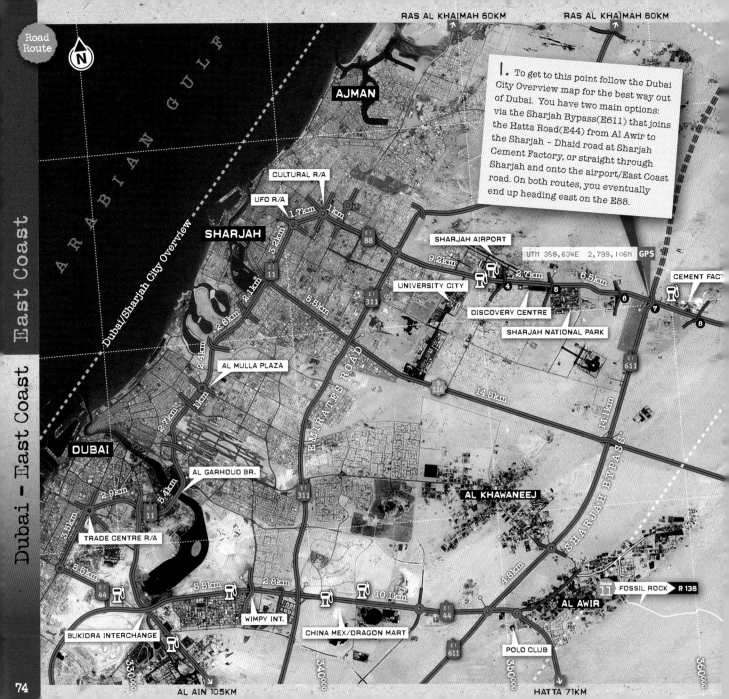

Road Route

N

RAS AL KHAIMAH 60KM   RAS AL KHAIMAH 60KM

ARABIAN GULF

AJMAN

Dubai/Sharjah City Overview

CULTURAL R/A

UFO R/A   1.7km   1km

SHARJAH

3.2km

E 88

E 11

2.1km

2.8km

5.5km

E 311

2.4km

AL MULLA PLAZA

1km

2.7km

DUBAI

AL GARHOUD BR.

2.9km

5.4km

3.5km

E 11

TRADE CENTRE R/A

5.5km

E 44

5.5km   2.8km

WIMPY INT.

10.1km

CHINA MEX/DRAGON MART

BUKIDRA INTERCHANGE

330000

340000

SHARJAH AIRPORT

UTM 358,634E   2,799,106N   GPS

9.2km   2.7km   6.5km   CEMENT FACT

UNIVERSITY CITY

4   5   6   7

DISCOVERY CENTRE   8

SHARJAH NATIONAL PARK

E 611

E 116   14.5km

14.1km

EMIRATES ROAD

AL KHAWANEEJ

SHARJAH BYPASS

E 311

4.8km

Route 11   FOSSIL ROCK   R 136

AL AWIR

E 44

E 611

POLO CLUB

350000

360000

AL AIN 105KM   HATTA 71KM

1. To get to this point follow the Dubai City Overview map for the best way out of Dubai. You have two main options: via the Sharjah Bypass(E611) that joins the Hatta Road(E44) from Al Awir to the Sharjah – Dhaid road at Sharjah Cement Factory, or straight through Sharjah and onto the airport/East Coast road. On both routes, you eventually end up heading east on the E88.

UMM AL QUWAIN 17KM

RAS AL KHAIMAH 45KM

Route 1 ► FALAJ AL MOALLA R 16

Route 5 ► WADI ASIMAH R 84

Route 10 ► WADI SIDR/SANA R 116

Road Route

E 18

MANAMA

2. Once you reach **Al Dhaid**, go left (3rd exit) at the first roundabout and then right (1st exit) at the second roundabout, to continue towards **Masafi** and **Fujairah**.

1.8km

1.7km

R 77

2800 000

3.3km

9.1km

E 88

SIJI

SHARJAH NATURAL HISTORY MUSEUM

AL DHAID

8.0km

E 88

6.0km

15.0km

9

10

11

12

UTM 387,040E 2,796,561N   GPS

SHARJAH ARAB CULTURE CAPITAL MONUMENT

E 55

2790 000

18.5km

S 116

16.2km

SHARJAH – KALBA ROAD

FOSSIL ROCK

14.0km

2780 000

0   Scale 1:200,000   10km

The maps are not an authority on international boundaries

S 116

2780 000

370 000

380 000

390 000

2780 000

MADAM 26KM / HATTA 65KM

KALBA 35KM

LE MERIDIEN AL AQAH BEACH RESORT

DADNA

SNOOPY ISLAND
11.8km

KHOR FAKKAN

HOLIDAY BEACH MOTEL

AQA'A

SHARM

E1 99

ROYAL BEACH AL FAQEET RESORT

RUL DADNA

SANDY BEACH MOTEL

BIDIYAH

15.4km

18km

BIDIYAH MOSQUE

THURSDAY MARKET

OCEANIC HOTEL

POT R/A

Route 9   WADI WURRAYAH   R 110

DOLPHIN R/A

3. The 'T-junction' roundabout in **Masafi** is the linking point of the **East Coast** loop. Turn right (1st exit) to go to **Fujairah**, or turn left (2nd exit, ignoring the military entrance) to go to **Dibba**. (We suggest going left first.)

E1 89

DIBBA

16km

WADI BIH   R 52
Route 4

OMAN

4. Head straight (1st exit) at Dolphin roundabout on the outskirts of **Dibba**, keeping on the main road. Then follow the main coast road all the way to **Fujairah**.

CEMENT FACTORY

S

GHUB

Route 10   WADI SIDR/SANA   R 116

AL HALA

12.1km

R

Route 6   WADI TAYYIBAH   R 90

TAYYIBAH

10km

ASIMAH

E1 89

MURE

MAIDAQ

Route 5   WADI ASIMAH   R 84

AL GHAIL

Scale 1:200,000   10km
0

The maps are not an authority on international boundaries.

RAS AL KHAIMAH 65KM

O   F   O   M   A   N

SOHAR →

QIDFA MURBA

QURAYYA

KHOR KALBA

KALBA

13.8km

17.8km

FUJAIRAH PORT

FUJAIRAH HILTON

FUJAIRAH

INTL AIRPORT

MADHAH

WADI MADHAH/SHIS R 102

1.3km

OMAN

NAHWA(UAE)

DAM

5. If you wish to bypass **Fujairah** and complete the loop, then turn right (1st exit) at the roundabout after **Fujairah Port**. At the peculiar bend in the road you have no choice but to bear left, passing **Fujairah Hospital** on your right. At the next roundabout turn right (1st exit), out of **Fujairah** heading towards Masafi. Alternatively, if you wish to visit **Fujairah** or **Khor Kalba**, go straight at the roundabout (2nd exit).

6. To visit Khor Kalba head south for about 16 km along the coast road, through **Kalba**. Go straight over the roundabouts to the outskirts of Kalba. Eventually you will be driving parallel to the khor and will come to a small bridge over the creek by a roundabout. Park here and explore on foot.

E1 89

Route 7 WADI HAYL R 96

BITHNAH

26.5km

GPS UTM 416,092E 2,798,371N

BLAYDAH

DIFTAH

U A E

MASAFI

FRIDAY MARKET

15km

E1 88

SIJI

SHARJAH 50KM R 75

SHARJAH 50KM R 75

Road Route

N

East Coast Highlights

The highway takes you from Dubai through the open desert to Al Dhaid and Masafi (source of the local bottled water), eventually climbing and twisting through the rugged Hajar Mountains and down to the Gulf of Oman. At Masafi, you have the choice of driving north to Dibba and then along the coast to Fujairah and Kalba and back to Masafi, or heading south towards Fujairah and making the loop in the other direction. Along the route are plenty of options for off-road driving, five-star beach hotels and cosy, family-style beach resorts, markets, forts, heritage and archaeological sites, and the oldest mosque in the UAE.

Sharjah Natural History Museum

Combining entertainment and learning in the most dynamic of atmospheres, Sharjah Natural History Museum (see Directory)

↑ Friday Market

unfolds through five exhibition halls, revealing the earth's secrets and the natural history of the area.

A highlight for all ages is the Arabian Wildlife Centre with a great selection of reptiles, mammals and creepy crawlies. This site is a breeding centre for endangered species – most famously the Arabian Leopard. There is also a children's farm, where youngsters have the chance to feed and pet animals such as donkeys, camels, goats and sheep.

The facilities are state-of-the-art and offer an enjoyable, interactive and educational experience. Picnic areas are available, as well as cafes and a shop. Great fun for all ages, and a place that you will want to visit time and time again. (Entrance fees – adults Dhs.15; family Dhs.30; Timings 09:00 - 19:00; Thursday 11:00 - 19:00; Friday 14:00 - 19:00; Closed Mon. Last tickets at 17.30).

Sharjah – Kalba Road

For a different route over to the east coast, the Sharjah – Kalba highway (completed only fairly recently), provides a quick, interesting and traffic-free route to the most south-easterly part of the UAE on the Indian Ocean. The road takes you through the desert past Jebel Maleihah (Fossil Rock) then through the Hajar Mountains, ending up near Khor Kalba, from where it is only a short drive north up the coast to Fujairah.

Also an interesting alternative route back to Dubai, this drive is more scenic than most roads in the country. It is possible to take this road (previously an off-road route but now paved all the way), from Kalba to Hatta via Munay. The hilly terrain, tunnels and superb views of the Hajars make this a great way to get to or from the east coast.

Friday Market

Even though it is open on other days, the Friday Market is aptly named for the special buzz generated there on Fridays.

The Hajar Mountains

Everything is available, including carpets, plants, local produce (ever tasted a crunchy palm heart?), and a wide selection of often-bizarre knick-knacks (such as an inflatable Santa Claus!).

Masafi

Masafi, in the emirate of Ras Al Khaimah, is the source of the popular mineral water of the same name. The water occurs naturally in a number of underground springs, and is packaged in a nearby facility that has the capacity to produce 34,000 bottles per hour.

Wadi Bashing

Criss-crossed with many wadis, this area was previously home to several excellent off-road routes. The construction of several new roads and quarrying has cut through some parts of it, but this is still a good place to explore your own

routes between the E88 to Sharjah-Masafi and the E89 Masafi-Fujairah road. Some quiet wadis still remain if you look hard enough, with remote spots not often visited by people – good places for camping and gentle hikes in the low hills.

Diftah

Diftah is an old abandoned village (4km south of Masafi Roundabout along the Fujairah road), with an oasis and a wadi that often has a stream with running water and pools. The inhabitants moved to a new village right beside the main road and left the old village, but they do still use the houses, so please don't try to get in! A nice place for exploring, and a very short detour off the main road on the way to Fujairah.

Bitnah

The village of Bitnah is notable chiefly for its fort and archaeological sites. The fort once controlled the main pass of Wadi Ham through the mountains from east to west and is still impressive, probably more so than the fort at Fujairah. The main archaeological site is known as the Long Chambered Tomb or the T-Shaped Tomb, and was probably once a communal burial site. It was excavated in 1988 and its main period of use is thought to date from between 1,350 and 300BC, although the tomb itself is older. Fujairah Museum (see Directory) has a detailed display of the tomb, and is worth visiting since the site itself is fenced off and covered as protection against the elements. The tomb can be found by taking a right off the main road at the turning for Bitnah, then a left before the village, near the radio tower.

Aerial Tours

Get a bird's-eye view of the stunning mixture of coastline, rugged mountains, beautiful valleys, villages and date plantations. Aerial tours are available every day through the Fujairah Aviation Centre (see Directory), and can last for anything from 30 minutes to several hours. Costs start at Dhs.100 per person .

Fujairah

Fujairah is a small city with a real mix of old and new. Being situated close to the Hajar Mountains, the Indian Ocean and many areas of natural beauty, it's an excellent base from which to explore the East Coast. In the city and the immediate surrounding area there are a number of heritage sites and attractions such as Fujairah Fort, Bitnah Fort, Fujairah Museum, Fujairah Heritage Village, Ain Al Madhab Gardens (which has its own hot springs), and Al Hisn Fort and Al Hisn Kalba a little further down the coast.

Further afield, the areas around Bidiyah and Al Aqah are popular stops on the east coast tour to see the oldest mosque in the UAE and the new developments on the beach near Le Meridien Al Aqah and Sandy Beach Hotel. These will soon be joined by a number of other hotels and resorts, as well as Fujairah's newest development, the Al Dana project, a man-made island stretching out into the sea from the shore just north of Bidiyah Mosque. It will be home to timeshare villas and is due to open in 2008.

Bidiyah watch tower

For more information contact the Fujairah Tourism Bureau (see Directory).

Bullfighting

One rather dubious attraction in Fujairah is the chance to see the emirate's unique form of bullfighting. Here the spectacle is not a gory man-against-beast struggle to the death, but a contest of strength between two great animals. The bulls can still occasionally be seen working on farms in the area and they are often pampered family pets. The fight itself is bloodless, as the bulls lock horns and wrestle until the weaker of the two gives up and turns away. It's a form of entertainment much loved by the local population.

Bullfights take place every Friday afternoon at about 16:30 (except during the summer) near the Fujairah – Kalba bridge area. Each fight lasts just a few minutes and the bulls suffer little or no injury, except for a few scratches and a bruised ego on the part of both the losing bull and his owner.

Khor Kalba

A beautiful tidal estuary, Khor Kalba is the most northerly mangrove forest in the world and home to a variety of plant, marine and birdlife not found anywhere else in the UAE. It is an excellent place for birdwatching in the spring and autumn since it is on the migratory route from Siberia to Central Asia, and 'twitchers' are drawn here to see the endangered white-collared kingfisher, a surprisingly common sight despite there being only around 50 pairs in existence. Khor Kalba is best seen from the water, and canoes are available to rent from Desert Rangers (04 340 2408).

Watersports

The rocky islands and coral reefs make the east coast a great spot for snorkelling, diving, fishing, sailing and other watersports. However, be careful of strong currents, rough seas and careless speed demons in boats and on jet skis.

Bidiyah Mosque

Bidiyah is best known as the site of the oldest mosque in the UAE. The mosque is officially called Al Masjid Al Othmani and is thought to date back 600 years to the middle of the 15th century, having been built in the year 20 Hijra in the Islamic calendar. The small building, made from gypsum, stone and mud-bricks, is surrounded by a 1.5m wall and is still used for prayer, so non-Muslim visitors will have to satisfy themselves with a photo from the outside. It has been recently reconditioned, now painted a slightly different shade than its original white, and there has been the addition of a Heritage Village next to the mosque, showing items from the traditional way of life.

The village of Bidiyah itself is one of the oldest settlements on the east coast having been inhabited, it is believed, since 3,000BC. It is a good place for a walk around in the area behind the mosque, passing hill-top watchtowers and through green plantations

Snoopy Island

This area is set to be the booming tourist region of Fujairah, with several new hotels planned alongside the existing Sandy Beach Hotel and Le Meridien Al Aqah Beach Resort. Sandy Beach is a friendly beach hotel and a great place to spend a lazy Friday afternoon, or the whole weekend, especially with a group of friends. It has the added bonus of being just a stone's throw away from Snoopy Island, one of the UAE's best spots for diving and snorkelling. It is possible to park on the public beach on either side of Sandy Beach for free, and then swim out to the island if you have your own snorkel. But for a Dhs.50 entry charge you get to use the hotel's facilities, including a chilled pool and shady grounds. For more luxurious accommodation, Le Meridien is a five-star property with matching service and facilities. The first of the new hotels, the Fujairah Rotana Resort, is set to open in spring 2007.

Dibba

The Hajar Mountains on the Mussandam side, rising in places to over 1,800m, are a wonderful backdrop to the village of Dibba. There is a great sandy beach at the end of the bay sheltered by the mountains – perfect for relaxing after a long drive. There's good snorkelling off the beach next to the rocks - and from the port you can charter a dhow or a fishing boat for trips to dive or just enjoy a picnic lunch on a secluded beach. The coastline is very attractive and there are quite a few gravel beaches to choose from. The snorkelling is good and you will often see dolphins and turtles. The area is generally

Bidiyah Mosque

very clean, but unfortunately you will sometimes have to avoid crude oil on the beach and in the water.

Burial Site

This area is rich in history and there are various burial sites throughout the region. Rumour has it that a vast cemetery with over 10,000 headstones can still be seen just outside Dibba on the rocky plains. These are the legacy of a great battle fought in 633AD, when the Muslim armies of Caliph Abu Baker were sent to suppress a local rebellion against Islam and to reclaim the Arabian Peninsula for Islam.

Mussandam – Dhow Charter

Large, independent groups can try chartering a dhow from the fishermen at Dibba to travel up the coast of the Mussandam to see the 'fjords'. Use your best bargaining skills to get a good deal – knowing a bit of Arabic may smooth things along. Expect to pay around Dhs.2,500 per day for a dhow large enough to take 20 - 25 people.

Visas aren't required since technically you won't be entering Oman. However, it is possible to arrange stops along the coast and is probably best to take camping equipment for the night, although you can sleep on board.

You'll need to take your own food and water as nothing is provided, except ice lockers that are suitable for storing supplies. Conditions are pretty basic. The dhow is also ideal for diving, but hire everything before reaching Dibba. Alternatively, spend the days swimming, snorkelling and lazing, or for an extra Dhs.800 hire a speedboat for the day.

Another way to visit Mussandam is via Khasab. See the Dubai - Khasab road route p.4 (Dhow/Boat trips).

'Grand Canyon'

It is well worth the stop, just off the main road, to admire the views in this area. Heading towards Masafi, near the top of the

hill, there is a small area on the left to park your car. You'll see various deep, narrow gorges with terraced cultivation, and further along is an even deeper gorge with folding hillsides that are spread out before you. For hikers, at the bottom of the hill near Etisalat tower, several tracks head east into the 'Grand Canyon' wadi itself. Try any of these tracks and explore the narrow wadis which often have streams, pools, greenery and cultivated plots.

The Road to RAK

This relatively new road provides a fast link to Ras Al Khaimah, allowing you to get over to the west coast much quicker than on the routes that existed previously. It's also a road worth taking if you're heading back to Dubai, as it cuts the corner off the old route, eventually bringing you out on the E88 near Al Dhaid.

Route 5

N

↗ RAS AL KHAIMAH

Route 4 WADI BIH R 52   RAK

DIBBA R 82

DIBBA

RAK INTL AIRPORT

E1 18

Route 1 FALAJ AL MOALLA R 16

Route 10 WADI SIDR/SANA R 116

E1 89

Route 6 WADI TAYYIBAH R 90

P.86

WADI ASIMAH

AL GHAIL

Route 9 WADI WURRAYAH R 110

↗ UMM AL QUWAIN

E1 55

KHOR FAKKAN

MASAFI

Route 8 WADI MADHAH/SHIS R 102

AL DHAID

E1 88

DIFTAH R 80

NAHWA(UAE)

MADHAH

↙ SHARJAH

FRIDAY MARKET R 78

OMAN

WADI BASHING R 80

E1 99

↙ SHARJAH

Route 11 FOSSIL ROCK R 136

↙ FUJAIRAH R 81

0   Scale 1:350,000   15km

E1 89

FUJAIRAH

84

↙ AL AIN   ↘ KALBA

The maps are not an authority on international boundaries

GULF OF OMAN

Wadi Asimah

From the village of Al Ghail on the edge of the desert, this route takes in secluded villages, small pools, quiet strolls and plentiful greenery. The driving gets interesting in a couple of places as the track meanders between falaj, dams and plantations, and over the solid rock bed, but the increased tarmac through Wadi Asimah has smoothed out the roughest parts.

Terrain: Oasis, Wadi
Water: Pools, Streams
Driving: A little tricky in parts
Activities: Camping, Hiking

Trip Info

Other Names:
Assimah, Asymah

Distances:

	Paved	Unpaved
Dubai to start of route	107km	–
Route	10.9km	16.8km
End of route to Dubai	119km	–

From Abu Dhabi: Add 300km for the round trip

Jeep

Route 5

East Coast

Wadi Asimah

E 18

2. Roughly 11 km after **Manama** take the tarmac road to the right, signposted **Ghail** – just after the speed humps. Drive 7.4 km into the village of **Al Ghail**.

4. Head downhill past the water tower, then once you've emerged from the narrow passageway into the wadi bed, head straight across the wadi intersection towards the plantations, keeping on the lower of the two tracks in front of you.

AL GHAIL YOUTH CENTRE

7.4km

3.1km

Wadi Al

GPS UTM 398,632E 2,810,950N
GEO 25°24'43"N 55°59'31"E

Speed Bumps

3.5km

E 18

AL GHAIL

1. Follow the East Coast route through Al Dhaid. After 3.3 km turn left at the roundabout. When you reach the main road, turn right then take the first U-Turn towards RAK.

3. At the end of the tarmac road, follow the track into **Al Ghail**, down and up through the initial dip, bearing left towards the mosque. Keeping left (mosque now on your right), follow the line of smaller telegraph poles on the left-hand-side towards the large water tower and palm trees in the distance.

Speed Bumps

398000 400000 402000 404000 406000

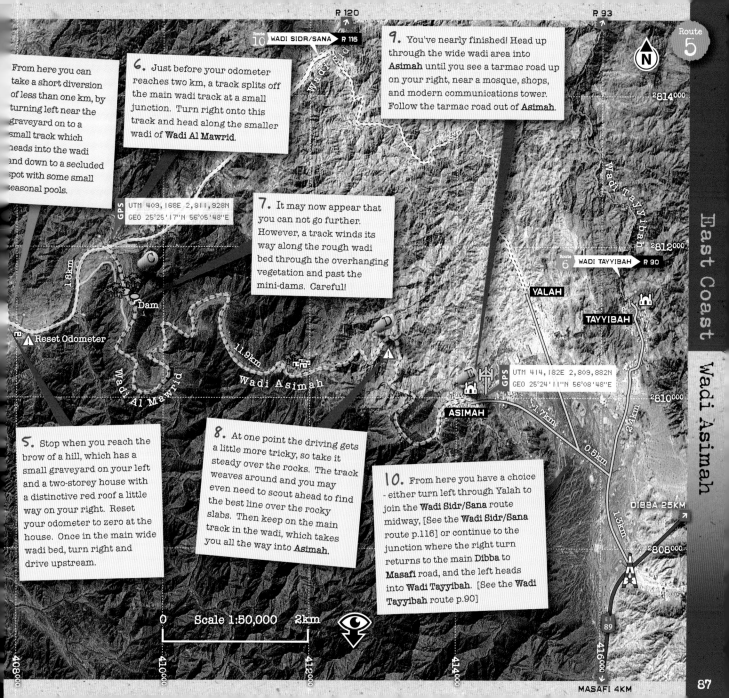

P 120

P 93

Route 5

Route 10 WADI SIDR/SANA R 116

From here you can take a short diversion of less than one km, by turning left near the graveyard on to a small track which heads into the wadi and down to a secluded spot with some small seasonal pools.

6. Just before your odometer reaches two km, a track splits off the main wadi track at a small junction. Turn right onto this track and head along the smaller wadi of **Wadi Al Mawrid**.

9. You've nearly finished! Head up through the wide wadi area into **Asimah** until you see a tarmac road up on your right, near a mosque, shops, and modern communications tower. Follow the tarmac road out of **Asimah**.

2814000

GPS UTM 409,168E 2,811,928N
GEO 25°25'17"N 56°05'48"E

7. It may now appear that you can not go further. However, a track winds its way along the rough wadi bed through the overhanging vegetation and past the mini-dams. Careful!

Wadi Tayyibah

2812000

Route 6 WADI TAYYIBAH R 90

YALAH

TAYYIBAH

1.8km

Dam

⚠ Reset Odometer

Wadi Al Mawrid

11.9km

Wadi Asimah

⚠

GPS UTM 414,182E 2,809,882N
GEO 25°24'11"N 56°08'48"E

ASIMAH

1.7km

2810000

2.4km

0.5km

5. Stop when you reach the brow of a hill, which has a small graveyard on your left and a two-storey house with a distinctive red roof a little way on your right. Reset your odometer to zero at the house. Once in the main wide wadi bed, turn right and drive upstream.

8. At one point the driving gets a little more tricky, so take it steady over the rocks. The track weaves around and you may even need to scout ahead to find the best line over the rocky slabs. Then keep on the main track in the wadi, which takes you all the way into **Asimah**.

10. From here you have a choice - either turn left through Yalah to join the **Wadi Sidr/Sana** route midway, [See the **Wadi Sidr/Sana** route p.116] or continue to the junction where the right turn returns to the main **Dibba** to **Masafi** road, and the left heads into **Wadi Tayyibah**. [See the **Wadi Tayyibah** route p.90]

DIBBA 25KM

1.3km

2808000

E 89

0   Scale 1:50,000   2km

👁

408000   410000   412000   414000   416000

MASAFI 4KM

87

Wadi Asimah Highlights

For many years the route through Wadi Asimah was on the main route from the east coast to the west, continuing on through Wadi Tayyibah. The highlights of this trip include some wonderful opportunities for camping near Al Ghail and a lovely short walk down Wadi Al Fara with its stream, seasonal pools and waterfall. Further along, Wadi Al Mawrid has some slightly more challenging driving through lush oasis scenery with an old falaj (irrigation system) built into the wadi walls. Even the village of Asimah is quaint and picturesque. This is a truly historic (if a little bumpy) trip down memory lane.

Camping

Rather unusually, this attractive area features sand dunes directly between stark rocky outcrops. It is an ideal place to stop for a photo, a picnic or just a break from driving, and peaceful spots are easy to find just a short distance from the road — head into the desert at any point you fancy, but keep away from people's property. Further into the dunes there are plenty of places suitable for camping, good for the day before or the evening after driving this route.

Hiking

From the hilltop graveyard, a small windy track takes you five minutes down the wadi to where you have to leave your car and explore on foot, (depending on the time of year, you may have to stop earlier due to the condition of the track). In the wet season the stream spills over the rocks and suckerfish wriggle their way up under a waterfall. Follow the stream past palm trees and greenery and enjoy a swim or some bouldering (climbing) above the small quiet pools.

Oasis

Full of greenery the length of the stream, this hidden wadi is a true oasis. The old falaj, which supplies the small palm groves and cultivated areas with water, is cut into the side of the wadi and often hidden behind vegetation. As the track weaves its way through the wadi, you will pass several dams which catch water during the rainy season.

Navigation

Keep following the meandering Wadi Al Mawrid, sticking to the main track in the wadi, and you can drive all the way to Asimah. The minor tracks that branch off to the sides all end at small villages, single houses, or farms and plantations. In some places, the track traverses rocky slabs, but stick with it and you'll get there.

Asimah

The village of Asimah is strikingly pleasant, clean and peaceful. There is still a very laid-back way of life evident here. Friendly children run around the street and wave as you pass by, while in the afternoons, people sit in shady courtyards or just outside their gates under the trees, chatting and generally relaxing in the slow pace of village life.

Water splash in Wadi Al Mawrid

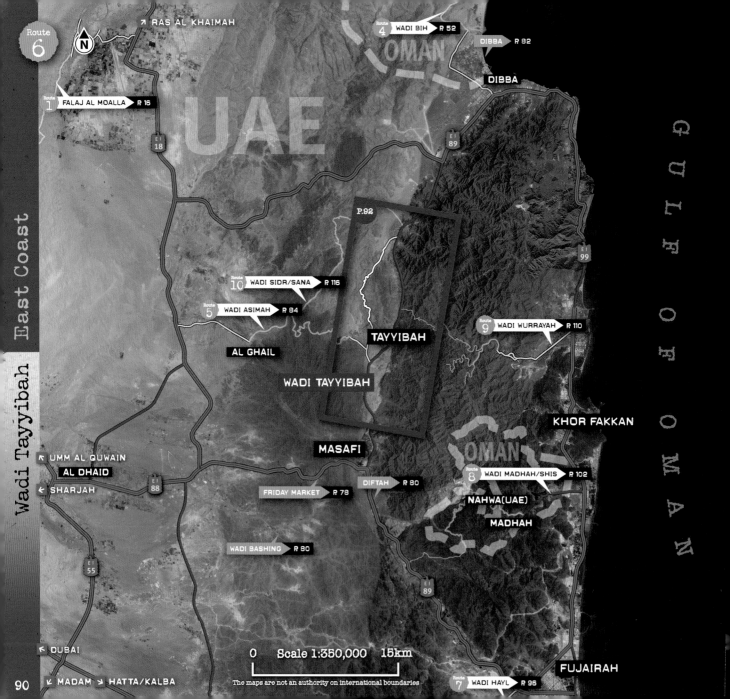

↗ RAS AL KHAIMAH

N

Route 4   WADI BIH   R 52

OMAN

DIBBA   R 82

DIBBA

Route 1   FALAJ AL MOALLA   R 16

UAE

E I 18

E I 89

P.92

G U L F   O F   O M A N

Route 10   WADI SIDR/SANA   R 116

E I 99

Route 5   WADI ASIMAH   R 84

TAYYIBAH

Route 9   WADI WURRAYAH   R 110

AL GHAIL

WADI TAYYIBAH

KHOR FAKKAN

MASAFI   OMAN

↖ UMM AL QUWAIN

Route 8   WADI MADHAH/SHIS   R 102

AL DHAID

DIFTAH   R 80

NAHWA(UAE)

← SHARJAH   E I 88   FRIDAY MARKET   R 78

MADHAH

WADI BASHING   R 80

E I 55

E I 89

← DUBAI

0   Scale 1:350,000   15km

FUJAIRAH

↙ MADAM   ↘ HATTA/KALBA   The maps are not an authority on international boundaries   Route 7   WADI HAYL   R 96

Wadi Tayyibah

Part of the old road that used to link Dubai and the east coast, this route winds down through the mountains from the pass near the village of Tayyibah. Sections of the disintegrating tarred highway are still visible in places. If nothing else, it is enjoyable just to be surrounded by the green of plantations and fruit trees. Driving can be quite tricky at any time of year, and serious floods running down the track can block it completely for some time.

Terrain: Oasis, Wadi
Water: Pools, Stream
Driving: Tricky, can become impassable after heavy rains
Activities: Hiking, Picnicking

Trip Info

Other Names:
Wadi Al Uyaynah

Distances:

	Paved	Unpaved
Dubai to start of route	119km	–
Route	9.3km	6.4km
End of route to Dubai	131km	–

From Abu Dhabi: Add 300km for the round trip

Jeep

R 87

Route
5   WADI ASIMAH   R 84

ASIMAH   YALAH

TAYYIBAH

2.4km

2. As you enter the village of **Tayyibah** keep as straight as possible, winding down past the mosque which is perched up on your right. Keep driving down through the village and plantations, along a wadi bed.

1.3km

GPS   UTM 416,381E 2,807,673N
GEO 25°23'00"N 56°10'07"E

MASAFI 3KM

E1
89

1. Unless you're coming from **Wadi Asimah**, follow the **East Coast** road route to **Masafi**. At the roundabout take a left (2nd exit) towards **Dibba**. Keep on the main road for 10km until you see a signpost to **Asimah/ Tayyibah**. Take this left. Alternatively, this turn is 28km from the Dibba side.

'GRAND CANYON'

C

0   Scale 1:50,000   2km

420000   2802000   2804000   2806000   2808000   422000

R 87

WADI SIDR/SANA ▸ R 116

EAST COAST ROAD

A

Wadi Tayyibah

1.8km

.8km

4. Once up and out of the wadi, the tarmac road at **Al Hala** village takes you back to the main **Dibba** - **Masafi** highway.

4.1km

AL HALA

1.5km

3. After the initial plantation area near the village of Tayyibah, you come across another area roughly 4.5km further on, where the wadi bends around to the right. At this point, you can wander up to your left to a small pond and an interesting falaj system.

UTM 418,662E 2,818,502N
GEO 25°28'53"N 56°11'26"E

GPS

E
89

DIBBA 10KM ↗

12km

GORGE

418000

420000

2820000

422000

424000

2812000

2814000

2816000

2818000

Wadi Tayyibah Highlights

This route can either be taken as a diversion on the way from Masafi to the east coast or as a continuation of the Wadi Asimah route. Driving can be testing, especially in the winter, when heavy rains can make picking your way down the wadi quite a challenge.

Old East Coast Road

In some places you can still see the remnants of paved sections along the track - the leftovers of the old road. This was part of the main road between the east and west coasts before the modern highway was cut through the mountain, (now linking Masafi to Dibba.)

Walk

There are plenty of opportunities to stop and explore the falaj system, take the short hike up to the pools, or enjoy a picnic in the shade of the palm trees.

Falaj - This is the Arabic word for a channel used to irrigate palm plantations and farm fields. Often these channels run for many kilometres, from the source of the water upstream in a wadi to the site of the plantation.

Originally many of these channels ran underground for long distances. According to local legend, they were carved out of the rock by a tribe of men of small stature. A well or shaft was dug and a canal built at a gentle angle, with another well every 30m or so, until the canal eventually reached the surface. Another method was to build a wall across an underground river, so that the water would dam up behind it and be forced to the surface. The wall did not block the river entirely, so the overflow could escape and continue underground down the wadi - very eco-friendly!

It's not known how the falaj systems were built so accurately, since the original builders are long gone. Nowadays, people calling themselves 'falaj builders' simply repair the existing falaj system. There are no real falaj north of Al Ain, since the area is generally too dry. Remnants of the shafts belonging to the famous falaj of Buraimi, which dates from around 1,000BC, can still be found near the Hilton Hotel in Al Ain.

'Grand Canyon'

It is well worth the stop, just off the main road, to admire the views in this area. Heading towards Masafi, near the top of the hill, there is a small area on the left to park your car. You'll see various deep, narrow gorges with terraced cultivation and further along is an even deep gorge with folding hillsides lying spread out before you. For hikers, at the bottom of the hill near Etisalat tower, several tracks head east into the "Grand Canyon" wadi itself. Try any of these tracks and explore the narrow wadis which often have streams, pools, greenery and cultivated plots.

RAS AL KHAIMAH ↑

DIBBA ↗

DIBBA ↑

Route 5 WADI ASIMAH ▶ R 84

Route 9 WADI WURRAYAH ▶ R 110

E 18

KHOR FAKKAN

UMM AL QUWAIN

MASAFI

OMAN

E 99

AL DHAID

DIFTAH ▶ R 80

NAHWA(UAE)

E 88

FRIDAY MARKET ▶ R 78

MADHAH

SHARJAH

Route 8 WADI MADHAH/SHIS ▶ R 102

WADI BASHING ▶ R 80

E 89

UAE

E 55

FUJAIRAH

◀ SHARJAH/DUBAI

FUJAIRAH ▶ R 81

5 116

◀ MADAM/AL AIN

P.98

KALBA

WADI HAYL

KHOR KALBA ▶ R 81

SHARJAH-KALBA ROAD ▶ R 78

116

OMAN

Gulf of Oman

0   Scale 1:350,000   15km

◀ DUBAI

The maps are not an authority on international boundaries

↓ HATTA/SOHAR

↓ HATTA

↓ SOHAR

Wadi Hayl

Route 7

A short route recently paved all the way in, the trip to Wadi Hayl is a must-do during your time in the Emirates purely for a visit to the fascinating Fort Hayl, one of the finest old forts in the UAE. As well as the fort, the wadi and the surrounding mountains offer some excellent places for exploring.

Terrain:	Mountains, Wadis
Water:	Pools (Seasonal)
Driving:	Tarmac to the fort
Activities:	Camping, Hiking
Culture:	Fort

Trip Info

Other Names:
Wadi Hail, Fort Hayl

Distances:

	Paved	Unpaved
Dubai to start of route	135km	–
Route (round trip)	19.8km	–
End of route to Dubai	135km	–

Abu Dhabi Timings:
From Abu Dhabi: Add 300km for the round trip

3. After passing a dam in the wadi, head straight through the new village of Hayl and keep going until you reach the fort.

UTM 422,020E 2,774,565N
GEO 25°05'05"N 56°13'36"E

GPS

Wadi Sanam

Wadi Hayl

A

B

0.8km

HAYL

5.1km

FORT HAYL

Wadi Hayl

C

Wadi Hayl

Wadi Lib

QUARRY

⚠ Once the main way into Wadi Hayl, this route has now been blocked off in both directions by the quarry.

0   Scale 1:50,000   2km

👁

2768000

420000

422000

2770000

424000

426000

MASAFI 22KM R 77

WADI HAM DAM

HERITAGE VILLAGE

KHOR FAKKAN 20KM

E1 89

2. At the second roundabout carry straight on, following the signs to Al Hayl.

GPS UTM 429,667E 2,778,823N
GEO 25°07'25"N 56°18'08"E

POLICE STATION

FUJAIRAH MUSEUM

MILITARY BASE

0.8km

2.5km

0.7km

1. Follow the East Coast road route. Just before the outskirts of Fujairah, take the right hand turn opposite the police station, just past the signs for 'crushers'. Follow the signpost to Hayl Castle / Palace.

FUJAIRAH

E1 89

QUARRY

FUJAIRAH INTERNATIONAL AIRPORT

AIN AL GHAMOUR/KALBA

KALBA 7KM

428000 430000 432000 2774000 2776000 2778000 2780000 2782000 434000 2772000 2776000

Wadi Hayl Highlights

Wadi Hayl is home to the best preserved of all the mountain forts in the UAE. The ruins of the main buildings and watchtower are located on a hillside, while the fertile oasis in the wadi bottom offers hiking and a range of other opportunities to explore further. Although not irrigated and farmed to the extent it was in the past, there are still green plantations and fields through which it is very pleasant to stroll. As this route is such a short drive from the main Fujairah road, it is ideal to combine with a day out on an east coast beach or with one of the other routes in the area.

Fort Hayl

Once the home of the ruling Al Sharqi family of Fujairah, Fort Hayl is one of the best preserved historical buildings in the UAE.

Inside the Fort's Tower

While the fort's history remains rather vague, it is commonly believed to be not more than one to two hundred years old. As the headquarters of the ruler it was most likely used as a base for surveillance and defence of the neighbouring areas. Made of stone and mud bricks mixed with straw, and with wooden planks and earth for the floors, it remains a tantalising glimpse of how life used to be.

The fort is surrounded by small houses, with more in the oasis below, and a watchtower perches on the hill above. Both the fort and the watchtower are great to poke around in, and it is still possible to climb to the top floor of the fort for a view of the surroundings and to take some photographs.

Hayl Village

The old village of Hayl is situated in the valley in a cultivated oasis that still has evidence of the many crops once grown here. There are some old wells, and the area is also home to a wide variety of plant and animal life. Small pools can be found in the bottom of the valley (at the right time of year) and exploring along the course of the wadi among all the greenery can be good fun.

Explore

The track continues after passing the fort, although it doesn't really go anywhere, just mainly serving as an access road for the quarries. However, there are plenty of places to explore – either up the wadi or into the mountains for complete seclusion.

Bitnah

If the fort in Wadi Hayl has awoken an archaeological interest in you, the village of Bitnah situated just off the Fujairah - Masafi highway is a good place to stop at on the way home to see Bitnah Fort and the other archaeological sites around the village. See p.80 for more details.

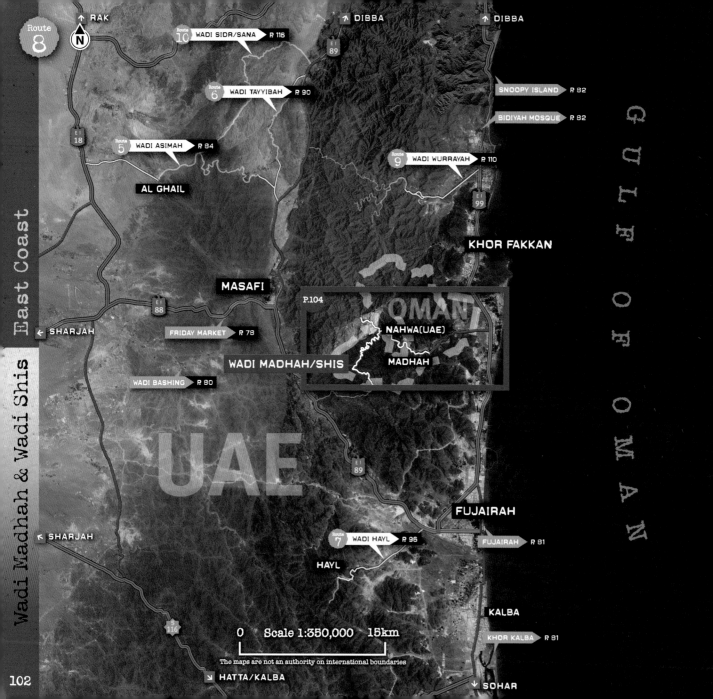

↑ RAK

N

↑ DIBBA

↑ DIBBA

Route 10 WADI SIDR/SANA R 116

E 89

SNOOPY ISLAND R 82

Route 6 WADI TAYYIBAH R 90

BIDIYAH MOSQUE R 82

E 18

Route 5 WADI ASIMAH R 84

Route 9 WADI WURRAYAH R 110

AL GHAIL

E 99

KHOR FAKKAN

MASAFI

P.104

OMAN

← SHARJAH

E 88

NAHWA(UAE)

FRIDAY MARKET R 78

MADHAH

WADI MADHAH/SHIS

WADI BASHING R 80

UAE

E 89

FUJAIRAH

← SHARJAH

Route 7 WADI HAYL R 96

FUJAIRAH R 81

HAYL

KALBA

S 116

KHOR KALBA R 81

0   Scale 1:350,000   15km

The maps are not an authority on international boundaries

GULF OF OMAN

↓ HATTA/KALBA

↓ SOHAR

Wadi Madhah & Wadi Shis

Route 8

Two contrasting wadis with some of the best scenery on the east coast. Visit the shady pools in Wadi Shis in Omani (no visa required) territory where, if you manage to climb the slippery falls, you'll see the fascinating falaj that passes high above the pools. Alternatively, follow the winding river bed of Wadi Madhah (UAE) until you reach the open plateau with some great areas to explore. If you are hiking or biking, it is possible to reach the Fujairah - Masafi Road from the Wadi Madhah side.

Terrain:	Mountains, Oases, Wadis
Water:	Pools, Waterfall
Activities:	Camping, Hiking, Mountain Biking, Swimming
Warning:	Oman Car Insurance

Trip Info

Other Names:
Wadi Madah

Distances:

	Paved	Unpaved
Dubai to start of route	155km	–
Route (round trip)	17.4km	45.8km
End of route to Dubai	155km	–

From Abu Dhabi: Add 300km for the round trip

View from Wadi Shis ↗

Jeep

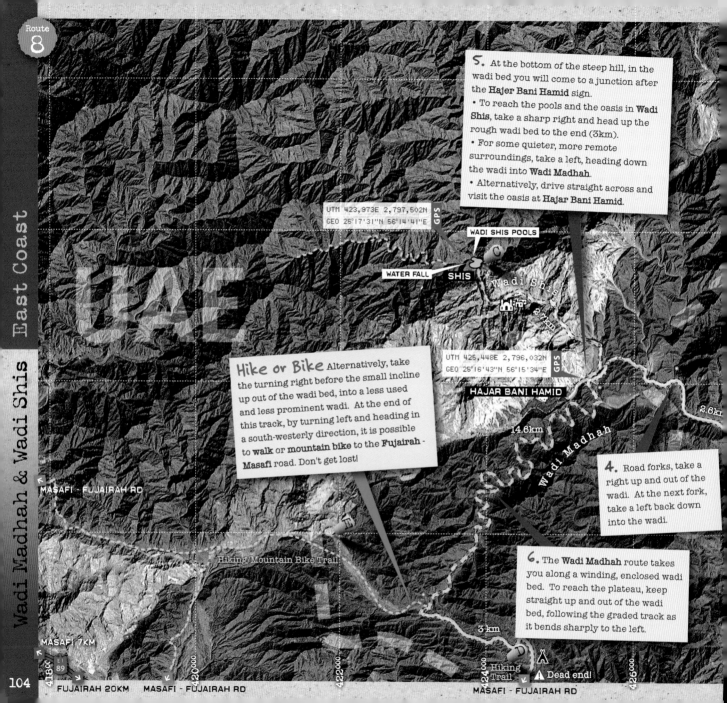

5. At the bottom of the steep hill, in the wadi bed you will come to a junction after the **Hajer Bani Hamid** sign.
• To reach the pools and the oasis in **Wadi Shis**, take a sharp right and head up the rough wadi bed to the end (3km).
• For some quieter, more remote surroundings, take a left, heading down the wadi into **Wadi Madhah**.
• Alternatively, drive straight across and visit the oasis at **Hajar Bani Hamid**.

UTM 423,973E 2,797,502N
GEO 25°17'31"N 56°14'41"E
GPS

WADI SHIS POOLS

WATER FALL

SHIS

Wadi Shis

2.75km

UTM 425,448E 2,796,032N
GEO 25°16'43"N 56°15'34"E
GPS

HAJAR BANI HAMID

2.6km

14.6km

Wadi Madhah

Hike or Bike Alternatively, take the turning right before the small incline up out of the wadi bed, into a less used and less prominent wadi. At the end of this track, by turning left and heading in a south-westerly direction, it is possible to walk or **mountain bike** to the **Fujairah - Masafi** road. Don't get lost!

4. Road forks, take a right up and out of the wadi. At the next fork, take a left back down into the wadi.

6. The **Wadi Madhah** route takes you along a winding, enclosed wadi bed. To reach the plateau, keep straight up and out of the wadi bed, following the graded track as it bends sharply to the left.

Hiking/Mountain Bike Trail

3 km

Hiking Trail

⚠ Dead end!

MASAFI - FUJAIRAH RD

MASAFI 7KM

E89

418000   420000   422000   424000   426000

QIDFA

OMAN

2800000

2798000

3. Take a right at the **T-junction** heading towards **Sa'd**, and ultimately to **Hajar Bani Hamid**. The road is now tarmac until the village of Al Nahwa when it changes to a good graded track.

A'SHAHNA'A

MADHAH

3.4km

2.7km

UTM 435,707E 2,796,483N
GEO 25°17'00"N 56°21'41"E

0.5km

AL HARAH

0.6km

2.6km

1.8km

MURBAH

2796000

AL ARDIYAH

1.8km

1. Follow the **East Coast** road route. In the town of **Murbah**, (14km north of Fujairah, 5km south of Khor Fakkan) follow signs towards **Madhah**.

AL NAHWA

1.1km

AL EHUNAH

PARK

A'SAROUJ

Wadi Madhah

2.8km

SA'D

2. Go left (2nd exit) at the **roundabout** and keep on the main paved road, which winds up through various small villages. **Warning**: The road gets narrow in places so take care.

2794000

UAE

0   Scale 1:50,000   2km

The maps are not an authority on international boundaries

GULF OF

2792000

Wadi Madhah & Wadi Shis Highlights

The journey through this pocket of Oman is an attractive drive through oasis villages, all of which are wonderful spots to explore further. In Wadi Shis you are in Oman and in Wadi Mahdah you are actually back in the UAE. It is always interesting to note on a first visit that although there are no visible borders there's quite a striking difference between the Omani villages and those of the UAE. All of a sudden the street signs, architecture and phone booths change style. In addition, most of the people you see are Omani locals, as opposed to the variety of nationalities you come across in Dubai and the other emirates. Remember, to be on the safe side, you may need to extend your car insurance to cover Oman for this trip. However, there are no checks so the risk is yours.

The highlight is, without doubt, the pools and falls at Wadi Shis. Plan to spend a while here relaxing between your energetic explorations.

Omani Fort

This hilltop fort is still used by the Omani military, so it's not open to visitors. Notice that the watchtowers are whitewashed; unlike the 'au natural' look of those in the UAE.

Shahna'a Oasis

Shahna'a is a very old oasis with a well-preserved irrigation system. Some of the trees here are huge. At the Y-fork at the end of the oasis, an enticing track bends around to the right to the next wadi and small village.

Wadi Shis Pools

Such an idyllic spot! Even if you do not intend to work your way to the top of the gorge, it is worthwhile swimming or wading across the first pool that you come to and clambering across the rocks. It's best to keep your shoes on - a good pair of water-shoes or sandals come in handy. You will then come to a deep dark pool with a waterfall flowing into it - a brilliant spot for swimming. If you want to explore further, you can climb up and beyond the waterfall and after a few more pools you will reach the wadi and plantations, fed by the falaj system, at the top.

On your way back, you can either descend the gorge the way you climbed up, or follow the falaj to the left of the gorge against the side of the wadi. This will take you back to above where you left your car. From here the walk passes through a very narrow gap in the rocks, then over a 'bridge' which you should negotiate one by one as we're not sure how much weight it can bear! Just after this are some stairs which take you between the plantations back to the wadi below.

⌐Fields near Al Harah

Wadi Madhah

Although this road ends in a strangely inexplicable dead-end, it is a great drive if you are in the mood. It starts by winding its way through a narrow wadi — keep your eyes on the mountain-tops to spot the old Omani fort peering down on your progress. There is also an interesting well and a cave-dwelling on your right. Once out of the wadi the track takes you over undulating plains to the top of a plateau with some amazingly peaceful and remote sites for camping. The track eventually ends at the head of another wadi, down which it is possible to walk or bike just a few kilometres to the Masafi - Fujairah road near Bitnah.

Hike or Mountain Bike

Just before the track climbs up out of the wadi to the plateau, a right fork takes you onto a rougher track through a narrower wadi. At the end of this, there's a good hike or mountain-bike ride of about two to four kilometres (depending on how far you drive down the wadi), up and over the hills, turning left in a south-westerly direction. This then leads down to various tracks, which eventually join the Fujairah - Masafi road, near the Diftah area. Don't get lost!

Shame about the car. Perhaps you could do a two-car trip, leaving a vehicle at either end of the route?

Note
- The local farmers strongly dislike anyone swimming in the upper pools, as this is their drinking water.

The road into Wadi Madhah

Mountain bike trail

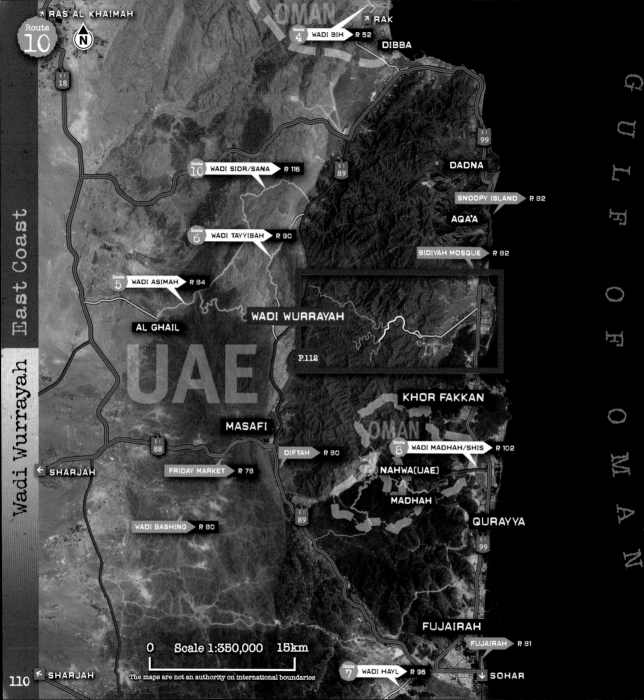

N

E1 18

OMAN

RAK

Route 4 WADI BIH R 52

DIBBA

E1 99

Route 10 WADI SIDR/SANA R 116

DADNA

E1 89

SNOOPY ISLAND R 82

AQA'A

Route 6 WADI TAYYIBAH R 90

BIDIYAH MOSQUE R 82

Route 5 WADI ASIMAH R 84

WADI WURRAYAH

AL GHAIL

UAE

P.112

KHOR FAKKAN

MASAFI

OMAN

Route 8 WADI MADHAH/SHIS R 102

E1 88

DIFTAH R 80

NAHWA(UAE)

SHARJAH

FRIDAY MARKET R 78

MADHAH

QURAYYA

E1 89

E1 99

WADI BASHING R 80

FUJAIRAH

Scale 1:350,000

0   15km

FUJAIRAH R 81

SHARJAH

The maps are not an authority on international boundaries

WADI HAYL R 96

SOHAR

Route 7

GULF OF OMAN

Wadi Wurrayah

A short, easy drive to one of the UAE's most visited waterfalls. It's a great spot for swimming all year round, but one that is unfortunately, year by year, being spoiled visitors. However, a little effort to get up and away from the main falls will take you to some beautiful, secluded pools and hiking areas that have been less affected by the thoughtless few.

Ras Al Khaimah

Dubai

Fujairah

Abu Dhabi · UAE · Hatta

Al Ain

OMAN

Arabian Gulf · Gulf of Oman

Terrain:	Mountains, Wadis
Water:	Pools, Waterfall (UAE style!)
Activities:	Hiking, Swimming
Warning:	Graffiti, Litter

Trip Info

Other Names:
Wurayyah Waterfall

Distances:

	Paved	Unpaved
Dubai to start of route	178km	–
Route (Round Trip)	16.6km	8.8km
End of route to Dubai	178km	4.5km

From Abu Dhabi: Add 300 km for the round trip

Wurrayah waterfall ↗

Jeep

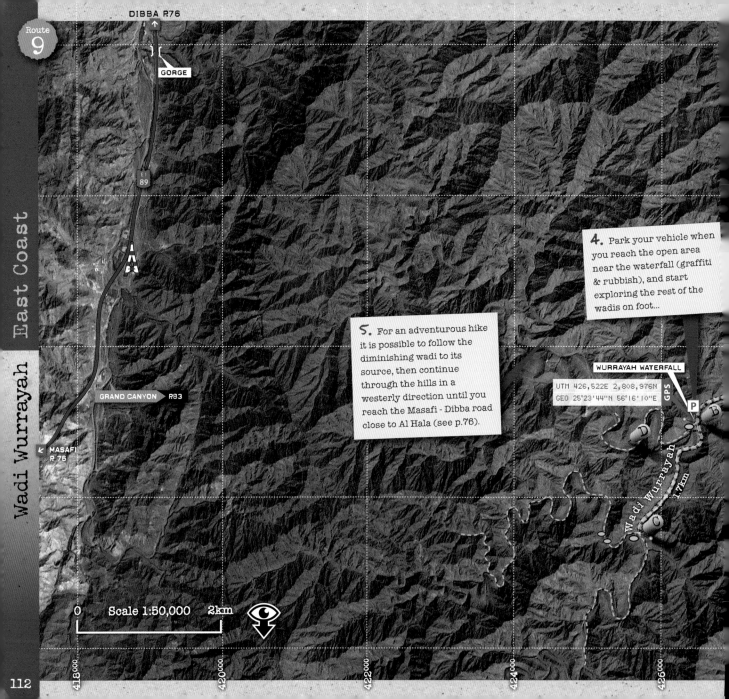

DIBBA R76

GORGE

E1
89

4. Park your vehicle when you reach the open area near the waterfall (graffiti & rubbish), and start exploring the rest of the wadis on foot...

5. For an adventurous hike it is possible to follow the diminishing wadi to its source, then continue through the hills in a westerly direction until you reach the Masafi - Dibba road close to Al Hala (see p.76).

GRAND CANYON R83

MASAFI
R 76

WURRAYAH WATERFALL

UTM 426,522E 2,808,976N
GEO 25°23'44"N 56°16'10"E

GPS

P

B

Wadi Wurrayah

0   Scale 1:50,000   2km

DIBBA 25KM R 76

BIDIYAH MOSQUE ▸ R 82

THURSDAY MARKET

BIDIYAH

N

1. Follow the East Coast road route.
• From **Fujairah** 4.7km from Khor Fakkan Oceanic Hotel Roundabout, take the U-turn. 700m later take the next paved right at the end of the shops near the mosque.
• From **Dibba** 2.4km from Bidiya Roundabout, take the paved road right at the end of the shops near the mosque.

GPS UTM 434,627E 2,810,711N
     GEO 25°24'42"N 56°21'00"E

SHOPS

3. While you are in the second major dip in the wadi, 1km after the roads join up, take a right turn into the wide wadi bed.

2.7km

1.0km

1.5km

1.2km

1.7km

4.3km

0.4 km

0.7km

1km

2. At the **junction** take either the left or right fork - they join up after about 1km.

2km

E1 99

OCEANIC HOTEL

KHOR FAKKAN

FUJAIRAH 24KM R 76

GULF OF OMAN

2812000

2810000

2808000

2806000

428000 430000 432000 434000 436000

113

Wadi Wurrayah Highlights

Largely because of its waterfalls and pools, Wadi Wurrayah is one of the most popular places on the east coast for picnickers and wadi bashers, especially at weekends. Even in summer, water flows over the high falls to feed the main pool.

Sadly, the increasing number of visitors is starting to have a serious effect on the wadi and the normally clear water. Compared to just a few years ago, the area is in an appalling state with litter finding its way into the pool, and graffiti spreading over the rocks around the pool like a rash. At the time of writing, even the new municipality sign to discourage littering had been ripped up and dumped by the water.

Having said this, the drive up the wadi is still enjoyable and there are some lovely walks above the waterfall and further up the main wadi that are less touched (polluted) by man where it's possible to find clean, smaller pools inside the snaking canyons for a dip.

Wadi Wurrayah

The wadi is a slightly bumpy, but picturesque, drive as you twist and turn between its narrowing sides. There is a fair amount of plant life along the edges as well as interesting curves carved by years of rushing floodwaters.

Wurrayah Waterfall

When you arrive at the waterfall, the wadi widens into an open area perfect for parking your car. Rocky outcrops rise steeply on your right and the waterfall and pools are found in the gap in the rocks (the main pool is surprisingly deep). At certain times of the year Rock Martins build their nests on the sides of the wadi.

Hike – Along Wadi

In the main wadi, the track after the waterfall becomes much rougher and a bit trickier to negotiate. For the hardy, it is possible to drive to its conclusion where the walk up the canyon starts, or for a less bumpy journey, head up on foot. From here there is a magnificent hike that follows the course of the stream, which flows all year round. The first hour is the most interesting, but you can continue exploring as far as you like, as the wadi takes you in and out of shallow water, wading and swimming through pools and climbing up or sliding down small waterfalls. Look out for the small cave, pictured opposite, home to small brown bats, up to your left along the route.

Hike – Above Falls

The steep sides of the wadi shade most of this walk and because you are often in the water wading or swimming, it can be done even in the height of summer.

Above the waterfall, the stream runs along a small tributary of Wadi Wurrayah. If you are prepared to walk for one or two hours you are in for a treat, eventually arriving at a quiet and secluded second pool, also with a waterfall.

Pools above the waterfall

Cave along the hiking route

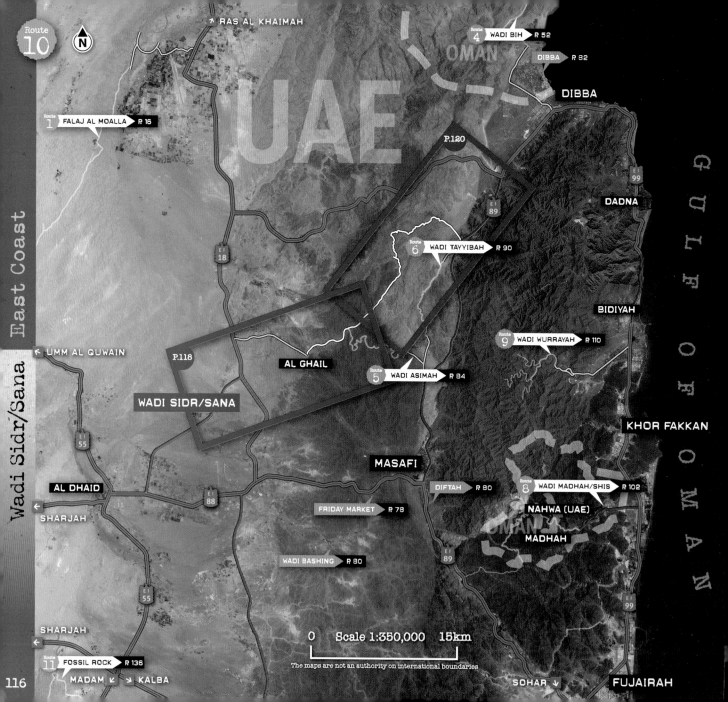

N

Wadi Sidr/Sana · East Coast

RAS AL KHAIMAH

UAE

OMAN

DIBBA

Route 4 WADI BIH ▶ R 52

DIBBA ▶ R 82

Route 1 FALAJ AL MOALLA ▶ R 16

P.120

E I 99

DADNA

E I 89

Route 6 WADI TAYYIBAH ▶ R 90

BIDIYAH

Route 9 WADI WURRAYAH ▶ R 110

E I 18

P.118

AL GHAIL

Route 5 WADI ASIMAH ▶ R 84

UMM AL QUWAIN

WADI SIDR/SANA

KHOR FAKKAN

E I 55

MASAFI

AL DHAID

DIFTAH ▶ R 80

Route 8 WADI MADHAH/SHIS ▶ R 102

E I 88

FRIDAY MARKET ▶ R 78

NAHWA (UAE)

SHARJAH

OMAN

MADHAH

WADI BASHING ▶ R 80

E I 89

E I 55

E I 99

SHARJAH

0 Scale 1:350,000 15km

Route 11 FOSSIL ROCK ▶ R 136

The maps are not an authority on international boundaries

MADAM ↙ ↘ KALBA

SOHAR ↓

FUJAIRAH

G U L F   O F   O M A N

Wadi Sidr/Sana

An alternative route to the east coast from the village of Al Ghail on the Wadi Asimah route or a different way home from Dibba. Instead of turning off into Wadi Al Mawrid (which leads into Wadi Asimah), it keeps to the main wadi, Wadi Sidr, and then heads up into the mountains. The highpoint on the plateau has a great spot for camping, some interesting, easy hikes and fantastic views all the way down to Dibba on the Gulf of Oman.

Terrain: Wadi, Mountains

Driving: Mostly good tracks, but go steady on the descent to Sana

Activities: Camping, Mountain Biking

Trip Info

Other Names:
Wadi Sanaa

Distances:

	Paved	Unpaved
Dubai to start of route	107km	–
Route		
End of route to Dubai	7.4km	25.4km
	132km	–

From Abu Dhabi: Add 300km for the round trip

Jeep

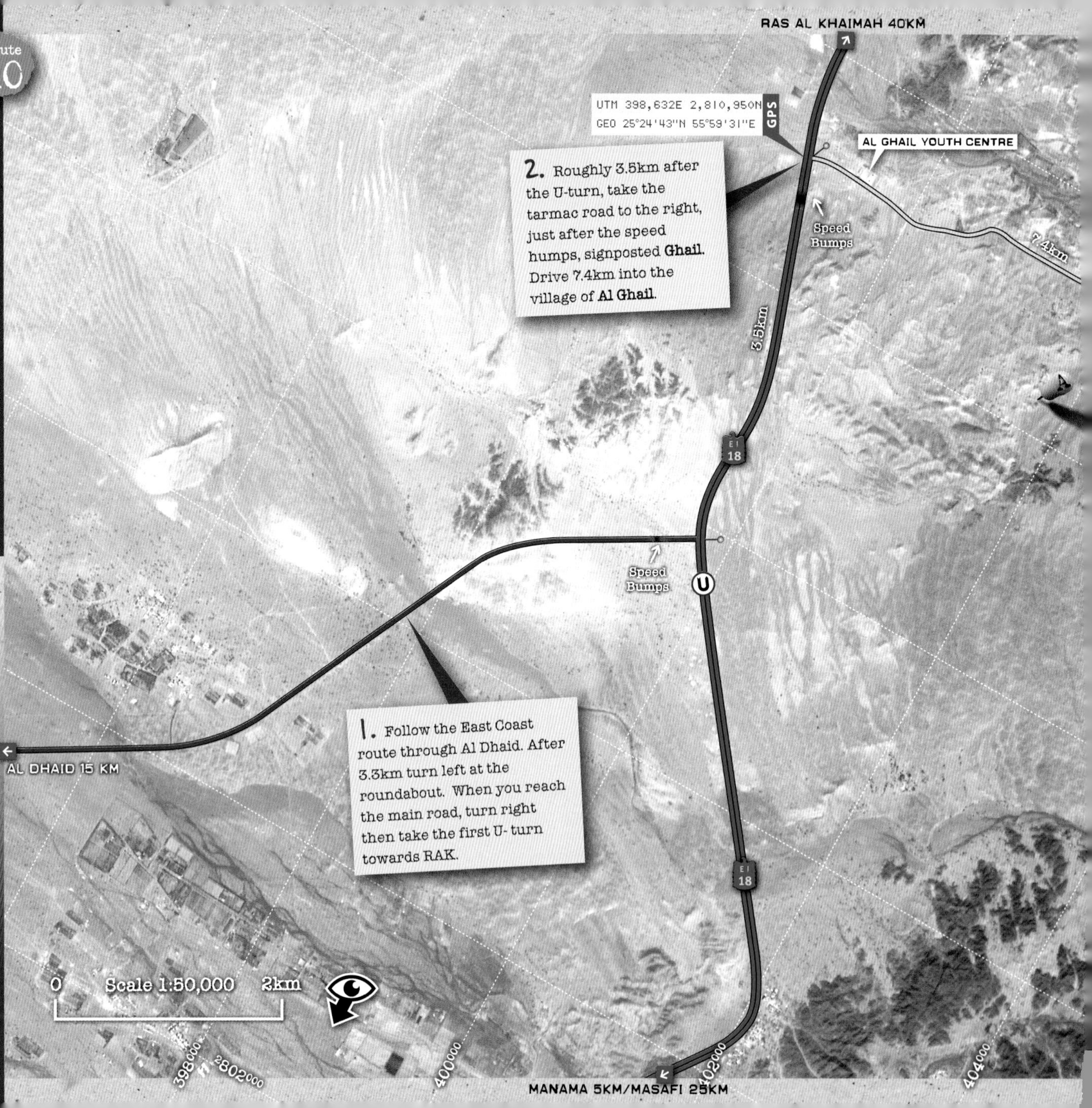

East Coast

Wadi Sidr/Sana

RAS AL KHAIMAH 40KM

UTM 398,632E 2,810,950N
GEO 25°24'43"N 55°59'31"E

GPS

AL GHAIL YOUTH CENTRE

2. Roughly 3.5km after the U-turn, take the tarmac road to the right, just after the speed humps, signposted **Ghail**. Drive 7.4km into the village of **Al Ghail**.

7.4km

Speed
Bumps

3.5km

E 1
18

Speed
Bumps

U

1. Follow the East Coast route through Al Dhaid. After 3.3km turn left at the roundabout. When you reach the main road, turn right then take the first U-turn towards RAK.

AL DHAID 15 KM

E 1
18

0   Scale 1:50,000   2km

398 000   2802000   400 000   402000   404 000

MANAMA 5KM/MASAFI 25KM

4. Head downhill past the water tower, then once you've emerged from the narrow passageway into the wadi bed, head straight across the wadi intersection towards the plantations, keeping on the lower of the two tracks in front of you.

From here you can take a short diversion of less than 1km, by turning left near the graveyard on to a small track which heads into the wadi and down to a secluded spot with some small seasonal pools.

6. At the junction around 2km from the house, continue straight up the main Wadi Sidr lined with palm plantations.

GPS UTM 409,168E 2,811,928N
GEO 25°25'17"N 56°05'48"E

R 120

3.1km

Wadi Al Fara

Wadi Sidr

1.6km

AL GHAIL

2.2km

Route
5 WADI ASIMAH R 84

3. At the end of the tarmac road, follow the track into **Al Ghail**, down and up through the initial dip, bearing left towards the mosque. Keeping left (mosque now on your right), follow the line of smaller telegraph poles on the left-hand side towards the large water tower and palm trees in the distance.

5. Stop when you reach the brow of a hill, which has a small graveyard on your left and a two-storey house with a distinctive red roof a little way on your right. Once in the main wide wadi bed, turn right and drive upstream.

Wadi Al Mawrid

Wadi Asimah

ASIMAH

R 87

10. At a split in the tracks just in front of a small farm, take the right fork past a sign in Arabic. Follow this track up the hill between the rocks and along the ridge above the fertile little valley on your left. Continue climbing until you reach the plateau on top of the hill.

9. 300m from the T-junction turn left just before the small shop. Then follow the road around to your right as it winds up the valley (don't go up the hill to your left).

UTM 413,284E 2,818,547N
GEO 25°28'53"N 56°08'14"E

7. Continue straight along the wadi, past several groups of houses and Wadi Sidr Dam, until you reach a village. At the centre, keep in the wadi bed and follow the track to the left of the mosque, again heading along Wadi Sidr.

11. Upon reaching the top of the hill, a smaller track off to the left takes you to the edge of the plateau – a great place for camping or picnics with views down to the sea at Dibba. Alternatively, the trees on the right of the track offer shelter if it's hot.

FARM
Pass
TOP OF HILL
0.6km
1.2km
Plateau
DAM
2.0km
3.0km
SHOP
1.0km
3km
0.9km
Pass

WADI SIDR DAM
1.5km
DAM
1.6km
0.8km
Wadi Sidr 1.4km
UTM 412,228E 2,814,513N
GEO 25°2'42"N 56°07'37"E
R 119   1.6km

8. Continue through the wadi to a small village. The track then starts winding up to a pass through the mountains. Ignore the left turn and head straight down the hill for 1km to a T-junction with a main track and turn right.

Route
6   WADI TAYYIBAH   R 90

12. From the plateau it's 3km downhill to the valley bottom. Quite steep and rough in places - advisable to engage 4WD and use engine braking. Fantastic downhill for mountain bikers! Once at the bottom it's a simple drive out of the wadi and straight across the plain to meet up with the Dibba-Masafi road.

SANA

E 87

CEMENT FACTORY

DIBBA 14KM R 76

DAM

1.7km

0.8km

1.7km

E 1
89

7.0km

13. Turn right to Masafi, left to Dibba.

HALA

1.3km

E 1
89

GPS UTM 419,255E 2,819,590N
GEO 25°29'28"N 56°11'47"E

0   Scale 1:50,000   2km

Wadi Sidr/Sana Highlights

If you're looking for new scenery in this area and a different option to the more-often travelled Wadi Asimah, or just for a straightforward route through the mountains, this could be the one. Starting off along the same track into Wadi Sidr as the Wadi Asimah route, it follows the wadi until the end, then up into the mountains with spectacular views, before descending to the Masafi-Dibba road. Mountain bikers also frequent this area for a full-on downhill from the plateau to the main road.

Camping

Rather unusually, this attractive area features sand dunes directly between stark rocky outcrops. It is an ideal place for a photo-stop, a picnic or just a break from driving, and peaceful spots are easy to find just a short distance from the road —

head into the desert anywhere you like the look of, but keep away from people's property. Further into the dunes there are plenty of places suitable for camping, good for the day before or the evening after driving this route.

Hiking

From the hilltop graveyard a small windy track takes you five minutes down the wadi to where you have to leave your car and explore on foot, (depending on the time of year, you may have to stop earlier due to the condition of the track). In the wet season the stream spills over the rocks and suckerfish wriggle their way up under a waterfall. Follow the stream past palm trees and greenery and enjoy a swim or some bouldering (climbing) above the small quiet pools.

Yalah

For a quick way into the middle of Wadi Sidr, or an escape route, this track links to the Dibba-Masafi road via the village of Yalah. Very useful if you want to combine two or more of these nearby routes, it's a good way into Wadi Sidr from the end of Wadi Asimah and the beginning of Wadi Tayyibah.

The Plateau

The area at the top of the hill is great for camping, or a picnic if you're only daytripping. Camping at the edge of the plateau offers great views over the wadi below, and for early birds the experience of watching the sun rise is hard to beat.

There are plenty of rocky summits beside the main track that can be reached by trekkers (and non-trekkers) of all ages and abilities. Just a five-minute climb will reward you with great views across the plateau and surrounding mountains, and even as far as the coast towards Dibba. You can also investigate the stone cairns that have graced many of these peaks for generations. Perhaps the best time to make these mini climbs is in the last hour or so before sunset, when you'll see the surrounding mountains take on a beautiful, golden hue. Just watch your footing on the way back down, as once the sun sets, the light goes very quickly.

Bike or Hike

The descent is an awesome downhill for mountain bikers - only 3km but fast and pretty gnarly in some places. If you're feeling fit, riding up is a real challenge, but it's definitely worth doing at least two runs on the downhill while you're there. Otherwise, take turns doing shuttle runs in a 4WD or get a friend to ferry you to the top for the next time down.

For hikers, the old track to the top is visible from the current one, starting from Sana Village and heading up the other side of the valley it can be a nice way to arrive at the campsite at the top.

The Road to RAK

This relatively new road provides a fast link with Ras Al Khaimah, allowing you to get over to the west coast much quicker than on the routes that existed previously. It's also worth taking if you're heading back to Dubai, as it cuts the corner off the old route, eventually bringing you out on the E88 near Al Dhaid.

Stunning mountain scenery, temperature-controlled swimming pools, international cuisine, deluxe chalet-style rooms, archery, clay shooting, driving range, mini-golf, children's activities and more.

Expect Nothing Less.

Hatta

Jeep

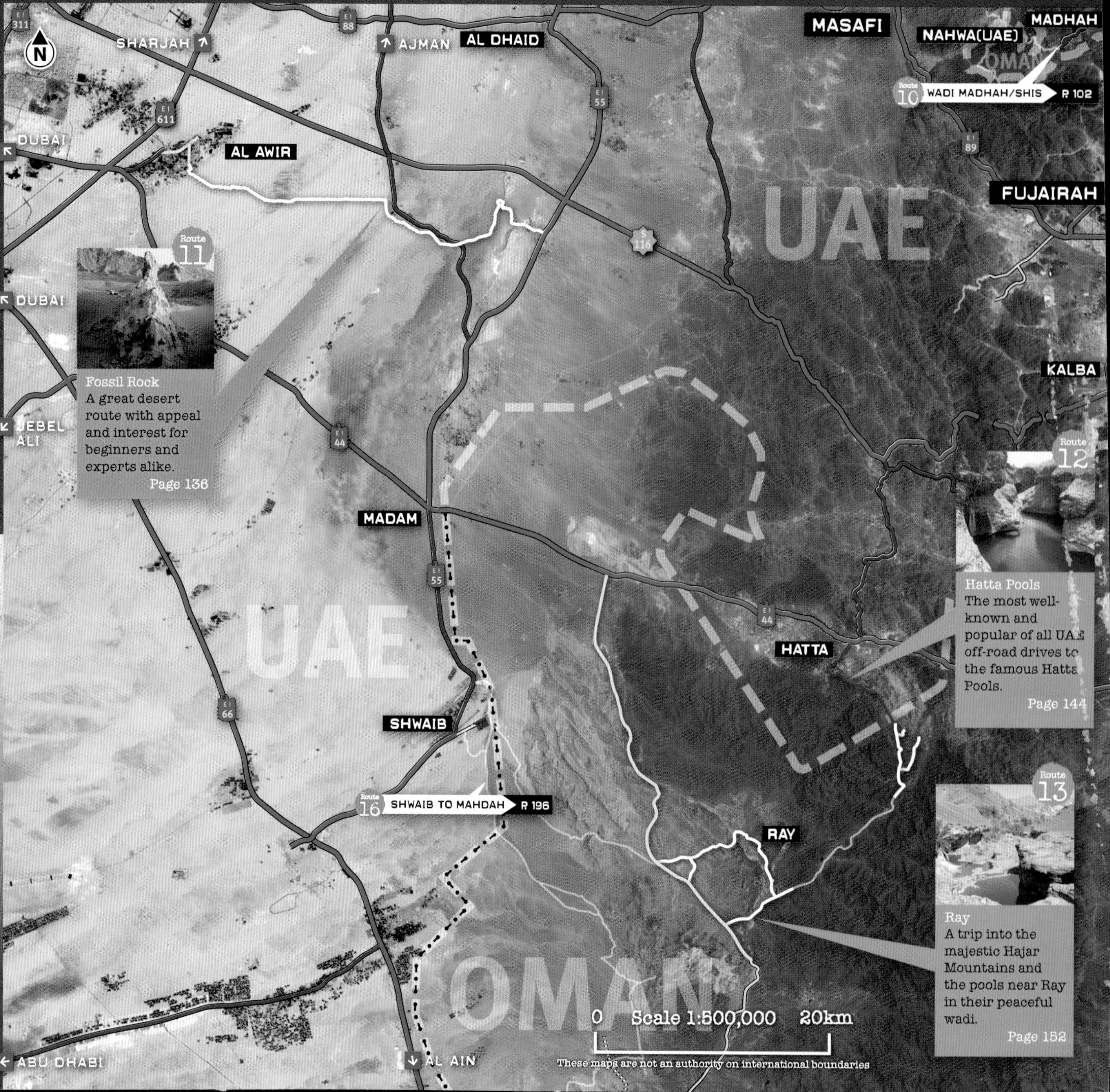

N

311
SHARJAH ↑
88
↑ AJMAN
AL DHAID
MASAFI
NAHWA(UAE)
MADHAH

OMAN
Route 10
WADI MADHAH/SHIS
R 102

611
55

DUBAI ↖
89

AL AWIR
FUJAIRAH

116
UAE

Route 11
Fossil Rock
A great desert
route with appeal
and interest for
beginners and
experts alike.
Page 136

DUBAI ↖

KALBA

JEBEL ALI ↖

44

Route 12

MADAM
UAE
44
HATTA
Hatta Pools
The most well-
known and
popular of all UAE
off-road drives to
the famous Hatta
Pools.
Page 144

55

66

SHWAIB
Route 13

Route 16
SHWAIB TO MAHDAH
R 196

RAY

Ray
A trip into the
majestic Hajar
Mountains and
the pools near Ray
in their peaceful
wadi.
Page 152

OMAN

0   Scale 1:500,000   20km

↓ AL AIN
These maps are not an authority on international boundaries

Hatta Route Overview Table

Route	Name	Page	Total Dist. (km)	Total Unpaved (km)	Terrain Mtn	Desert	Wadi	Camp	Climb	Hike	Bike	Swim	Route Combinations
	Hatta Road Route	128	100	–									
11	Fossil Rock	136	39.9	32.2		✓		✓					12 + 13 + 5
12	Hatta Pools	144	32.6	10.8	✓		✓	✓		✓	✓	✓	11 + 13 + 16
13	Ray	152	80.6	26.4	✓		✓	✓		✓	✓	✓	11 + 12 + 16

Hatta Route Combinations

One-Day Trips

Hatta Pools P.144 ▶ Ray P.152

Although the Hatta Pools is somewhere people sometimes manage to spend the whole day, it's also nice to extend the route to a full day of off-roading by continuing into the mountains. After a morning at Hatta Pools, you have a choice of the quick main track to Shuwayhah village then to the Ray Pools, or from Ray you can take the more adventurous route cross country to the same wadi. You will then end up at the perfect spot for lunch on the sandy ground under the trees in the small plantation The route home is the Ray route in reverse out to the Hatta – Dubai road.

Fossil Rock P.136 ▶ Wadi Asimah P.84

The Fossil Rock route offers a great all-round desert experience, and can be tackled by any level of driver (although you'll find some challenging dunes off the main track). The drive through Wadi Asimah then provides completely different scenery and driving, with mountains, farms, plantations and villages where life hasn't changed in decades.

Two-Day Trips

Hatta Pools P.144 ▶ Ray P.152 ▶ Shwaib to Madhah P.196

To extend the Hatta Pools/Ray route described above, to a weekend trip, follow the same plan described above on the first day, but take more time over it, then spend the night in the wadi. On the second day, head to the road on the way home, then turn off to go through the Sumayni gap and the Omani border post, before heading straight across the plains to join up with the Shwaib – Madhah route at the edge of the dunes. After enjoying this fantastic area of dunes, head out of the desert to Madhah to re-inflate your tyres, then back on the Hadf road to join the Hatta – Dubai road.

Fossil Rock P.136 ▶ Wadis Mahdah & Shis P.102

Combine this classic desert route with a trip into the Omani enclave just off the east coast for the two contrasting wadis of Mahdah and Shis. While at the coast you should explore Kalba, either on foot or by hiring a canoe. Then head up the coast where good camping can be found in Wadi Mahdah if you get there in time, or in among the foothills of the Hajar near Kalba.

N

UMM AL QUWAIN

↗ RAK ↗ RAK ↑ RAK DIBBA

A R A B I A N   G U L F

AJMAN

SHARJAH

MASAFI

DUBAI

AL DHAID

OMAN

Route 11 FOSSIL ROCK R 136

P.130

FUJAIRAH

KALBA

← ABU DHABI

DUBAI - HATTA

MADAM

Route 13 RAY R 152

Route 12 HATTA POOLS R 144

HATTA

SHWAIB

Route 16 SHWAIB TO MAHDAH R 196

SOHAR

UAE

OMAN

0   Scale 1:750,000   30km

These maps are not an authority on international boundaries. AL AIN ↓

Dubai - Hatta

The drive to Hatta offers picturesque views of the desert on the way, as you pass the popular 'Big Red' dune, and finishes at the peaceful town of Hatta, nestling in the foothills of the Hajar Mountains just a few kilometres from the border with Oman. On the way there, a number of areas of the desert are worth checking out, while from around Hatta there are options for off-roading or road trips through the Hajars.

Terrain: Desert, Mountains, Oasis, Wadi

Water: Pools, Streams, Waterfalls

Driving: Varied, desert and mountains

Activities: Swimming, Hiking, Picnics, Sandboarding

Trip Info

Distances:
Dubai to Hatta   100km

From Abu Dhabi: Add 300km for the round trip

Dunes near Big Red ↗

Road Route

AJMAN

SHARJAH

I. Follow the **Dubai City Overview** map for the best way to **Bu Kidra Interchange** at the end of the creek, where you have two options:
• For the quickest way, follow the signs for **Al Ain** onto the E66. At the 5th main interchange, (6th bridge) take the slip road off and head left towards **Hatta/Oman** on the E77 joining the E44 at the Lahbab R/A, then turn right to Hatta.
• For the simplest way, follow the signs for **Hatta/Oman** onto the E44. Keep on this, going straight through all the roundabouts and follow the signs to **Hatta**.

Route 11 · FOSSIL ROCK · R 136

AL AWIR

E 44
18km

DUBAI

LAHBAB
9km

TRADE CENTRE R/A

E 44

DRAGON MART

3km

6km

SHARJAH BYPASS

Dubai/Sharjah City Overview (p.xx)

E 311

GPS UTM 429,667E 2,778,823N

5km

4km

E 77

15km

DEFENCE I/C

BU KIDRA I/C

4km

4.3km

1

2.6km   3

4.6km   4

E 66

7.9km

5

4km

6

E 44

0 — Scale 1:275,000 — 10km

AL DHAID 4KM   SHARJAH   KALBA 36KM

MILEIHA

MUNAY

3. Arrived! Take a right (1st exit) at **Hatta Fort** R/A to head up into the small town. For more details on **Hatta**, refer to the **Hatta Pools** route.

FILI

D. For a walk to the summit of **Jebel Rawdah**, turn left off the main road 10km after **Madam R/A** and follow the paved road leading into the quarry. The track bends to the right behind the mountain into a valley, at the end of which various walking routes to the top are possible.

SOHAR 81KM

HATTA FORT HOTEL

UTM 412,454E 2,745,127N   GPS

8.1km

HATTA

10km

C. You are now passing through an Omani enclave, so it is important to ensure that your car insurance covers Oman.

Jebel Rawdah 10.1km
692m

E I 44

Route 12   HATTA POOLS   R 144

R 146

17.9km

RED'

15km

MADAM

E I 44

MADAM R/A

From the new roundabout at the Shell petrol station, if you turn right this road takes you to Mahdah and Al Ain.

E. For the **Jebel Hatta** hike, 28 km after **Madam R/A**, turn right between some shops onto a dual carriageway and head for the communication tower. Follow the wadi track as far as possible.

Jebel Hatta

2. At the Madam R/A, head straight across (2nd exit).

Jebel Sumayni

Route 16   SHWAIB TO MAHDAH   R 196

SHWAIB

Route 13   RAY   R 152   R 126

AL AIN 59KM

Dubai to Hatta Road Route Highlights

There is something very tranquil and peaceful about the Hatta area, and in the village itself the pace of life is relaxed and unhurried. You can visit the Hatta Fort Hotel for an alfresco lunch surrounded by beautiful scenery or, if you want more action, the Hajar Mountains and the Hatta Pools are on your doorstep waiting to be explored.

Alternatively, the desert you pass through on the way to Hatta has off-road options, such as the route from Al Awir to Fossil Rock (good for all levels of drivers), or the desert playground near 'Big Red'. This area close to the main road has some gentle undulating tracks through the flatter dunes, and a lot more big thrills on huge, clean dunes for the more experienced driver.

Ras Al Khor Wildlife Sanctuary

At the end of the creek, the Ras Al Khor Wildlife Sanctuary is a great place to see flamingos, as well as other shore birds and waders. Several thousand Greater Flamingos (the only pink flamingo to occur regularly in Arabia), arrive here each winter from the north-west of Iran.

To protect the reserve you are only allowed to enter it with special permission. But there are three hides located around the end of the creek, looked after by wardens, where it is possible to easily observe the birds with the binoculars and telescopes provided. Sometimes you can also sometimes spot the birds from the road. For an official permit contact the Environmental Protection Department of the Dubai Municipality, or Birdwatching Tours for further details (see Directory).

Big Red

Over 100m high, the Big Red sand dune is a popular spot for practising dune driving in 4 WDs, dune buggies or on quad bikes, as well as for trying sand skiing. Quad bikes are available for hire on either side of the road, as well as camel and horse rides. Alternatively, take a walk to the top which takes about 20 minutes (not advisable on Fridays when there are too many maniacs racing up the dunes)

Oman Enclave

Be aware that you are now passing through an Oman enclave. Make sure that your car insurance covers Oman, because knowing how life goes, if you're going to hit a camel, it'll probably happen here. Also, for routes such as Hatta Pools and Ray, most of the routes are well inside Oman so it is useful to have insurance for these anyway.

↑ Falcon at Big Red Tourist Spot

Jebel Rawdah Hike

More of a large hill than a mountain, Jebel Rawdah is the first peak to be seen on the left side of the road on the way to Hatta, and the base is easily accessible by two-wheel-drive vehicles. At the end of the valley, various routes are possible to the top – the centre one is the easiest (but all routes can be completed in about two hours). The views are definitely worth it. Remember to take enough water, even on a short walk like this, as well as appropriate footwear for the loose rock.

Jebel Hatta Hike

Another great walk is the hike up Jebel Hatta, which rises to a height of 1,311m. It's the highest mountain in the area and is made more prominent by the large communication mast on the summit. The climb can take around 10 hours, even for experienced hikers, so it's definitely not for beginners, but the views from the top are amazing.

After leaving your car, walk up the wadi bed for about 15 minutes to a fork and turn left up the wadi. Follow the wadi bed for about two hours, occasionally detouring to avoid pools or short rock sections, until you get to the first palm tree. Some of the pools have enough water for swimming (depending on the rains), but perhaps leave this as a treat for the journey back. After another half an hour take the wadi to the left, heading in a NE direction. The wadi narrows after about three hours and swings right into more of a gully. At 3½ hours you should get your first view of the mast on the summit. From here the route gets steeper. Follow the gully as it leads up a steep slope up to an obvious col at the top (about 1¼ hours).

Descend from the col into a gully below and traverse around to the next gully, which leads directly to the summit (one hour). The route is very steep and has very loose rocks/scree in places. The best route down is to retrace your steps to the col, half the time it takes to ascend this section.

Note – Unless you are prepared to walk to the start of this hike, you will need a 4 WD. From leaving the road it is about a 20 minute drive in the wadi to the start of the hike. Drive along the right-hand side of the wadi, then into the wadi itself until you can't drive any further.

Carpet Market

If you are in the mood for bargaining, the small shops lining the main road offer an interesting selection of clay pots and carpets — everything from Iranian silk and kilims from Afghanistan, to carpets that look like they've been there for years.

Hatta Fort Hotel

The Hatta Fort Hotel is a relaxing oasis of pleasure. Great for a leisurely lunch, a day by the pool or an overnight stay. Sports facilities include archery, clay-pigeon shooting, golf, horse riding or tennis.

Hatta

This ancient mountain village offers a slightly more peaceful way of life than other towns in the UAE. Visit the traditional Hatta Heritage Village, explore the ancient watchtowers, or visit one of Hatta's two dams (the one on the far side of the village is more scenic). For further information on Hatta, refer to the Hatta Pools route.

Hatta - Kalba Road

Previously an off-road route, but now paved all the way, this drive is one of the more interesting roads in the country. As it curves and twists its way through passes and tunnels cut into the rock, heading north into the mountains from Hatta offers grand views over endless jagged peaks (a refreshing change from the usual flat, straight highways found in the UAE). The road is easy to follow and is a suprisingly quick and enjoyable way to get to Kalba on the east coast. It is also possible to turn left towards Sharjah at Munay for the drive out of the mountains and through the desert near Fossil Rock. It's also a good place for cyclists, as the roads are generally quiet.

N

↗ UAQ / RAK   ↗ RAS AL KHAIMAH   RAS AL KHAIMAH ↑

AJMAN

Route
1 FALAJ AL MOALLA ► R 16

Route
5 WADI ASIMAH

E I
11

SHARJAH

E I
311

SHARJAH NATURAL HISTORY MUSEUM ► R 78

AL DHAID

MAS

E I
88

DUBAI

RAS AL KHOR WILDLIFE SANCTUARY ► R 132

S
116

E I
55

FOSSIL ROCK

SHARJAH - KALBA ROAD

AL KHAWANEEJ

P.138

P.140

E I
311

116

KAL

JEBEL ALI

E I
66

E I
44

LAHBAB

JEBEL ALI

BIG RED ► R 132

UAE

OMAN

E I
66

MADAM

E I
44

JEBEL RAWDAH HIKE ► R 134

Route
13 RAY ► R 152

HAT

0   Scale 1:400,000   15km

These maps are not an authority on international boundaries

AL AIN ↓   SHWAIB ↓

Fossil Rock

The closest route to Dubai, and a great desert drive for beginners or experts alike. Initially heading along a sandy track from Al Awir via camel farms and Wadi Faya, it's an easy introduction to sand driving, which becomes as challenging as you want to make it when you get near Fossil Rock. Officially called Jebel Maleihah, this large outcrop is more widely known as Fossil Rock, after the abundance of marine fossils that can be found on its slopes.

Terrain: Desert, Rocky Outcrops
Activities: Camping, Dune Driving, Fossil Hunting, Hiking

Trip Info

Other Names:
Jebel Maleihah

Distances:

	Paved	Unpaved
Dubai to start of route	31km	-
Route		
End of route to Dubai	7.7km	32.2km
	67.5km	-

From Abu Dhabi: Add 300km for the round trip

Jeep

Route
11

Sharjah Bypass

E 611

4.8km

3. Less than 2km later, you will come across a huge compound wall. At the far corner of the wall, turn right and continue to follow the wall.

2. Driving into Al Awir, take the right turn just before the prominent mosque, almost as if you are driving into the petrol station. Head past this and straight on past the shops.

1.3km

1.3km

Large walled compound

1.8km

Start of sandy track

Small walled plantation

GPS UTM 355,618E 2,783,798
GEO 25°09'47"N 55°34'02"

2.7km

AL AWIR

Gazelle!

4. Keep going straight along the wall until the road turns into a sandy track. Follow this alongside the smaller compound, around the corner to the right and then up among the dunes to your left in a southerly direction (SSE). You may want to deflate your tyres here.

1.6km

0.8km

GPS UTM 427,517E 2,831,266N
GEO 25°35'49"N 56°16'41"E

DUBAI 29KM

5. Keep on the main track heading towards the powerlines, which you will see in the distance after a short while. You will eventually be driving under them or parallel to them for the next part of the route.

1. Follow the Dubai - Hatta road route. At 31km outside Dubai, just after the roundabout for the E611 Sharjah Bypass, you will reach a smaller roundabout. Take a left (2nd exit) into Al Awir.

E 44

Powerlines

348 000
350 000
352 000
354 000
356 000

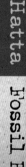

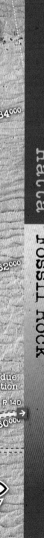

Hatta · Fossil Rock

2786 000

2784 000

2782 000

2780 000

On clear days you will be able to make out the distinctive v-cut of shape of 'Fossil Rock' in front of you (over 25km away). Bear this in mind if you get lost along the way! If you stray from the main track, you can follow any one of the many tracks heading in the same direction to reach it. If a track does not seem to be going in the direction you want, try another one, or read the rest of the route instructions!

6. Once you reach the camel farms, you will notice a gravel service track running alongside the powerlines. This track, heading east, points in the perfect direction. For a more adventurous, (and smoother), route you can drive on the twisting sand track which runs parallel to these tracks, starting a short way from the farms. Start by heading along the gravel track, then when you see the sand track off to the right, head over to it and follow it all the way to the edge of the dunes.

At the time of writing, starting at 2km on from the farms, a new set of pylons is under construction, also with a service track. Don't worry which track you take, as either of these, or the sandy route, all end up in Wadi Faya.

To liven up this part of the drive, head up onto the ridges following alongside the track. Here you can pick a little more challenging route, while still staying in easy sight of the main track.

⚠ Coordinates may be inaccurate in this area due to satellite image distortion

R 140 →

7 km

8.1km

Powerlines

CAMEL FARM

CAMEL FARM

GPS

UTM 362,480E 2,781,435N
GEO 25°8'34"E 55°38'09"N

0   Scale 1:50,000   2km

358 000

360 000

362 000

364 000

366 000

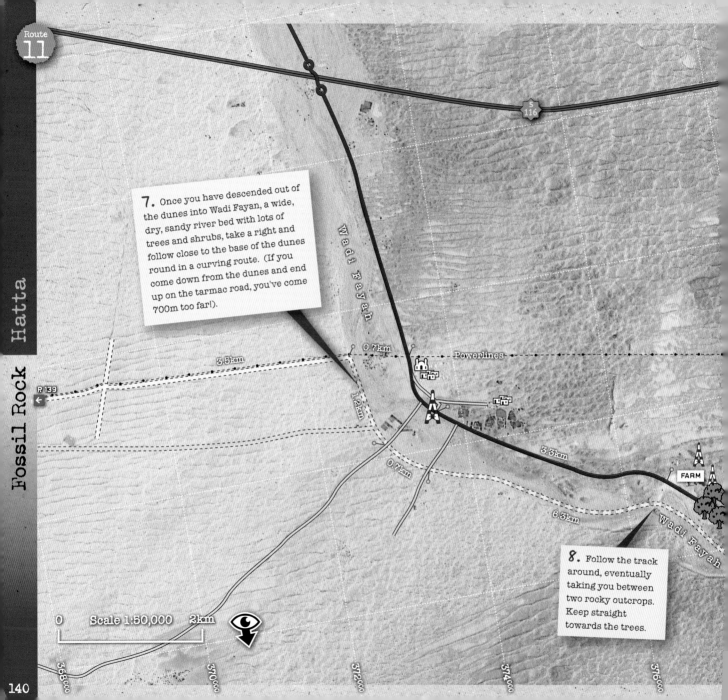

S
116

7. Once you have descended out of the dunes into Wadi Fayan, a wide, dry, sandy river bed with lots of trees and shrubs, take a right and follow close to the base of the dunes round in a curving route. (If you come down from the dunes and end up on the tarmac road, you've come 700m too far!)

W a d i   F a y a n

0.7km

Powerlines

3.5km

R 139
←

1.2km

3.5km

0.7km

FARM

6.3km

W a d i   F a y a h

8. Follow the track around, eventually taking you between two rocky outcrops. Keep straight towards the trees.

0   2km
Scale 1:50,000

368000   370000   372000   374000   376000

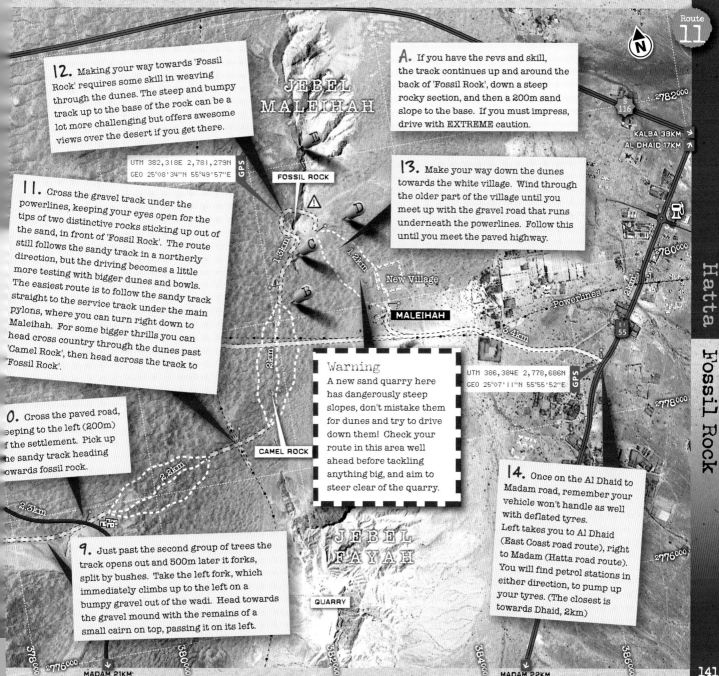

JEBEL MALEIHAH

FOSSIL ROCK

New Village

MALEIHAH

CAMEL ROCK

JEBEL FAYAH

QUARRY

Powerlines

KALBA 39KM
AL DHAID 17KM

S 116

E 55

12. Making your way towards 'Fossil Rock' requires some skill in weaving through the dunes. The steep and bumpy track up to the base of the rock can be a lot more challenging but offers awesome views over the desert if you get there.

A. If you have the revs and skill, the track continues up and around the back of 'Fossil Rock', down a steep rocky section, and then a 200m sand slope to the base. If you must impress, drive with EXTREME caution.

UTM 382,318E 2,781,279N
GEO 25°08'34"N 55°49'57"E
GPS

13. Make your way down the dunes towards the white village. Wind through the older part of the village until you meet up with the gravel road that runs underneath the powerlines. Follow this until you meet the paved highway.

11. Cross the gravel track under the powerlines, keeping your eyes open for the tips of two distinctive rocks sticking up out of the sand, in front of 'Fossil Rock'. The route still follows the sandy track in a northerly direction, but the driving becomes a little more testing with bigger dunes and bowls. The easiest route is to follow the sandy track straight to the service track under the main pylons, where you can turn right down to Maleihah. For some bigger thrills you can head cross country through the dunes past 'Camel Rock', then head across the track to 'Fossil Rock'.

Warning
A new sand quarry here has dangerously steep slopes, don't mistake them for dunes and try to drive down them! Check your route in this area well ahead before tackling anything big, and aim to steer clear of the quarry.

UTM 386,384E 2,778,686N
GEO 25°07'11"N 55°55'52"E
GPS

10. Cross the paved road, keeping to the left (200m) of the settlement. Pick up the sandy track heading towards fossil rock.

14. Once on the Al Dhaid to Madam road, remember your vehicle won't handle as well with deflated tyres.
Left takes you to Al Dhaid (East Coast road route), right to Madam (Hatta road route). You will find petrol stations in either direction, to pump up your tyres. (The closest is towards Dhaid, 2km)

9. Just past the second group of trees the track opens out and 500m later it forks, split by bushes. Take the left fork, which immediately climbs up to the left on a bumpy gravel out of the wadi. Head towards the gravel mound with the remains of a small cairn on top, passing it on its left.

1.3km
1.2km
2km
2.2km
2.3km
3.4km

MADAM 21KM
MADAM 22KM

Fossil Rock Highlights

A distinctive solitary mountain rising from a surrounding sea of sand, Fossil Rock gets its name from the abundance of marine fossils found on its flanks. It is also an interesting example of how dunes form when wind blows sand up against an obstruction - in this case the large lump of rock that is Jebel Maleihah.

This enjoyable desert trip is a good chance for novice dune drivers to gain experience and learn some valuable lessons. A little care is needed as you near Fossil Rock as the track is less straightforward, but it remains drivable all the way, even for first timers. If you haven't driven in sand before, check the Driving section of the book before setting out (p.265)

The second part of the route also gives proficient drivers the chance to head off the track and find some great bowls and ridges, as well as the challenge of trying to make the climb up to Fossil Rock, and even up and over the ridge next to the rock itself.

Plant Life

The dunes between Al Awir and Fossil Rock are full of a broom-like bush. To find out why it's called 'Firemaker Bush' by the Bedu, check out the Natural World section (p.239).

Insects

You'll see no end of tracks in the desert, made by insects, reptiles and mammals. Look for those made by beetles such as the Unicorn Beetle (*Phyllognathus excavatus*).

Animals

Animals you should look out for are the Cape Hare and the Yellow-spotted Sand Lizard (recognised by the elliptical shaped cream spots on its flanks). If you're lucky, you may see a Blue-headed Agame.

View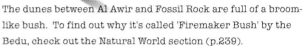

The presence of iron oxide gives the sand in this area a lovely rich, orange-red colour. The dunes around Fossil Rock are especially spectacular in the late afternoon and at sunset.

Jebel Maleihah (Fossil Rock)

Like Fossil Valley near Al Ain (see Hanging Gardens, Al Ain p.181), this area is rich with the fossils of shells and small sea creatures that were on the ocean floor millions of years ago when water covered much of Arabia.

It's great fun to explore and search for the fossils, which are quite easy to find. Try identifying your discoveries in the Natural World section of the book (p.239).

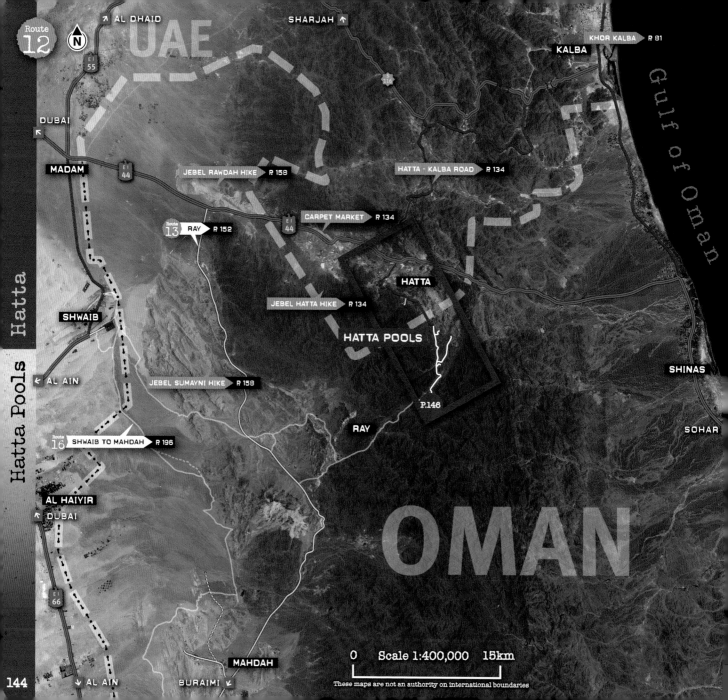

Route 12

N

UAE

↗ AL DHAID   SHARJAH ↑   KHOR KALBA ▶ R 81

KALBA

Gulf of Oman

E1 55

DUBAI ↖

MADAM
E1 44

JEBEL RAWDAH HIKE ▶ R 158   HATTA - KALBA ROAD ▶ R 134

E1 44   CARPET MARKET ▶ R 134

Route 13 ▶ RAY ▶ R 152

SHWAIB

JEBEL HATTA HIKE ▶ R 134

HATTA

HATTA POOLS

↙ AL AIN   JEBEL SUMAYNI HIKE ▶ R 158

SHINAS

P.146

Route 16 ▶ SHWAIB TO MAHDAH ▶ R 196   RAY

SOHAR

AL HAIYIR

↑ DUBAI

E1 66

OMAN

MAHDAH

0   Scale 1:400,000   15km

These maps are not an authority on international boundaries

↓ AL AIN   BURAIMI ↙

144

Hatta Pools

Definitely the most well-known and popular route for outdoor enthusiasts. The pools are easily accessible and full of water all year round. Apart from the obvious attractions of the pools, this is an interesting area with many opportunities to explore, either by car, on foot or by mountain bike.

Terrain: Mountains, Wadis
Water: Pools, Streams
Driving: 2 Wheel Drive Possible
Activities: Mountain Biking, Swimming, Hiking
Warnings: Flash Floods, Graffiti, Litter, Oman Car Insurance

Trip Info

Distances:

	Paved	Unpaved
Dubai to start of route	100km	-
Route (Round trip)	21.8km	10.8km
End of route to Dubai	100km	-

From Abu Dhabi: Add 300km for the round trip

Jeep

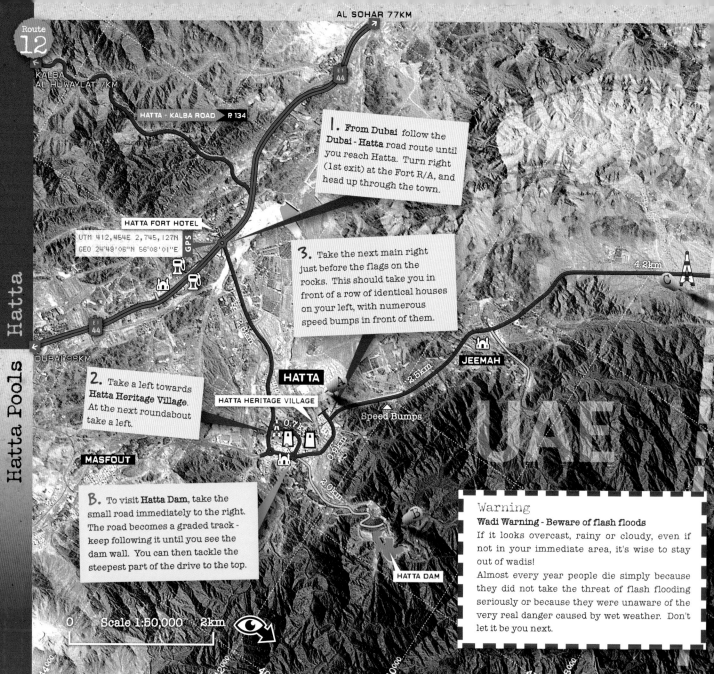

AL SOHAR 77KM

Route
12

KALBA
AL HUWAYLAT 7KM

HATTA - KALBA ROAD   R 134

E1
44

1. From Dubai follow the Dubai - Hatta road route until you reach Hatta. Turn right (1st exit) at the Fort R/A, and head up through the town.

HATTA FORT HOTEL
UTM 412,454E 2,745,127N
GEO 24°48'06"N 56°08'01"E
GPS

4.2km

C

E1
44

JEEMAH

DUBAI 98KM

3. Take the next main right just before the flags on the rocks. This should take you in front of a row of identical houses on your left, with numerous speed bumps in front of them.

2.5km

UAE

2. Take a left towards Hatta Heritage Village. At the next roundabout take a left.

HATTA

HATTA HERITAGE VILLAGE

0.7

Speed Bumps

0.9km

MASFOUT

2.0km

B

A

B. To visit Hatta Dam, take the small road immediately to the right. The road becomes a graded track - keep following it until you see the dam wall. You can then tackle the steepest part of the drive to the top.

HATTA DAM

Warning
Wadi Warning - Beware of flash floods
If it looks overcast, rainy or cloudy, even if not in your immediate area, it's wise to stay out of wadis!
Almost every year people die simply because they did not take the threat of flash flooding seriously or because they were unaware of the very real danger caused by wet weather. Don't let it be you next.

0   Scale 1:50,000   2km

2744,000   2742,000   408,000   2740,000   410,000   2738,000

146

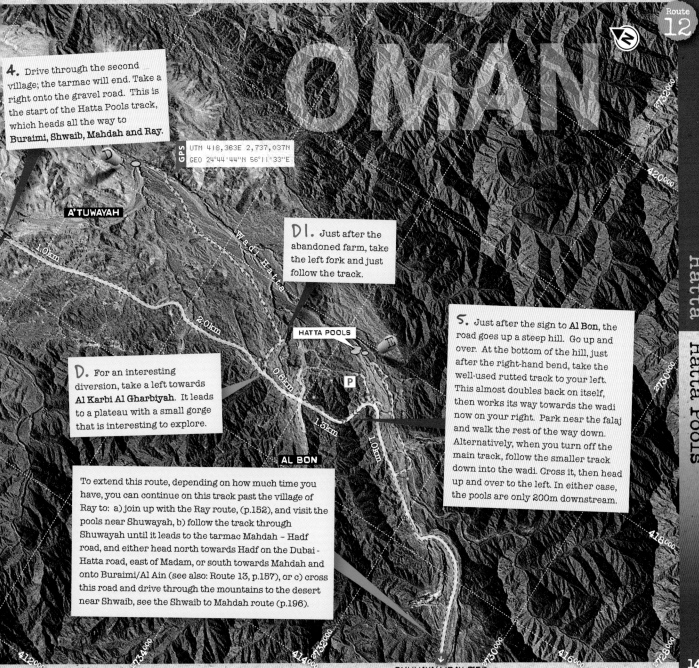

4. Drive through the second village; the tarmac will end. Take a right onto the gravel road. This is the start of the Hatta Pools track, which heads all the way to **Buraimi, Shwaib, Mahdah and Ray.**

GPS UTM 418,363E 2,737,037N
GEO 24°44'44"N 56°11'33"E

A'TUWAYAH

1.0km

Wadi Hatta

2.0km

D1. Just after the abandoned farm, take the left fork and just follow the track.

HATTA POOLS

0.6km

P

D. For an interesting diversion, take a left towards **Al Karbi Al Gharbiyah.** It leads to a plateau with a small gorge that is interesting to explore.

1.3km

1.0km

AL BON

5. Just after the sign to **Al Bon**, the road goes up a steep hill. Go up and over. At the bottom of the hill, just after the right-hand bend, take the well-used rutted track to your left. This almost doubles back on itself, then works its way towards the wadi now on your right. Park near the falaj and walk the rest of the way down. Alternatively, when you turn off the main track, follow the smaller track down into the wadi. Cross it, then head up and over to the left. In either case, the pools are only 200m downstream.

To extend this route, depending on how much time you have, you can continue on this track past the village of Ray to: a) join up with the Ray route, (p.152), and visit the pools near Shuwayah, b) follow the track through Shuwayah until it leads to the tarmac Mahdah – Hadf road, and either head north towards Hadf on the Dubai - Hatta road, east of Madam, or south towards Mahdah and onto Buraimi/Al Ain (see also: Route 13, p.157), or c) cross this road and drive through the mountains to the desert near Shwaib, see the Shwaib to Mahdah route (p.196).

Hatta Pools Highlights

One of the classic trips in the Emirates, the Hatta Pools route offers stunning views of the rugged Hajar Mountains. This is the land of leopards, gazelles, foxes and caracals (though you're rather unlikely to see them today). All along this route there are possibilities for walking, mountain biking, picnics and wadi exploration. The striated red rocks near the beginning of the track are particularly spectacular towards sunset.

The Hatta Pools are well known and visited, so unfortunately they suffer from the same fate as other popular spots - litter and graffiti. The local authorities clean the area from time to time and you can, of course, do your bit by leaving with everything, or even more than you arrived with.

The popularity of the area also means that you should take extra care when driving, because although the track is good, you'll meet regular oncoming traffic and the loose gravel makes it easy for the car to slip out of control when braking or turning suddenly.

This trip is possible in a two wheel drive until near the pools at which point, depending on how much you value your undercarriage, it is probably advisable to walk.

This is a simple but worthwhile route that can be continued through the mountains to the village of Ray and some more pools, then out on the new tarmac road to the Hatta - Dubai road. Alternatively it could be rounded off by heading back to the Hatta Fort Hotel for a reviving cappuccino or a sundowner on the terrace

> **Warning** - Care needs to be taken in and near wadis during unstable weather, as flash floods do occur. As you can see by the size of the wadis at Hatta, this is a massive catchment area and the water can come from seemingly nowhere. A traditional way used to detect imminent floods in wadis is to watch the ants. If you see them starting to make a hasty escape from a wadi en masse, chances are you had better do the same!

Hatta Heritage Village

Set in an oasis, Hatta Heritage Village was built as a traditional mountain village - visitors can explore narrow alleyways, a large central fort and discover traditional life in the mud and barasti houses. A falaj runs through out the village, and there are some with pleasant shaded seating areas. Near the entrance a house displays traditional products and handicrafts. Note - opening times of the village can be rather erratic.

Hatta is also the site of the oldest fort in the Dubai emirate, built in 1790. You'll also see several watchtowers on the surrounding hills.

Hatta Dam

Hatta Dam was built in 1989 to control the flow of water from the mountains to the village below. Some of the water also seeps through and replenishes the subterranean water table. A trip to the dam makes for a scenic and unusual visit in this generally arid country.

Hatta actually has two dams. The other is located nearer the Hatta Fort Hotel; refer to the map.

Emirati Borders

There's an interesting story of how the borders of the individual emirates were drawn up. In 1970, the British Trucial Oman Scouts made numerous trips around the country (apparently by camel), asking each Sheikh to whom he pledged his allegiance. They also asked people where the extent of

their territories were, to try and make the existing borders official without creating animosity. However, to this day there are still borders that are hotly disputed.

Interesting Diversion

If you have the time and are up for a challenging drive, this rocky track leads to a plateau, and then a further narrow track down to a very scenic wadi. After passing through the narrow gorge (and it really is narrow, and steep too - probably safest on foot!), you will find the best pools by strolling to your left down the wadi.

Park at the plateau for a picnic or to go mountain biking or walking. This is a great area, offering many different tracks to explore, plus it's a lot quieter than the rutted main route to the Hatta Pools.

While still on the gravel plains, it's a thrilling sight to peer over the edge of the plateau and see the riverbed far below.

Hatta Pools

There is always water in this wadi, which runs across the bedrock then plunges a few metres down a waterfall into a small pool and continues inside a steep-sided gorge. By walking downstream you can reach the start of the gorge. When the water is high, the pool and waterfall can only be reached by swimming through certain spots.

The track leads to a falaj system that runs along the side of the wadi to plantations further downstream. By following the falaj from this point, the Hatta Pools and waterfall can be reached on foot. At the pools you can see deep, strangely shaped canyons cut by rushing floodwaters. Even in the hot summer months the water keeps flowing, and it is always cool and refreshing (how this is possible during the long, unforgiving summers never ceases to amaze).

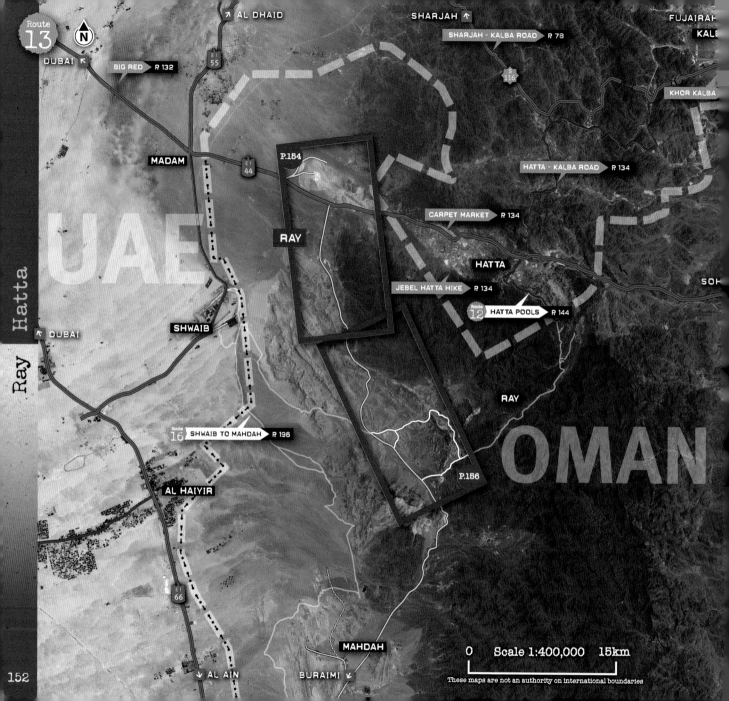

↑ AL DHAID

SHARJAH ↑

FUJAIRAH
KALB

SHARJAH - KALBA ROAD   R 78

DUBAI ↑

BIG RED   R 132

E 55

116

KHOR KALBA

MADAM

E 44

P.154

HATTA - KALBA ROAD   R 134

UAE

RAY

CARPET MARKET   R 134

HATTA

HATTA - KALBA ROAD   R 134

JEBEL HATTA HIKE   R 134

SOH

↑ DUBAI

SHWAIB

Route
12   HATTA POOLS   R 144

RAY

Route
16   SHWAIB TO MAHDAH   R 196

OMAN

AL HAIYIR

P.156

E 66

MAHDAH

↓ AL AIN

BURAIMI ↓

0   Scale 1:400,000   15km

These maps are not an authority on international boundaries

Ray

An enjoyable drive through the mountains that ends with the reward of a swim and a prime camping location next to the stream near Shuwayhah. The first part of the route from the Hatta highway is now paved, taking less time than the previous off-road route. Once off the smooth tarmac, the track along the wadi bed takes you into remote, rocky countryside before reaching the pools at the head of the valley. A great place to escape for a weekend of peace and quiet, and to explore the area.

Terrain:	Mountains, Wadis
Water:	Stream, Pools, Seasonal Floods
Activities:	Camping, Hiking, Mountain Biking, Picnics
Warnings:	Oman Car Insurance

Trip Info

Other Names:
Rayy, Shuwayhah

Distances:

	Paved	Unpaved
Dubai to start of route	80km	-
Route (Round trip)	54.2km	26.4km
End of route to Dubai	80km	-

From Abu Dhabi: Add 300km for the round trip

Jeep

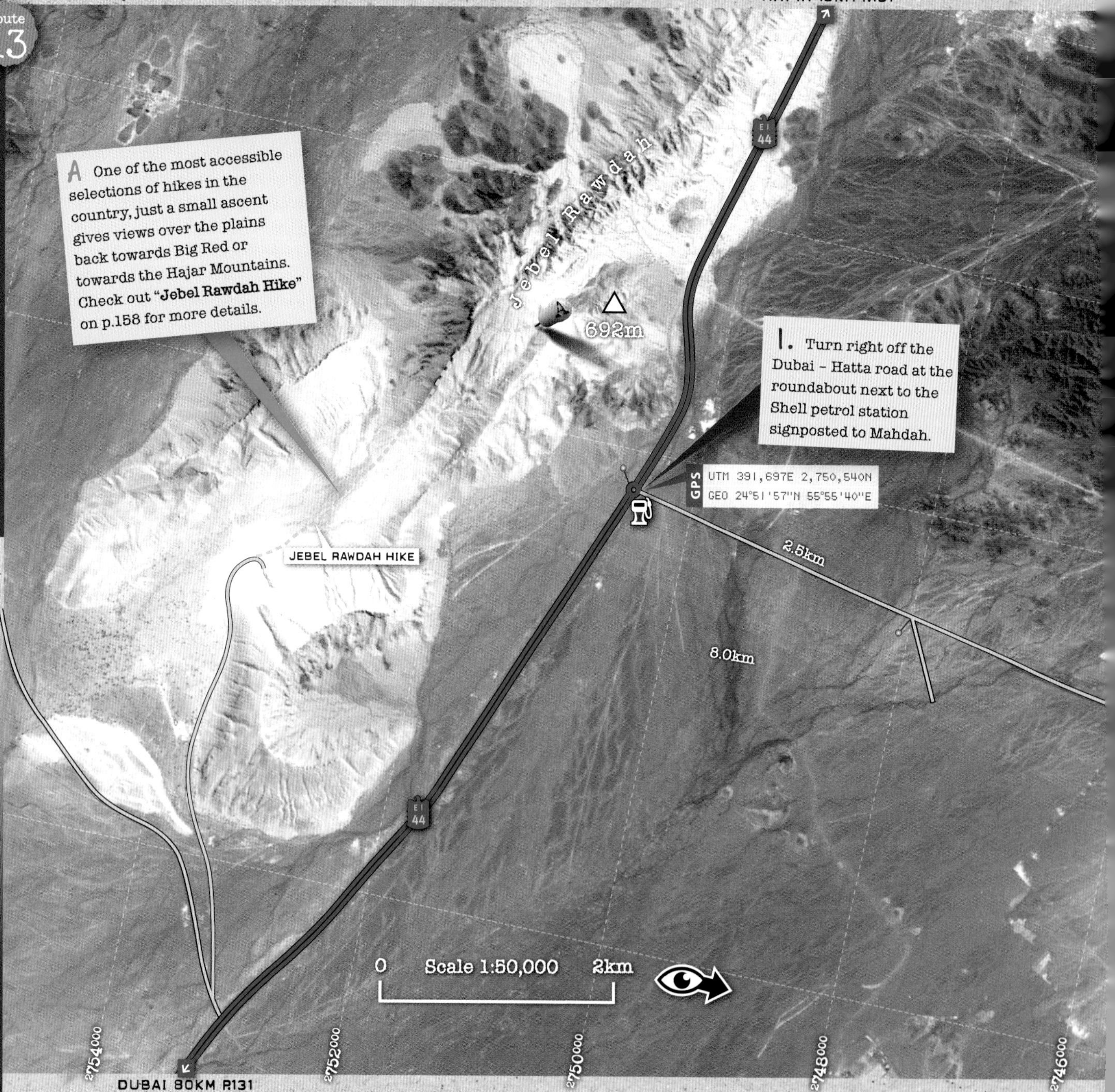

Ray Hatta.

A One of the most accessible selections of hikes in the country, just a small ascent gives views over the plains back towards Big Red or towards the Hajar Mountains. Check out "**Jebel Rawdah Hike**" on p.158 for more details.

J e b e l   R a w d a h

△ 692m

E 44

1. Turn right off the Dubai – Hatta road at the roundabout next to the Shell petrol station signposted to Mahdah.

GPS | UTM 391,697E 2,750,540N
GEO 24°51'57"N 55°55'40"E

2.5km

8.0km

JEBEL RAWDAH HIKE

E 44

0   Scale 1:50,000   2km

2754000
2752000
2750000
2748000
2746000

154

OMAN

396000

394000

2. This road takes you straight into the mountains. No need to concentrate too hard on the directions, just enjoy the view.

R 156

13.2km

392000

OMAN

5. When you approach the village, take the track that heads up a little rise, keeping up and to your right, and weave your way through the houses. Follow the obvious main track along the power lines. For an alternative route with a bit more adventure and bumps, stay to the right of the village and follow the wadi bed for another 2km.

R 155 FARM

11.4km

With the Oman/UAE border fence now splitting the Shwaib to Mahdah route (p.196), this route provides a great alternative way into the dunes. Take this track into Wadi Sumayni and through the Oman Check Point to join up with the route on p.199.

Jebel Sumayni

C

0   Scale 1:50,000   2km

Route
16 SHWAIB TO MAHDAH R 196

Wadi Sumay

SHWAIB R 199

Route
13

UTM 405,554E 2,726,448N
GEO 24°38'57"N 56°04'00"E

3km

GPS

406 000

8. Before you reach the pools at the end of the wadi, there are various shady camping spots in and out of the wadi. Stop, camp, walk and swim!

6. Pass between two traditional houses, and follow the road as it veers to the right, again following the power lines.

7. After a steep descent back into the wadi bed, take a left upstream towards the distinctive white rocks. At the rocks, the wadi bends right up to the pools.

3.5km

SHUWAYHAH

2722 000

406 000

5.2km

E. For an interesting alternative route out of the wadi, at the bend by the white rocks take the small track that heads off initially through gravel – this eventually joins the track from Shuwayhah to Hatta Pools near the village of Ray, (see route 12 p.147).

9. To get back to the road, either retrace your route from the pools, or turn left on exiting the wadi and drive 3km to the junction near Shuwayhah Village. Turning left there takes you on a spectacular drive through the mountains to the Hatta Pools route (p.144) and Hatta, turning right will take you back to the main road.

5.8km

4. Just after a group of trees, a track will join in from the right. Keep straight.

2720 000

404 000

2.7km

FOREST

2.3km

2722 000

3.0km

4.8km

MAHDAH →

3. Turn left off the tarmac road onto the track signposted A'Shega.

10. Head right to return to the Hatta road or left to Al Ain & Buraimi.

2724 000

398 000

2722 000

400 000

2720 000

402 000

Hatta

Ray

157

Ray Highlights

Just after the landmark peak of Jebel Rawdah, the Mahdah road turns in from the Dubai - Hatta highway and is a pleasant drive, heading into the impressive Hajar Mountains and passing Jebel Sumayni nearby on your right. The easy off-road drive takes you into a wadi where the pools (and usually a stream) are present all year round, along with a shady set of palm trees. This is an idyllic place for a chilled-out camp.

Several options are available for other routes on the way there or back — the Hatta Pools route (p.144) can be reached by the track from Shuwayhah village, or at the junction of the track to A'Shega with the tarmac road, another track heading west takes you through Wadi Sumayni to the Shwaib desert, p.199 on the Shwaib to Mahdah route.

Jebel Rawdah Hike

More of a large hill than a mountain, Jebel Rawdah is the first peak to be seen on the left side of the road on the way to Hatta, and the base is easily accessible by two-wheel drives. At the end of the valley, various routes are possible to the summit – the centre one is the easiest (but all routes can be completed in about two hours). The views are definitely worth it. Remember to take enough water, even on a short walk like this, as well as appropriate footwear for the loose rock.

Wet and Wild Wadis

In the rainy season, the small wadis only a short way off the left-hand side of the road can fill up with water if you want to explore. Alternatively, for some great short exploratory hikes, whenever you see a wadi weaving its way into the mountains or a hill worth checking out, drive in as far as you can, park the car, and step out!

Jebel Sumayni Hike

This walk, tackling the north-east face of Jebel Sumayni to a height of 1,073m, is fairly easy and a good introduction to some of the longer walks in the UAE. An added attraction is that close access can be made by car, leaving a three hour ascent to the summit.

To get to the trailhead, from the Madam roundabout on the Dubai–Hatta road, the mountain will be visible as a rounded summit in a group of peaks at 150 degrees south-east. Proceed towards Hatta for 17 km and turn right at the Shell petrol station on the road signposted Madhah. After 15 km turn right off the road at a group of palm trees and a farm on the right-hand side. Jebel Sumayni is now clearly visible about two km away. The actual summit is just visible behind the skyline ridge. The right-hand end of the ridge is sharply pointed.

After turning at the small white house with the large veranda and a vaguely Mediterranean style, Jebel Sumayni is now clearly visible in front of you. Follow a track past the small settlement that usually has lots of goats. It's advisable for those in 2WD vehicles to bear left after the settlement and to head about 300m to some trees and bushes that are hidden from the houses by a small ridge - park here. For those with 4WD vehicles, you can drive across the wide gravel plain towards an obvious wadi that lies in a line with the midpoint of the skyline ridge. Drive into the wadi as far as a large tree that provides good shade. The hike starts from here. For those who have parked their cars, it will take about 15 minutes to walk across the wadi to this spot.

From the tree head straight towards the mountain. When the ground rises more steeply, turn to the left behind a ridge. Follow the gully up to the left to a col (30 minutes). From the col go diagonally up to the left for about 300m to a gully that leads directly up to the skyline. Parts of the gully are quite steep and offer some scrambling in places (although this can be avoided). It's one hour to the top of the gully.

From here, walk diagonally to your left across the saddle between the mountains and continue curving your way to the right around the face of the next mountain. Once you reach the opposite ridge (20 minutes), there is one more gentle descent of about 100m before ascending the final summit.

The view from here is magnificent. Perched on top of the rocks, you will survey an endless sea of rippling red sand. What is so surprising is the distinct line created where the desert ends and the mountains begin. (UTM coordinates of the peak are 390,600E, 2,732,300N at 1,073m).

Choice of Routes

For other options, continuing straight along this road takes you to Mahdah then into Buraimi and Al Ain. Turning right onto the track to Sumayni takes you through the mountains and the Omani border to a large gravel plain, across which are some fantastic dunes, see Shwaib to Madhah (P.196).

Ghaf Trees

This area is home to a group of hardy Ghaf trees (*Prosopis Cineraria*). Reaching underground water with long taproots, these trees tend to grow in clusters just like they do here. The trees support a host of bird and small animal life, that feeds on the elongated pods.

Cross Country Routes to Hatta Pools

To link the Ray Pools with the Hatta Pools route (p.144), the alternative route from the easily recognisible white rocks heads off initially through gravel, then follows some 4WD tracks through very remote countryside. The driving can get a little tricky in places, and finding the way can be interesting, but it's a fun route and if you follow your nose to the village of Ray (or Rayy) it shouldn't be too much of a challenge.

Camping

Set in an unused, walled field of palms, the smooth sandy ground beneath the trees makes this a particularly comfortable spot to camp, with plenty of shade for the morning. As well as the walk up to the pools, try a hike up to one of the rocky peaks nearby for a great view over the area before sundown.

Pool

A gentle stroll up the wadi takes you to a lovely pool, suprisingly deep and cool even in summer, with a little shade afforded by it's token palm tree. For the more intrepid, it's great to swim through the narrow gorge and scramble over the rocks and pools beyond. You should see a number of toads and may even be fortunate enough to spot a snake — sometimes to be found sunning themselves on the rocks to digest their catch after a spot of a fishing!

DRIVE YOURSELF CRAZY

Bungee Jumping doesn't come close. This is bubbling, fizzing fun that lasts as long as you want it to.

You - your guts & 4 wheels

Gear up. Strap yourself in and let go. Be the brave explorer you always thought you were. Don't worry - we won't lose you. Our expert guides are always within reach.

We give safety the priority it deserves. We operate a tough, new fleet and our drivers guides are good, really good.

And that's just half the story. We've got a menu that's as wide as your appetite for excitement.

- CAMPING ■ TREKKING
- WADI BASHING ■ SAND SKIING
- CAMEL RIDING ■ ARABIAN NIGHTS
- 4 WHEELER COURSES

Speciality events for corporates

- TREASURE HUNTS
- UNIQUE PRODUCT LAUNCHES
- TEAM BUILDING EVENTS

Off-Road and You

Real 4 wheeling is an art that can be learned. We'll teach you well. We'll show you great spots to test your skills. And we can help you choose a 4WD that's right for you.

OFF-ROAD ADVENTURES

Where Nature Meets Adventure

We're the real deal adventure people. Call in to book or for more info.
T +971-4-343 2288   **Hotline** +971-4-32 11 377   **E** ora@emirates.net.ae

www.arabiantours.com

Al Ain

Jeep

Overview Al Ain

N

↖ DUBAI   DUBAI ↘   MADAM   KALBA ↗   FUJAIRAH ↘

E1 55   UAE   HATTA

Route 13 RAY ▸ R 152   E1 44   Route 12 HATTA POOLS ▸ R 144   SOHAR ↘

E1 66   OMAN

SHWAIB

Route 16

Shwaib to Mahdah
A fun and varied
drive on all types
of terrain and
through some
stunning desert.
Page 196

Route 14   Route 15

Khutwa
A short drive into
the inviting,
green Khutwa
oasis for walks
amid the shady
tranquility.
Page 188

Hanging Gardens
Spectacular area
for hiking with
amazing rock
formations and
stunning views.
Page 180

↙ ABU DHABI   UAE   E1 66   MAHDAH

KHUTWA

SOHAR ↗

AL AIN   BURAIMI   Route 17

22

↙ ABU DHABI

Wadi Madbah
The biggest
waterfall in the
UAE with
freshwater pools
to swim in and
explore.
Page 208

MADBAH

JEBEL HAFEET

0   Scale 1:800,000   30km

The maps are not an authority on international boundaries

↙ UMM AL ZAMOOL   ↓ IBRI/NIZWA

Al Ain Route Overview Table

Route	Name	Page	Total Dist. (km)	Total Unpaved (km)	Terrain			Activity					Route Combinations
					Mtn	Desert	Wadi	Camp	Climb	Hike	Bike	Swim	
	Al Ain Road Route	166	110										
14	Hanging Gardens	180	72.8	9	✓				✓	✓			15 + 16
15	Khutwa	188	40.4	2	✓		✓			✓			14 + 16
16	Shwaib to Mahdah	196	61.3	60.4	✓	✓		✓					14 + 15 + 12 + 13
17	Wadi Madbah	208	41.2	18.5	✓		✓	✓	✓	✓		✓	15

Al Ain Route Combinations

One-Day Trips

Ray P.152 ▶ Shwaib to Madhah P.196

The Ray route takes you into the mountains from the Hatta road, and to the Ray Pools for swimming and a perfect spot for lunch under the trees in the small walled plantation. This is also great place to camp if you want to extend this route to two days. In the afternoon, head back to the road then turn towards the Sumayni gap and through the Omani border post, to join up with the Shwaib-Madhah route for the fantastic area of dunes.

Wadi Madbah P.208 ▶ Khutwa P.188

These routes are short enough to be easily combined in a day offering different views of the area. Khutwa oasis offers shady walks under the wide variety of fruit trees in the tranquil plantations – a refreshing change to the usual dry terrain of the country. At Madbah, the freshwater stream and pools offer a cooling dip on the way to the largest waterfall in the UAE and some good exploring in the pools and canyons above the waterfall.

Two-Day Trips

Shwaib to Madhah P.196 ▶ Wadi Madbah P.208

Shwaib to Madhah P.196 ▶ Khutwa P.188

The route from Shwaib to Madhah offers interesting views of the UAE's varied landscape including desert right next to the mountains. If you plan for a whole day, you'll have plenty of time to play in the dunes, then pitch up by the dunes for the night on the way out of the route near the Madhah road. For a shorter drive on the second day, choose between the pools, waterfall and canyons at Madbah or the shady walks in the tranquil oasis of Khutwa.

Shwaib to Madhah P.196 ▶ Hanging Gardens P.180

Shwaib to Madhah, with its varied views, is a great introduction to the area, and ends conveniently near the 'Hanging Gardens' hike for the second day of this trip. Camping next to the dunes on the way out of the route near the Madhah road means only a 30 minute drive to the start point of the hike, leaving you fresh to enjoy one of the most interesting walks in the Emirates.

ARABIAN GULF

OMA

KHASAB ↑

RAS AL KHAIMAH

DIBBA

UMM AL QUWAIN

AJMAN

311

UAE

MASAFI

SHARJAH

FUJAIRAH

DUBAI

P.168

311

55

11

E
66

44

MADAM

HATTA

SOHAR

DUBAI - AL AIN

Route
16 SHWAIB TO MAHDAH ▶ R 196

AL HAIYIR

OMAN

P.170

ABU DHABI

UAE

ABU DHABI - AL AIN

Route
14 HANGING GARDENS ▶ R 190

BANI YAS

P.174

AL AIN BURAIMI

Route
15 KHUTWA ▶ R 188

11
22

Route
17 WADI MADBAH ▶ R 208

LIWA,
SAUDI ARABIA

0 Scale 1:1,250,000 50km

LIWA ↓

The maps are not an authority on international boundaries

IBRI/NIZWA ↓

P.172

Al Ain

Al Ain lies south-east of Dubai, east of Abu Dhabi, on the border with Oman in an area known as the Buraimi Oasis. Historically the area was important not only for its relative lushness, but also strategically, since it straddled the ancient trading routes between what are now the UAE and Oman. The town is actually split between the UAE and Oman, (the Emirati side is known as Al Ain and the Omani side as Buraimi) and Al Ain has a variety of sights to interest visitors, including its museum, forts, heritage and archaeological sites and camel and livestock souks. Outside the city, visit the imposing Jebel Hafeet for a dramatic view, especially at sunset.

Terrain: Desert
Driving: Easy, with great views
Activities: Picnics, Walks
Warning: New border fence being
             constructed between
             UAE and Oman

Trip Info

Distances:
Dubai to Al Ain   110km
Abu Dhabi to Al Ain   130km

Jeep

RAS AL KHAIMAH 85KM R6

AL DHAID 36KM R75 HATTA 36 KM R1

MADAM

E1 44

AL AWIR

MARGHAM

AL MAHA RESORT

LAHBAB

1. Take the E66 to
Al Ain until you
reach The 'Coffee
Pot' R/A at Al Oha,
just outside Al Ain.

WIMPY
INTERCHANGE

DUBAI

AL RUWAYAH

E1 66

7.9km

4km

7.2km

10km

6.5km

E1 66 13.0

4km

4.3km

2

4.6km

3

4

6

8

7

8

9

MURQUAB

1

NAD AL SHEBA

AL LISAILI

GPS UTM 330,355E 2,785,912N

E1
311

UMM NAHAD

Dubai/Sharjah City Overview (p.xvi)

11

0 Scale 1:320,000 10km

The maps are not an authority on international boundaries

2770000

310000

2760000

2750000

320000

2740000

2730000

330000

ABU DHABI 111KM R223

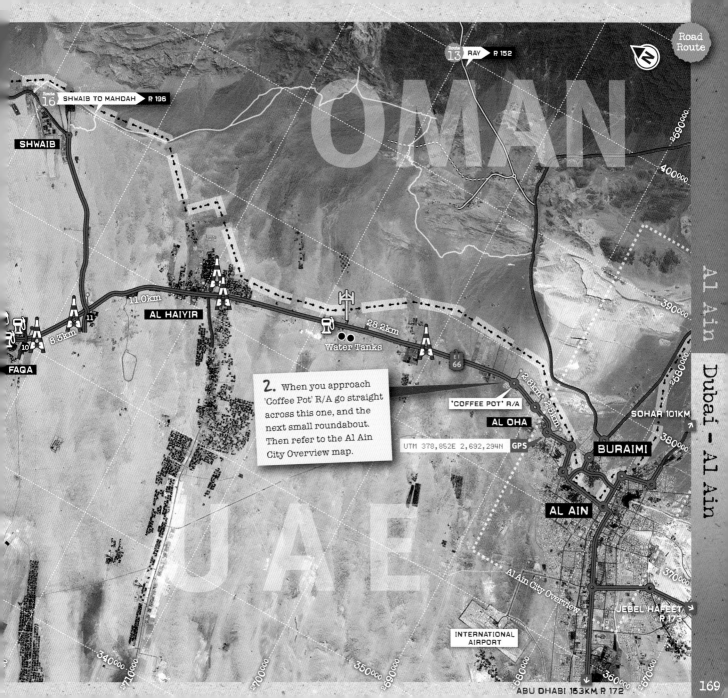

OMAN

UAE

Route 13 | RAY | R 152

Route 16 | SHWAIB TO MAHDAH | R 196

SHWAIB

FAQA

10   8.3km   11   11.0km   AL HAIYIR   28.2km   E1 66

Water Tanks

2.8km 2.5km

'COFFEE POT' R/A

AL OHA

SOHAR 101KM

BURAIMI

2. When you approach 'Coffee Pot' R/A go straight across this one, and the next small roundabout. Then refer to the Al Ain City Overview map.

UTM 378,852E 2,692,294N | GPS

AL AIN

Al Ain City Overview

JEBEL HAFEET
R 173

INTERNATIONAL
AIRPORT

ABU DHABI 153KM R 172

DUBAI 130KM R 222

SHAHAMAH

ARABIAN GULF

Abu Dhabi City Overview (p.xviii)

Khor al Baghal

LULU ISLAND

AL RAHA BEACH HOTEL

ABU DHABI INTERNATIONAL AIRPO

ABU DHABI

AL MAQTA BRIDGE

KHALIFA CITY

GPS UTM 246,887E 2,702,452N

Khor al Batin

2.1km

2.2km

MUSSAFAH BRIDGE

1. Leaving Abu Dhabi by any route, follow the signs for Al Ain (E22).

E 22

E 11

Khor Qirqishan

MUSSAFAH

AL MAFRAQ

BANI YAS

5.5km

7.0k

JARN YAPHOUR

BU KESHEISHAH

AL MAQATRAH

EMIRATES INT'L ENDURANCE VIL

E 11

220 000   230 000   240 000   250 000   260 000

LIWA 162KM R225/SAUDI/QATAR

N

2ᵍ700 000

320 000

RAMLAT
SWEIHAN

2ᵍ690 000

2ᵍ680 000

WATHBA

BU SAMARAH

AL KHATIM

12.0km

AL KHAZNAH

R 172

18.5km

3.5km

E
22

10.0km

Truck Road

2ᵍ670 000

R 172

0   Scale 1:250,000   10km

290 000

300 000

310 000

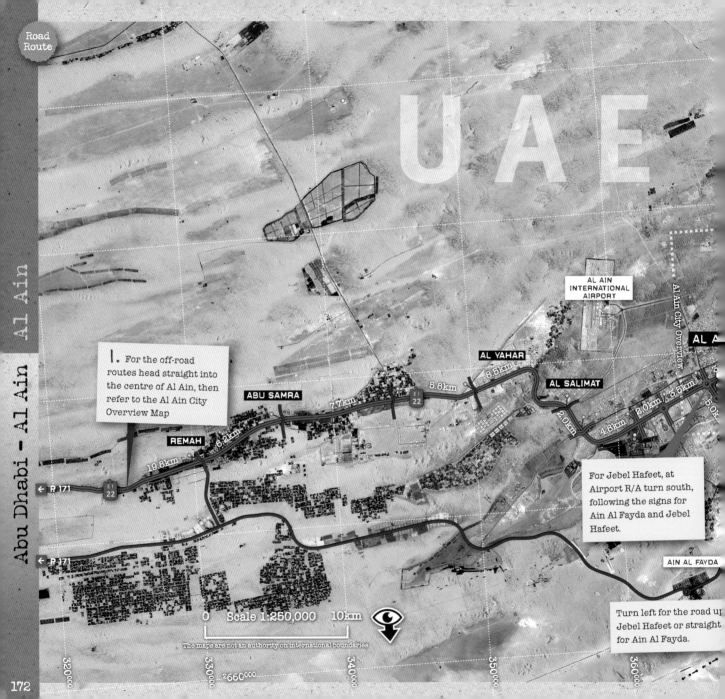

U A E

AL AIN INTERNATIONAL AIRPORT

Al Ain City Overview

AL A

1. For the off-road routes head straight into the centre of Al Ain, then refer to the Al Ain City Overview Map

AL YAHAR

8.5km

5.8km

AL SALIMAT

ABU SAMRA

7.7km

E 22

2.0km

3.5km

6.2km

REMAH

4.8km

2.0km

5.0k

19.8km

E 22

← R 171

For Jebel Hafeet, at Airport R/A turn south, following the signs for Ain Al Fayda and Jebel Hafeet.

← R 171

AIN AL FAYDA

Turn left for the road up Jebel Hafeet or straight for Ain Al Fayda.

0   Scale 1:250,000   10km

The maps are not an authority on international boundaries

320000   330000   2660000   340000   350000   360000

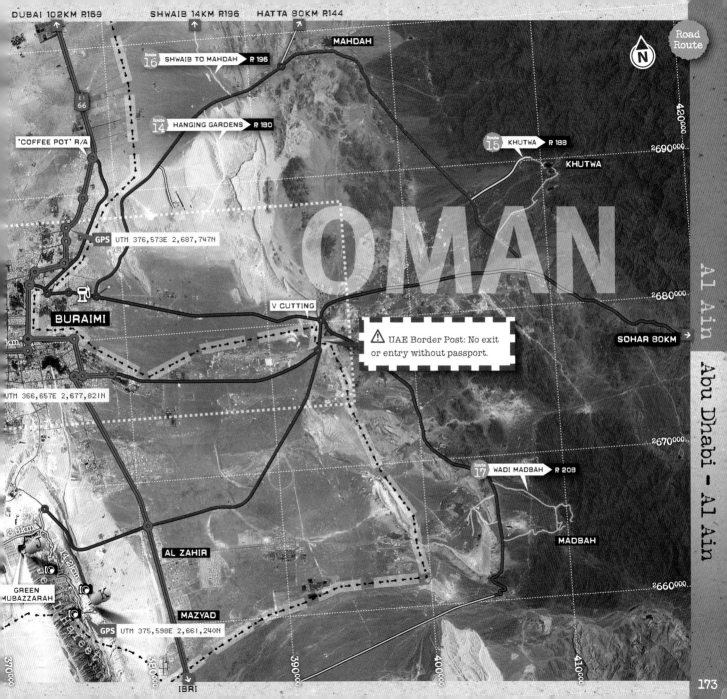

DUBAI 102KM R169   SHWAIB 14KM R196   HATTA 80KM R144

MAHDAH

Route **16** SHWAIB TO MAHDAH ▶ R 196

Route **14** HANGING GARDENS ▶ R 180

Route **15** KHUTWA ▶ R 188

KHUTWA

OMAN

N

Road Route

'COFFEE POT' R/A

E 66

GPS UTM 376,573E 2,687,747N

420000

2690000

2680000

BURAIMI

V CUTTING

⚠ UAE Border Post: No exit or entry without passport.

SOHAR 80KM ▶

UTM 366,657E 2,677,821N

km

2670000

Route **17** WADI MADBAH ▶ R 208

MADBAH

3.6km

AL ZAHIR

142km

2660000

GREEN MUBAZZARAH

K

MAZYAD

GPS UTM 375,598E 2,661,240N

370000   580000   390000   400000   410000

IBRI

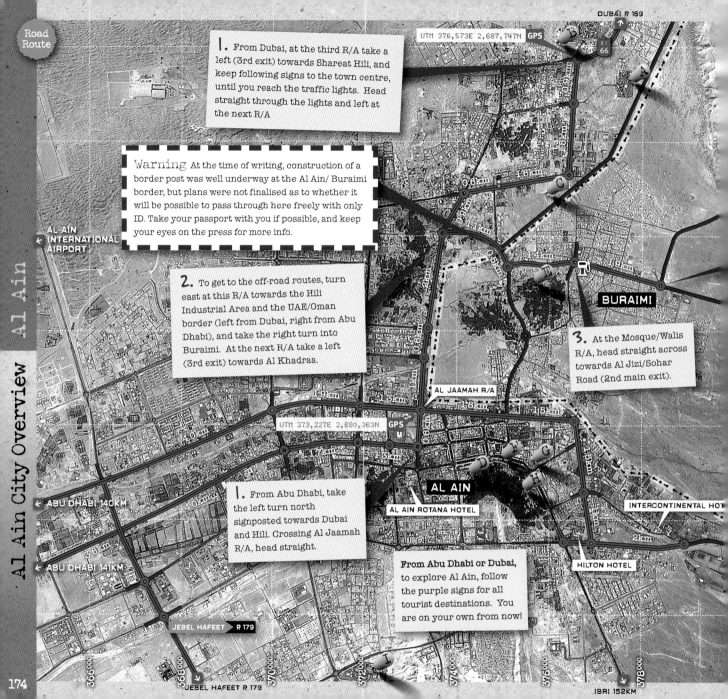

Road Route

DUBAI R 169

UTM 376,573E 2,687,747N **GPS**

1. From Dubai, at the third R/A take a left (3rd exit) towards Shareat Hili, and keep following signs to the town centre, until you reach the traffic lights. Head straight through the lights and left at the next R/A

Warning At the time of writing, construction of a border post was well underway at the Al Ain/ Buraimi border, but plans were not finalised as to whether it will be possible to pass through here freely with only ID. Take your passport with you if possible, and keep your eyes on the press for more info.

AL AIN INTERNATIONAL AIRPORT

2. To get to the off-road routes, turn east at this R/A towards the Hili Industrial Area and the UAE/Oman border (left from Dubai, right from Abu Dhabi), and take the right turn into Buraimi. At the next R/A take a left (3rd exit) towards Al Khadraa.

3. At the Mosque/Walis R/A, head straight across towards Al Jizi/Sohar Road (2nd main exit).

BURAIMI

0.6km   1.6km
0.9km
1.1km
0.5km   1.4km
0.5km   1.9km
2km
2km
0.6km

AL JAAMAH R/A

1.9km   3km
1.8km
1.5km
4.0km
UTM 373,227E 2,680,363N **GPS**
1.7km
3km
0.8km

AL AIN

1. From Abu Dhabi, take the left turn north signposted towards Dubai and Hili. Crossing Al Jaamah R/A, head straight.

AL AIN ROTANA HOTEL

INTERCONTINENTAL HOTEL

← ABU DHABI 140KM
5.6km
4.0km
← ABU DHABI 141KM

From Abu Dhabi or Dubai, to explore Al Ain, follow the purple signs for all tourist destinations. You are on your own from now!

2km

HILTON HOTEL

JEBEL HAFEET ▶ R 179

366000
368000
370000
372000
374000
376000
378000

JEBEL HAFEET R 179

IBRI 152KM

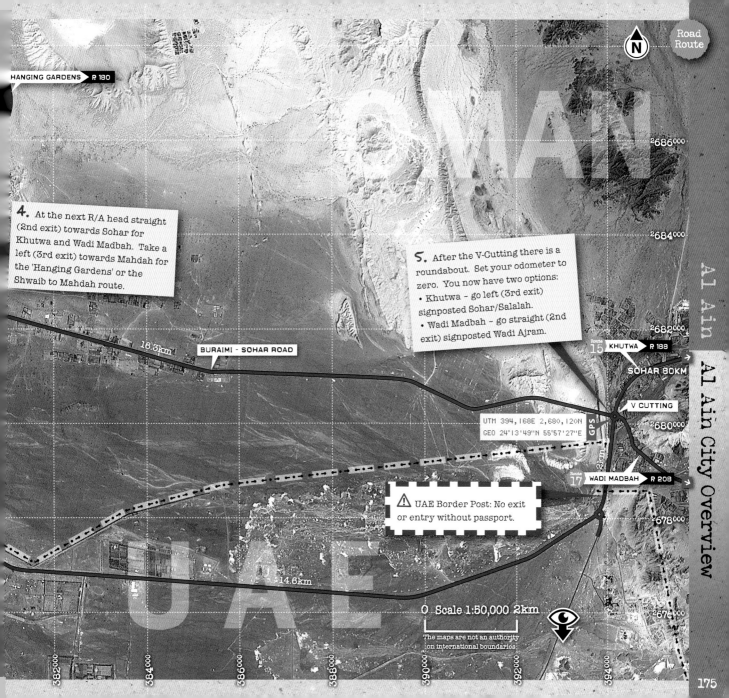

N

HANGING GARDENS ▶ R 180

4. At the next R/A head straight (2nd exit) towards Sohar for Khutwa and Wadi Madbah. Take a left (3rd exit) towards Mahdah for the 'Hanging Gardens' or the Shwaib to Mahdah route.

5. After the V-Cutting there is a roundabout. Set your odometer to zero. You now have two options:
• Khutwa – go left (3rd exit) signposted Sohar/Salalah.
• Wadi Madbah – go straight (2nd exit) signposted Wadi Ajram.

OMAN

²686 000

²684 000

²682 000

Route 15 KHUTWA ▶ R 188

SOHAR 80KM

16.3km

BURAIMI - SOHAR ROAD

V CUTTING

²680 000

UTM 394,168E 2,680,120N
GEO 24°13'49"N 55°57'27"E

GPS

Route 17 WADI MADBAH ▶ R 208

⚠ UAE Border Post: No exit or entry without passport.

²678 000

UAE

14.6km

0 Scale 1:50,000 2km

The maps are not an authority on international boundaries

²676 000

Al Ain

Al Ain City Overview

382 000 384 000 386 000 388 000 390 000 392 000 394 000

Al Ain Highlights

This is yet another area of the country that borders Oman, and some of the most enjoyable off-road trips will have you straying into foreign territory. You'll discover lovely scenery, cool hidden pools and ancient villages. Rich in leafy oases and winding wadis the region is also known for its ancient falaj (irrigation systems), the earliest of which dates back to around 1000BC. An unusual surprise is Jebel Hafeet, a monolith rising straight up out of the desert – take the road to the top for a spectacular view.

The town of Al Ain was once used as a summer retreat by people living on the coast, since the temperature and humidity here is often lower. In the days before, the trip here from Abu Dhabi took five days by camel! Today it takes about 1½ hours on a modern four-lane highway! Al Ain is amazingly green, and a very pleasant place to drive around with lush verges, roundabouts, parks and public areas .

Al Ain was also the birthplace of the first Ruler of the UAE, from 1972 to 2004, the late Sheikh Zayed bin Sultan Al Nahyan. The town is full of sites of interest , including 18 fortresses, a testament to the town's importance and its position on the ancient trading routes from Oman to the Arabian Gulf.

Up to 2005, it was possible to visit Buraimi from Al Ain, and all areas up to the Oman border post, without a visa. As this is about 40km from the UAE border in Al Ain/Buraimi, this included all the wadis, oases and off-road routes in the area. However, the building of the fence along the border right through the city and the construction of border controls on the UAE border has made it more difficult to move around this area. At the time of writing, it was still possible to cross between Al Ain and Buraimi, and while it looks set to stay that way, at least in the short-term, no official answer would be given as to whether it will be possible to pass through in the future with only ID, or whether passports and visa would be needed.

Also, with the completion of the UAE border post on the road from Al Ain towards the 'V-Cutting R/A', it is now impossible to get through here without passports, and without getting an exit stamp for the UAE. Therefore, you need to pass through the Oman border, and back, to be able to re-enter the UAE. So if you are travelling through the city for the off-road routes, make sure you take the Buraimi Road towards the 'V-Cutting', on which there are no such controls.

Keep your eyes on the press for more info. Also, if you are driving and decide to enter this part of the oasis, make sure that your car insurance covers Oman.

Hili Archaeological Garden

Off the Al Ain-Dubai road, about 10km outside of Al Ain, you will find Hili Archaeological Garden, which is both a public garden and an archaeological site. It's the source of some of the richest finds in the area, many of which are believed to be over 4,000 years old. The site includes the remains of a Bronze Age (2,000-2,500 BC) settlement, which was excavated and restored in 1995. There are other archaeological structures around the park, such as the famous Hili tomb, but the area is chiefly a garden. Keen archaeologists will probably find a visit to Al Ain Museum of more interest, since many of the finds from Hili are displayed there.

Hili Fun City

Opened in 1985, Hili Fun City and Ice Rink (see Directory for further details) is still one of the largest amusement parks in the Gulf with something for everyone. Renovated and added to in 1998, there are over 30 rides including bumper cars, a roller coaster, a merry-go-round and an ice rink.

Camel Market

Al Ain's camel market is well known throughout the country and is the last of its kind in the UAE. A visit here is an excellent opportunity to get up close to these 'ships of the desert' and to see and to hear the traders arguing over the price and merit of their animals. The market is only open in the mornings, but it's always busy and is a great place to enjoy some local colour.

Oases

Scattered throughout Al Ain are various pockets of palm plantations, many of which are still working farms. The shady palm trees provide a welcome respite from the heat and noise of the town, and visitors are welcome to wander around the main part near the Al Ain Museum (but stick to the paved areas that weave between the low walls). The farms have

Al Ain Oasis

plenty of examples of falaj (the ancient irrigation system), used for centuries to tap into the underground wells and to control scarce water resources.

Buraimi

There's less to see and do in the Buraimi part of the oasis and it's noticeably less affluent than Al Ain. (As part of the Abu Dhabi emirate, Al Ain has benefitted from the extensive oil revenues).

The Buraimi Souk is worth a visit though to sample the atmosphere. It sells a mixture of food and household goods. There is also a small selection of souvenir shops selling pottery and silver jewellery. Behind the souk is Al Hilla Fort, which is an interesting starting point from which to explore the oasis. The other main fort in town is Al Khandaq Fort, believed to be about 400 years old. Like many of Oman's forts, it has been extensively restored, and although there are no displays it is enjoyable to wander around and admire the view from the battlements.

Al Ain Museum

Opened in 1971, the Al Ain Museum (see Directory) is housed in a low modern structure standing on the edge of the main Al Ain Oasis. There is a variety of displays on life in the UAE, all well laid out with labelling in both Arabic and English. Of particular interest is the selection of photographs of Al Ain, Abu Dhabi and Liwa taken in the 1960s. These are striking illustrations of just how much the country has changed and developed in such a short space of time. Other exhibits include Bedouin jewellery, weapons and musical instruments, as well as a reconstruction of a traditional majlis, which, it appears, is just waiting for guests to arrive before coffee and dates are served! For those interested in archaeology, there are extensive displays from the nearby Hili Archaeological Gardens (a visit to the museum before going to the gardens is very informative), and from Qarn Bint Saud, a site 12km north of Hili, where there are more than 40 tombs dating from the 1st millenniumBC.

There's also a reconstruction of everyday life before the arrival of oil revenues. It's interesting to note that the figures are dressed with Omani turbans, instead of the traditional head-dress (gutra) of the Gulf Arabs. The area around Buraimi was a source of contention between Abu Dhabi, Oman and Saudi Arabia for many years. The museum shares the same compound as the Sultan bin Zayed Fort, or Eastern Fort as it is also known. Built in 1907, it is open to visitors, although there's little to see beyond the cannon in the courtyard.

Al Ain Souk

Also known as the Central or Old Souk, Al Ain Souk is a great place to explore and practise your bargaining skills. On sale are a mixture of household goods — pots and pans, plastic buckets of every size and colour, and fruit and vegetables. The souk itself is a rather ramshackle affair, but it is certainly different from the modern, rather sterile, air-conditioned markets found elsewhere.

Livestock Souk

Definitely the place to go if you need to find a goat or a sheep at a bargain price! Watch the locals arrive in pick-ups laden with animals. Arrive early (before 09:00, although there are people milling around all day), to soak up the atmosphere of this large, bustling market which attracts traders from all over the UAE. Be prepared, however, to be the object of a certain amount of curiosity. Don't be surprised by the rough treatment of the livestock.

Al Ain Zoo and Aquarium

Opened in 1969 and spread over 400 hectares, Al Ain Zoo & Aquarium is the largest zoo in the Gulf region. It's home to a wide variety of both rare and common animals, some indigenous to the Middle East and many from Africa and India. Local species include the Arabian oryx and gazelle, and there are also kangaroos, hippos, monkeys, big cats, reptiles, and a

⌐ Al Ain Museum

large aquarium. Be warned that international standards are not always met with regard to the treatment of, and facilities provided for, the animals.

Jebel Hafeet

One of the highlights of Al Ain is a visit to Jebel Hafeet, a mountain that lies 15km to the south of the city, rising abruptly from the flat countryside. From the summit, the views of the surrounding wadis, desert plains and oases are stunning. The city of Al Ain, which can be seen in the distance, lies at about 300 metres above sea level, so the height of the mountain at 1,180 metres is quite impressive. The road to the top is excellent, with lighting most of the way and numerous viewing points with plenty of car parking. The energetic could try cycling – only an hour or two up, then 20 minutes down! A new hotel, Mercure Grand Jebel Hafeet Al Ain, was opened at the end of 2002 near the top of the mountain and could be the best place in the area for sundowners. Near the base of the mountain there are hot springs, a visit to which can be combined with a stay at Ain Al Fayda Resthouse or Green Mubazzarah (see Directory on p.315).

Green Mubazzarah

Right at the bottom of Jebel Hafeet lies one of the most surprising sights in the UAE. Green Mubazzarah is a park of undulating rocky terrain that has been landscaped, giving the impression of rolling grassy hillsides. Accommodation is available in chalets (one or two bedrooms available). Running streams, waterfalls, hot springs and plants and trees make it look totally different to the normal mountain scenery of the Emirates, while play areas or the hills themselves keep children entertained.

Chalets are located either inside or outside the park, or around a man-made lake where you can rent pedalos. Many of the chalets are new, all have good facilities and are kept clean. Reception is open 24 hours, but reservations can be made in advance (03 783 8310), and prices range from Dhs.250 for a one-bedroom chalet during the week to Dhs.650 for a two-bedroom chalet for per night at the weekend. Even if you are only day-tripping, stop to enjoy the views down onto the park from the various viewpoints on Jebel Hafeet, and visit it on the way back down for a look around.

N

DUBAI

DUBAI-HATTA ROAD

HATTA

AL HAIYIR

← ABU DHABI

E1
66

Route
16   SHWAIB TO MAHDAH   R 196

OMAN

MAHDAH

UAE

KHUTWA

HANGING GARDENS

P.182

Route
15   KHUTWA   R 188

AL AIN

BURAIMI

← ABU DHABI

E1
22

V Cutting

AL AIN   R 176

MADBAH

GREEN MUBAZZARAH   R 179

Route
17   WADI MADBAH   R 208

0   Scale 1:400,000   16km

JEBEL HAFEET   R 179

The maps are not an authority on international boundaries.

↓ UMM ZAMOOL

↓ NIZWA

Hanging Gardens

This is not a day in the car route, but rather the route to an area for hiking. The famous hike in the area, after which it is named, ascends to the base of the cliff of Jebel Qatar where there are various routes to tackle, all offering spectacular views over the surrounding area. The focal points are some strange rock formations and the wonderful gardens.

Hike

Ras Al Khaimah

Arabian Gulf

Dubai

UAE

Abu Dhabi

Hatta

Fujairah

Al Ain

OMAN

Gulf of Oman

Terrain:	Desert, Mountains
Water:	Occasional Waterfalls
Driving:	2 Wheel Drive Possible
Activities:	Camping, Fossil Hunting, Hiking
Warnings:	Hike within your limits, Oman Car Insurance

Trip Info
Other Names:
Jebel Qatar, Fossil Valley
Distances & Start Times:

Distances:

	Paved	Unpaved
Dubai to start of route	110km	-
Route (Round Trip)	63.8km	9km
End of route to Dubai	110km	-

From Abu Dhabi: As Above

Al Ain

Hanging Gardens

DUBAI 109KM
AL OHA

UTM 378,852E 2,692,294N
GEO 24°20'20"N 55°48'20"E

GPS

UAE

E1 66

2. Take a left (3rd exit) towards Shareat Hili, and keep following the signs to the town centre, until you reach the traffic lights.

HILI FUN CITY

2.7km

1.3km

2.5km

3. Head straight through the lights then left at the next R/A. At the next R/A take another left and head towards the Hili Industrial Area and the UAE/Oman border, turning right through the border into Buraimi.

AL KHALEEF

1. Follow the Dubai-Al Ain road route until you reach the 'Coffee Pot' roundabout at Al Oha, just outside Al Ain. Go straight over this R/A and the next, (2nd exits).

1.1km

0.95km

HILI ARCHAEOLOGICAL PARK

AL AIN

1.8km

1.5km

9.4km

10.0km

10.4km

1.4km

BURAIMI

Hanging Gardens

Warning At the time of writing, construction of a border post was underway at the Al Ain/Buraimi border, but plans were not finalised as to whether it will be possible to pass through with only ID, or whether passports and visa would be needed. Keep your eyes on the press for more info.

AL BURAIMI INDUSTRIAL AREA

F O S S

Jebel Huwayyah

4. At the next R/A take a left (3rd exit) towards Al Khadraa. At the Mosque/Walis R/A, head straight across towards Al Jizi/Sohar road (2nd main exit).

AL BURAIMI HOTEL

1.2km

1.9km

5. At the next roundabout take a left (3rd exit) towards Mahdah. After approximately 16km, you will take a track to the right.

0   Scale 1:50,000   2km

The maps are not an authority on international boundaries.

378000

380000

2682000

AL JIZI/SOHAR 90KM

382000

2684000

384000

2686000

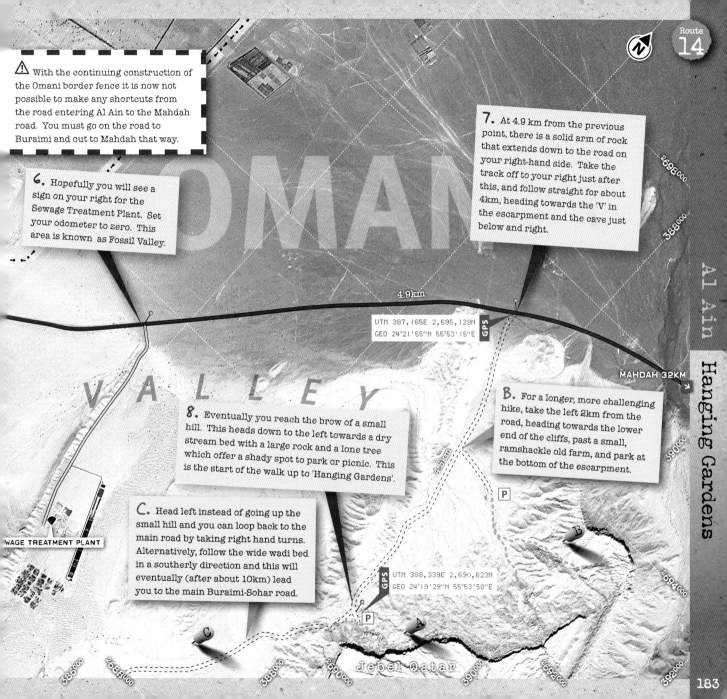

⚠ With the continuing construction of the Omani border fence it is now not possible to make any shortcuts from the road entering Al Ain to the Mahdah road. You must go on the road to Buraimi and out to Mahdah that way.

6. Hopefully you will see a sign on your right for the Sewage Treatment Plant. Set your odometer to zero. This area is known as Fossil Valley.

7. At 4.9 km from the previous point, there is a solid arm of rock that extends down to the road on your right-hand side. Take the track off to your right just after this, and follow straight for about 4km, heading towards the 'V' in the escarpment and the cave just below and right.

OMAN

4.9km

UTM 387,165E 2,695,129N
GEO 24°21'55"N 55°53'15"E
GPS

MAHDAH 32KM

V A L L E Y

8. Eventually you reach the brow of a small hill. This heads down to the left towards a dry stream bed with a large rock and a lone tree which offer a shady spot to park or picnic. This is the start of the walk up to 'Hanging Gardens'.

B. For a longer, more challenging hike, take the left 2km from the road, heading towards the lower end of the cliffs, past a small, ramshackle old farm, and park at the bottom of the escarpment.

C. Head left instead of going up the small hill and you can loop back to the main road by taking right hand turns. Alternatively, follow the wide wadi bed in a southerly direction and this will eventually (after about 10km) lead you to the main Buraimi-Sohar road.

WAGE TREATMENT PLANT

P

P

UTM 388,339E 2,690,623N
GEO 24°19'29"N 55°53'58"E
GPS

C

A

Jebel Qatar

Hanging Gardens Highlights

Located just outside Al Ain, 'Hanging Gardens' is one of the most unexpected finds imaginable. It is quite unlike anything that you will have seen during your stay in the Emirates.

After passing the bleakness of Fossil Valley, turn towards a horizontal band of rock visible in the distance. This is predominantly a hiking route - you will be leaving your car at the base of the mountain next to a small stream. Be sure you have a partner, an appropriate amount of water and are reasonably fit and active.

As you begin the walk, it seems just like any other mountainside in the UAE. Then you spot the cave and some of the strange rock formations above, but it is only when you reach the gardens themselves that you realise the full wonder of this very unusual place.

The area was named 'Hanging Gardens' by botanist and founder of the Arabian Leopard Trust, Marycke Jongbloed. The correct name is actually Jebel Qatar.

'Hanging Gardens Hike'

For the start of the hike up to Hanging Gardens, it is recommended that you set your sights on the escarpment of Jebel Qatar and walk straight up the steep scree slope on your right, heading directly away from the streambed and the lone tree. You should be able to find a small path that zigzags its way up a fair way from the bottom, then as the gradient eases, head across the rocky open hillside to the steeper slope into the cave. This route gets the hardest part of the climb over with right at the beginning, so while it may seem a tough slog to start with, don't worry... it will only get easier!

As you near the top of the rocky slope head into the cave (taking care not to disturb the bats), where you will find an amazing panorama over the tracks across the gravelly plains and the red desert, stretching as far as the eye can see.

When you've explored or rested enough, walk down to the right and follow the base of the cliff along to the north-east. Smooth faces decorated with bizarrely shaped rock, carved by many years of wind and sand, eventually lead to a steep slope descending to the 'gardens'. With water seeping through the rock almost all year round, this small shady area is unusually verdant and has a rarely visited air about it. Huge lumps of a rock similar to coral, as well as regular square-shaped features, make it a good place for some exploratory climbing as you meander along the cliff.

During rainy periods, water gushes from the rock like a waterfall, collecting in pools at the base and drizzling a fine spray over all the plants. The water doesn't remain for very long though, so you will be lucky to see a pool before it soaks into the ground. Also, the water is rather murky, so it is unsuitable for a swimming, even when the pools are deep enough.

Past the gardens, several impressive pillars of rock have become separated from the main rock face and you can squeeze through the narrow gaps. If you would like a longer walk, carry on along the base of the cliff for as long as you wish. Then, either retrace your steps for the choice of descent routes from the gardens, or make your way down from the escarpment onto the plain below where it's possible to join the track that you drove in on.

For the descent from the gardens there are several options depending on how quick you want to get back, and how much adventure you want! The tamest route is the path along the top edge of the wadi, which gently makes its way down to the starting point – just follow the snaking wadi on the right until you see the lone tree and the stream. For a wilder way down, an excellent route follows the wadi bed offering a very enjoyable challenge. The walk is easy enough to start with, but becomes increasingly extreme and you end up scrambling under, over and dropping down between boulders that are up to 20m in size, all the way back to the tree where you started.

Alternative Route: The simple return route described above can also be used as an alternative hike in. Walk up the left of the wadi to near the base of the cliffs, and head straight into the 'Hanging Gardens'. This way you reach the gardens directly, and it's a much shorter hike.

Ridge Hike

An alternative hike for those who have already done the 'Hanging Gardens', or just want to go that little bit higher, starts from the left and lower side of the escarpment, way before you reach the previously described car parking spot.

After passing the old, ramshackle farm, head into the corner of the L-shaped rock escarpment and park your car. You can then follow the rocky side ridge up to where it joins the main escarpment. From there it is possible to walk up to the highest point and all the way along the top of Jebel Qatar.

Ascending and descending the same route is the quickest way to gain height and get even better views of this area, and it's the simplest route to walk. If you choose to go all the way along the top of the escarpment, the route crosses many wadis, some shallow and inconsequential, but some serious propositions, with walls of up to 20m to scale down and then up the other side. A good head for heights and a good leader are required for this route, especially the last descent off the southern end of the Jebel as it can be hard to find a route down. Take your time, check out each section of the route before starting everyone down it, and be prepared for a fair bit of weaving on the way down. Once down, turn right and head along the flat track back to your car.

Onward Journey

For the journey home or further afield, this is a different route through to Fossil Valley. Turn left instead of going up the small hill and you can loop back to the main road by taking right-hand turns.

Alternatively, you could follow the wide wadi bed in a southerly direction and this will eventually (after about 10km) lead you to the main Buraimi-Sohar road, just before the V-cutting. This is a very useful shortcut if you are intending to explore any of the other routes in this area.

Fossil Valley

Before or after the walk, you may wish to explore Fossil Valley and Jebel Huwayyah, which was a reef millions of years ago when the ocean covered most of the Arabian Peninsula. Like Fossil Rock (see Fossil Rock, Hatta Area, p.136), this region is packed with the fossils of ancient shells and small sea creatures. These were created when limestone formed around them on the ocean bed, making a mould which then solidified to leave a perfect imprint.

Ridge Hike

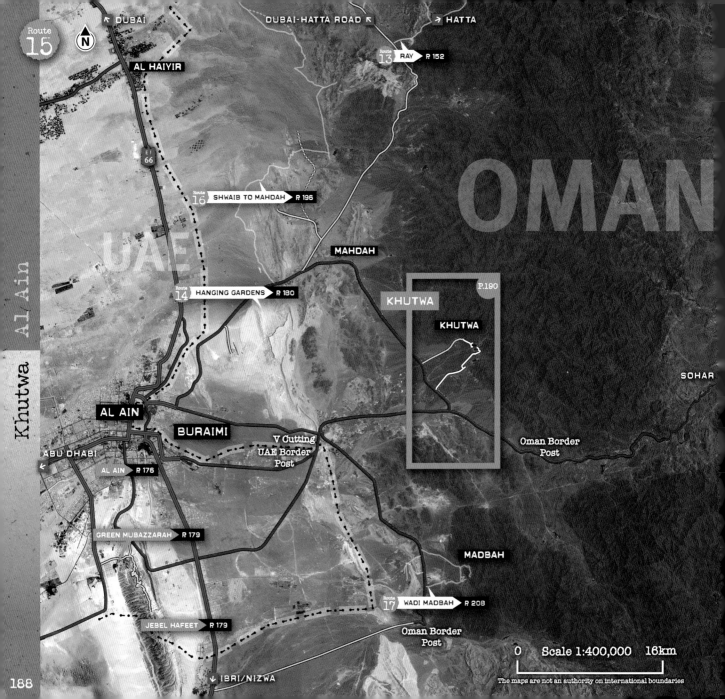

Route
15

↑ DUBAI

N

AL HAIYIR

DUBAI-HATTA ROAD

→ HATTA

Route
13 RAY R 152

OMAN

E1
66

Route
16 SHWAIB TO MAHDAH R 196

UAE

MAHDAH

Route
14 HANGING GARDENS R 180

KHUTWA

P.190

KHUTWA

SOHAR

AL AIN

BURAIMI

V Cutting
UAE Border
Post

Oman Border
Post

ABU DHABI
←

AL AIN R 176

GREEN MUBAZZARAH R 179

MADBAH

Route
17 WADI MADBAH R 208

JEBEL HAFEET R 179

Oman Border
Post

0   Scale 1:400,000   16km

↓ IBRI/NIZWA

The maps are not an authority on international boundaries

Khutwa

Situated alongside a deep gorge, Khutwa is a tranquil oasis with well-maintained plantations irrigated by falaj. The main attractions are the shady walks along the falaj through a wide variety of plants and trees, and the views from the narrow bridges that lead over the canyon to Al Khabbayan.

Terrain:	Gorge, Oasis, Wadi
Water:	Pools (Seasonal)
Driving:	2 Wheel Drive Possible
Activities:	Walking, Hiking
Warnings:	Oman Car Insurance, Secure your car!

Trip Info

Other Names:
Khatwa

Distances:

	Paved	Unpaved
Dubai to start of route	160km	-
Route (Round Trip)	38.4km	2km
End of route to Dubai	160km	-

From Abu Dhabi: As above

Jeep

Al Ain

Khutwa

11. Follow the Dubai-Al Ain road route until you reach Al Ain. Then using the Al Ain City Overview map, follow directions towards Buraimi then Sohar (Buraimi-Sohar road). After driving through the distinctive V-cutting on the Buraimi-Sohar road, take a left at the roundabout (3rd exit) signposted Sohar/Salalah. Follow the tarmac road straight.

Bridge

3.2

4.0km

3.0km

3.6km

Bus

UTM 408,099E 2,682,441N
GEO 24°15'07"N 56°05'40"E

GPS

2. Take the left turn signposted Mahdah, next to the mosque. This is about 16km from the last roundabout near the V-cutting. Take this left and head straight towards Mahdah.

F. For the Khabbayan side of the oasis, turn off the Mahdah road by the first bus stop, (3km), then drive up the track to the left-turn signposted to Khabbayan (3.6km).

0   Scale 1:50,000   2km

Route
15

For an alternative way to
Dubai avoiding Al Ain and
the UAE/Oman border,
follow this road to
Mahdah, then head up to
the Hatta-Dubai highway.

3. The turn off to Khutwa is the
third signposted turn on the right
near the bus shelter. Head
straight through the new village
of Khutwa, then onto the track up
and over the hill into the oasis.

Bus

5km

406 000

408 000

KHUTWA

4. At the fork head left,
quickly reaching an open
space where you can
park your car. Start your
walk here.

410 000

GPS UTM 410,979E 2,689,581N
GEO 24°19'00"N 56°07'21"E

P

'OLD' KHUTWA

KHABBAYAN
Bridges

⚠ Take care when parking your car: leave it
in the open, take all valuables with you and
try to leave it looking as empty as possible.
Break-ins have occurred in the past, but if you
leave nothing on show, you should be safe.

412 000

Khutwa Highlights

A short, straightforward drive off-road takes you to the serene and tranquil surroundings of the Khutwa oasis. There are many oasis villages in the area, but this one has a particularly special feel about it. The oasis farms overflow with dates, mangoes, papaya, avocados, bananas, pomegranates and figs. Just outside the oasis, on the rocky wadi, you'll find an impressive gorge and little footbridge — well worth exploring further.

Khutwa Old and New

Drive through the new village of Khutwa and up the gravel pass over the mountain behind. The first surprise is the spectacular view from the ridge over the beautiful green oasis nestled in the arid mountains.

Once through the pass the track winds its way left round narrow gaps in the palm trees and fields, to an open area before the old village. (This is a good place to leave your vehicle and start exploring on foot). The shady peace and abundant greenery are a wonderful contrast after the usually dry, harsh landscape of the UAE.

Gorge

After meandering through the peaceful plantation beneath shady palm trees, you should reach the small mosque in the old village of Khutwa. Adjacent to the mosque, follow the falaj upstream, past the gardens until the path bears right and drops down into the wadi. You will reach two narrow bridges crossing a deep gorge. On the far side of the wadi lies the small oasis village of Khabbayan. See (F).

Falaj Walk

From the mosque follow the falaj all the way through the plantation passing the turn off to the right down to the gorge. (Be careful not to knock any vegetation or rocks into the falaj that may then block it). Once you are out in the open, you will see the next oasis village further up the wadi. You can follow the falaj system which runs next to the narrow, tortured gorge all the way there. A true falaj actually taps the water from underground and feeds it to the surface. Here however, it acts as a simple canal, carrying the water from one area to another.

Flora and Fauna

In a year when there are good rains, some rare wild flowers can be found at Khutwa Oasis. In particular, look out for the buttercup (Ranunculus muricatus). Swallowtail butterflies (Papilio machaon) abound since their caterpillars feed on the citrus trees that grow underneath the date palms.

Wadi

In the smaller wadi near Khabbayan, a small canyon twists its way through curved rocks and water pools. Getting down to the bottom of the main wadi should only be attempted by those into extreme adventuring. There's just one place, a small walk downstream from the bridge, where the 20m high walls have collapsed and it's possible to make the challenging descent.

Falaj - This is the Arabic word for an irrigation channel used to irrigate palm plantations and farm fields. Often these channels run for many kilometres, from the source of the water upstream in a wadi to the site of the plantation.

Originally many of these channels ran underground for long distances. According to local legend, they were carved out of the rock by a tribe of men of small stature that specialised in this work. A well or shaft was dug and a canal built at a gentle angle, with another well every 30m or so, until the canal eventually reached the surface. Another method was to build a wall across an underground river, so that the water would dam up behind it and be forced to the surface where it was drawn off into a falaj system. The wall did not block the river entirely, so the overflow could escape and continue underground down the wadi – very eco-friendly!

It's not known how the falaj systems were built so accurately, since the original builders are long gone. Nowadays, people calling themselves 'falaj builders' simply repair the existing falaj system. There are no real falaj north of Al Ain, since the area is generally too dry. Remnants of the shafts belonging to the famous falaj of Buraimi, which dates from around 1,000 BC, can still be found near the Hilton Hotel in Al Ain.

Khabbayan

If you've done the lot on the Khutwa side of the wadi, a drive to Khabbayan can give a different view of the oasis. Park a little way from the houses and try not to walk through any private land, but there are paths which take you across the rocks towards the oasis and are particularly good for exploring the downstream section in the bottom of the wadi. See (E).

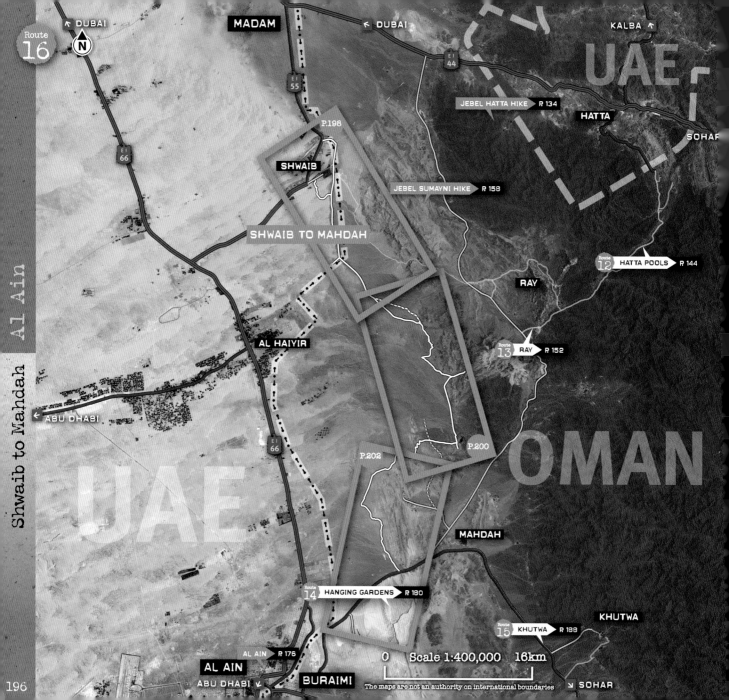

N

↑ DUBAI

MADAM

← DUBAI

KALBA ↑

E1
44

UAE

JEBEL HATTA HIKE ▶ R 134

HATTA

SOHAR

E1
55

P.198

E1
66

SHWAIB

JEBEL SUMAYNI HIKE ▶ R 158

SHWAIB TO MAHDAH

Route
12 HATTA POOLS ▶ R 144

RAY

AL HAIYIR

Route
13 RAY ▶ R 152

← ABU DHABI

P.200

OMAN

P.202

UAE

E1
66

MAHDAH

Route
14 HANGING GARDENS ▶ R 180

KHUTWA

Route
15 KHUTWA ▶ R 188

AL AIN ▶ R 176

0   Scale 1:400,000   16km

AL AIN

ABU DHABI ↓

BURAIMI

The maps are not an authority on international boundaries

↓ SOHAR

Shwaib to Mahdah

This route offers a delightful mix of desert driving, on both the sandy flats below some fantastic dunes and in the dunes themselves, as well as on rocky tracks across the plains beside the mountains. The driving and scenery are both very mixed, making this route an interesting view of the UAE's varied landscape.

Terrain: Desert, Mountains
Activities: Camping, Picnics
Warnings: Oman Car Insurance
New Border Fence

Trip Info
Other Names:
Shuaib, Ash Shuayb
Distances:

	Paved	Unpaved
Dubai to start of route	88km	-
Route	0.9km	60.4km
End of route to Dubai	110km	

From Abu Dhabi: As Above

⚠ STOP PRESS!
As the UAE/Oman border fence has now been completed all the way to the Dubai - Hatta road, it is now not possible to start this route from Shwaib as the fence cuts the route in two. Instead, see p.198 on how to start the route from the Hatta road near Madam.

Jeep

1. To start this route from the Dubai-Hatta road, at Madam head straight towards Hatta then just after the border fence, take a right onto the track heading straight along the fence towards Shwaib.

2. After reaching the dam, keep heading southwards, keeping your eye on the border fence as a guide.

DAM

MADAM 15KM
DUBAI 87KM

E1
55

GPS

UTM 381,377E 2,735,908N
GEO 24°43'59"N 55°49'37"E

SHWAIB

FARM

• Rubbish Tip / Landfill

0.9km

5.7km

Cattle Grid

D1. At the roundabout, head straight (2nd exit) towards the mountains.

SAND QUARRY

Previously the start of this route, this is now just a nice diversion to some nice undulating dunes for camping. To get here, at the signs for Fujairah/Dhaid/ Shwaib off the Dubai – Al Ain road, take the slip road, turn left over the bridge and head into Shwaib.

NEW SHWAIB

E1
55

D2. After the cattle grid, take the first right, a slip road running past a building with a green roof. Head towards the dunes. At the first bend in the road, carry straight on along the graded track, up and into the dunes – good camping can be found south of the sand quarry. You shouldn't need to deflate your tyres.

2738 000

376 000

2736 000

AL AIN 63KM/DUBAI 86KM

2734 000

378 000

2732 000

Route 16

Route 12 — HATTA POOLS ▸ R 144

Route 13 — RAY ▸ R 152

OMAN CHECK POINT

C

390000

2726000

Diversion As either an alternative route out of (or into) the dunes without following the border fence track or to link this route with one of the routes in the Hatta section (p.127), head to the Oman Check Point (ID required, preferably passports or driving licences) and then drive out through Wadi Sumayni. This then links up with the Ray route on (p.156).

OMAN

388000

4. Even though they are pretty tempting, unless you're really itching to get into the dunes it's worth holding off until a little bit further into the route. There's plenty to come, and it's best to not get too "bounced out" so you can enjoy the big stuff ahead.

R 200

386000

3. At the corner where the fence changes direction and goes up into the dunes, pick up the small track which follows the edge of the dunes south-eastwards.

Border Fence

2724000

7.0km

6.0km

UAE

GPS   UTM 382,287E 2,729,067N
       GEO 24°40'17"N 55°50'11"E

Border Fence

0   Scale 1:50,000   2km

The maps are not an authority on international boundaries

2730000   380000   382000   2726000   384000

2728000   382000   2724000

6. Follow the track beside the mountains, through a gap in the rocks, and out into a wide open area. Alternatively gun for the first major climb up into the dunes on your right, then drop down the other side into the same open area. Then, play around to your heart's content!

7. To continue on the route, head up the climb from the flat area at the bottom of the biggest dune, and weave your way in a south-easterly direction. At the edge of the dunes, there are a couple of drops which take you down to the gravel plain.

Rock

2.0km

1.1km

0.7km

FARM

FARM

2.3km

FARM

OMAN

6.3km

6.0km

8. From the base of the dunes, follow the track towards two small farms. Just after the first farm, turn left at the fork and go straight past the second farm on your right. When you reach the main track, turn left and follow it all the way to the cutting in the mountains.

5. Either go left, following the winding track alongside the dunes, or head right and make your own way through the gentle dunes. Just keep heading towards the mountains, and you'll meet up with the same track.

← R 199

0   Scale 1:50,000   2km

Al Ain

Shwaib to Mahdah

2724000

2722000

2720000

386000

2718000

2716000

9. As soon as you reach the track entering the pass into the mountains (with some marker posts 100m away to the left), cross straight over and head to the other side of the pass. Then follow the track next to the mountains out away from the pass.

GPS | UTM 394,555E 2,716,742N
GEO 24°33'39"N 55°57'31"E

2.6km

1.4km

5.3km

UTM 395,390E 2,709,746N
GEO 24°29'52"N 55°58'03"E | GPS

0.6km

3.1km

10. At the junction by a distinctive white rock, head straight on, and straight again at the second junction. When you reach a wide wadi, go straight across all tracks and continue towards the village.

11. Just before the village, go past the first small right turn by some trees, then take the next right, just before a walled enclosure. After 0.8km this joins another larger track, onto which you should turn right. Follow this until it crosses the new road, then head for the dunes.

New Road

Wadi Bed

13. Down the other side there is a great snaking trail where you can really put your foot down. After a few hundred metres cross over the small track then head onto another track following the mountains to the right.

12. At the right-hand end of the dunes a sandy track ascends diagonally up to the left by the rocks. Make your way up and continue around the rocks to the high point. From here you'll see a tree on the left-hand end of the highest ridge next to some rocks (See photo!). Head to the tree - a perfect shady spot for a lunch break - then drive over the ridge between the rocks and the tree.

1.2km

Tree

UTM 391,110E 2,709,406N
GEO 24°29'40"N 55°55'31"E | GPS

UTM 390,921E 2,708,832N
GEO 24°29'21"N 55°55'24"E | GPS

2714000 388000

2712000

2710000

390000 2708000

R 201

14. Follow the most obvious windy track – (fun driving!) and after passing the fenced field head across the open grey sandy area alongside the dunes to a capped water pipe. From here pick your way through the small dunes, (trickier than they look due to soft sand in some places), in the general direction of the mountains.

15. Once out of the dunes onto the brown sand plain, you have two options: head through the trees and camel farms and take the track south-east beside the mountains, or drive due south across the plain towards Jebel Qatar. Either way, you will end up at the road.

5.3km

● CAMEL FARM

Field

GPS | UTM 387,746E 2,706,884N
GEO 24°28'17"N 55°53'32"E

UTM 385,457E 2,703,882N
GEO 24°26'39"N 55°52'11"E | GPS

End of Dunes

WATER PIPE

2.0km

3.5km

2708000

386000

2706000

2704000

2702000

38

MAHDAH

Route 13 RAY R 152

GPS   UTM 389,478E 2,696,081N
      GEO 24°22'26"N 55°54'36"E

Route 14 HANGING GARDENS R 180

Route 16

8.8km

16. Turn right to join the 'Hanging Gardens' route (p.180) or to head to Al Ain and Buraimi. Left is the quickest way back to Dubai, with options to join the Hatta Pools route (p.144) or Ray route (p.152).

OMAN

BURAIMI/AL AIN P 169

Al Ain Shwaib to Mahdah

0   Scale 1:50,000   2km
The maps are not an authority on international boundaries

UAE

Shwaib to Mahdah Highlights

Amid the stark contrast of the red desert with the spectacular, rocky Hajar Mountains, this varied route takes you from the edge of the desert near Shwaib to two areas of dunes, separated by sandy flats and rocky plains. The first area of dunes in particular is a great place for playing around, with some challenging climbs, massive drops, and plenty of places for camping and picnics sheltered by rocky outcrops below the dunes. After leaving this area, tracks across a flat gravel plain lead to the second set of dunes. Having crossed these dunes you head out of the desert on a fun drive along twisting sand tracks, open flats and over tricky smaller dunes. The Oman border fence has now split this route at Shwaib, meaning it has to be accessed from the Dubai-Hatta road instead, but it's still definitely worth the detour!

Dams

In the past dams were never a feature of the UAE landscape, mainly because of the problem of evaporation — it's better to keep things underground. However, over recent years the water table has been decreasing as more water is pumped up to irrigate farmland. To combat this, numerous dams have been built in the foothills of the mountains. These are in areas where the water flows after rains and the ground is most permeable. You will rarely find water behind the dams, since they are simply designed to control flash floods long enough for some of the water to seep into the ground. Without the dams the water would quickly dissipate and be lost. They also reduce the damage that can be caused by flash floods to buildings and farms in the wadis.

UAE/Oman Border

During 2006 the border fence was completed from Al Ain to the Dubai-Hatta road and although there is one check point south of Shwaib, it seems that there will be no access for non-Emiratis. To get into the dunes, the track alongside the fence allows access from the Hatta road, and it is still possible to get to the same area of desert from the Hadf-Mahdah road, see the Ray route (p.156).

Scenic Detour

To combine the dunes with a change of scenery, head through the Oman checkpoint at the edge of the mountains, after which the track through the pass takes you to the Hadf-Madhah road. From here it is possible to join up with the Ray route (p.152), or the back of the Hatta Pools route (p.144).

Playtime!

This is a great place for some fun driving, with plenty of challenging climbs and massive drops. The biggest climb, directly in front of you from the flat area at the bottom, heads up then right and round to the top of the highest dune. When you're tired out, or when your car needs a rest, the tops of the dunes are a great place to enjoy some views of the surrounding jagged peaks, so typical of the Hajar Mountains looming attractively in the distance. At the base of the dunes there are plenty of places to tuck yourself away between the rocks for a picnic, or even camping.

Be warned though, the challenging dunes here are a popular spot for drivers, and riders, to practise their off-road skills. Therefore, it might not be the quietest camping spot you have ever found.

Detour

For a detour to some really rugged driving, from the narrow gap between the mountains and the rocky outcrop, a track leads you up a small wadi to a couple of farms and collections of bee-hives. There are several rough tracks here, descending through wadis and climbing to viewpoints over the mountains and desert, all offering real challenges to both driver and vehicle. Afterwards, the smooth sandy terrain back on the route will feel like driving on velvet.

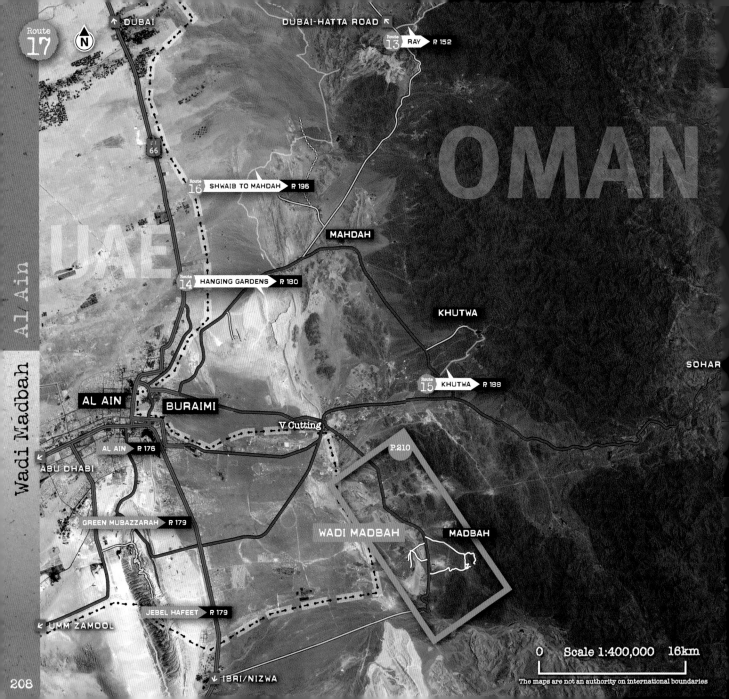

N

↑ DUBAI

DUBAI-HATTA ROAD ↗

Route
13 RAY ▶ R 152

66

OMAN

Route
16 SHWAIB TO MAHDAH ▶ R 196

UAE

MAHDAH

Route
14 HANGING GARDENS ▶ R 180

KHUTWA

SOHAR

Route
15 KHUTWA ▶ R 188

AL AIN BURAIMI

V Cutting

AL AIN ▶ R 176

P.210

ABU DHABI

GREEN MUBAZZARAH ▶ R 179

WADI MADBAH MADBAH

JEBEL HAFEET ▶ R 179

↙ UMM ZAMOOL

0 Scale 1:400,000 16km

↓ IBRI/NIZWA

The maps are not an authority on international boundaries

Wadi Madbah

A straightforward drive into the mountains, with pools and waterfalls. A short stroll up the wadi leads to the first pool and just around the next corner is the main pool and a waterfall, quite hidden and secluded. If you drive or walk around to the top of the cliff above the falls, there is a fantastic view and some more pools that are worth discovering. Far more impressive than the better-known falls at Wadi Wurrayah on the east coast, sadly this area is also starting to suffer from the same problem of litter.

Terrain: Mountains, Wadi
Water: Pools, Waterfall, Stream
Driving: Short but sometimes rough
Activities: Camping, Hiking, Rock Climbing, Swimming
Warnings: Oman Car Insurance.

Trip Info

Other Names:
Wadi Madabbah, Madbah Falls

Distances:

	Paved	Unpaved
Dubai to start of route	160km	-
Route (Round Trip)	22.7km	18.5km
End of route to Dubai	160km	-

From Abu Dhabi: As Above

Jeep

Al Ain

Wadi Madbah

OMAN

QUARRY   QUARRY

1. Follow the Dubai-Al Ain road route until you reach Al Ain. Then use the Al Ain overview road map to reach the V-Cutting. Go straight across at the roundabout (2nd exit) signposted Wadi Agram. After 13km you will reach a small distinctive mosque on the left. You are now on the map...

0.6km

2.2km

AL AIN/BURAIMI 27KM
V-CUTTING 8KM

QUARRY

Truck Road

1.2km

4.2km

1.1km

Truck Road

GPS   UTM 401,620E 2,670,487N
GEO 24°08'37"N 56°11'54"E

2. There is a fork in the road and a sign to Al Jeelat to the left, carry straight on to your right.

QUARRY

0   Scale 1:50,000   2km

396000   2672000   2670000   398000   2670000   2668000   400000   2666000

D2. After 1.5km, take the right at the fork and head towards a smaller oasis and plantation. Drive straight through the smallholding, then turn right at the fork just after the palm plantation. Follow this track to the end. **Warning:** Approach the cliff edge with extreme caution.

2.9km

Cliff Edge ⚠

GPS UTM 410,495E 2,664,632N GEO 24°05'29"N 56°07'09"E

Waterfall

MADBAH

5. Once you can drive no further, park your car near the Arabic sign and walk up the wadi the rest of the way.

0.9km

0.6km

Wadi Hamad

5.0km

GPS UTM 409,791E 2,664,362N GEO 24°05'20"N 56°06'45"E

D1. For breathtaking views from the plateau above the waterfall, stay left at the fork (triangle with tree) and take your next immediate left.

4.6km

4. Take a right at the fork (triangle with tree) down into the wadi, then immediately left upstream towards the palms, keeping to the left of the wadi bed. Be careful of the cables strung rather low over some parts of the track.

A. For the diversion to Wonderwall, turn right, double back on the truck road then take the immediate left towards the mountains. Just after another track joins from the right, head through the gap and take the next left towards the unexpected sand and greenery in the distance. Alternatively, you can reach it by the older route which heads across the truck road and follows the telephone cables up and over the hill. Then join the other track and turn left towards the escarpment.

1.9km

Truck Road

1.4km

2.3km

GPS UTM 405,767E 2,664,011N GEO 24°05'08"N 56°04'22"E

3. Carry on until you see the sign marked 'Madbah 4km' to your left. Take this track.

OMAN BORDER CHECK POINT

Wonder Wall

JEBEL HAFEET P.179

412,000

410,000

408,000

2,666,000

2,660,000

2,658,000

2,664,000

2,662,000

2,660,000

404,000

406,000

402,000

Wadi Madbah Highlights

The Wadi Madbah route makes a lovely trip into a relatively unspoilt area. The tracks off both sides of the paved road leading to Madbah provide short routes to the points of interest. The small village of Madbah has some pools that have water in all year round, the UAE's highest waterfall and in addition, the interestingly coloured stream and pools on the way in making it a very picturesque place. On the other side of the tarmac road there is a great track that takes you through a cutting in a ridge of mountains. Once through the gap, a large basin completely surrounded by mountains lies at your feet. Here you will find opportunities for rock climbing, general scrambling and exploring. From Madbah it is possible to explore further into the mountains, finding even more remote streams and pools.

Diversion and Rock Climbing

As you drive through the cutting in the rocks into a bowl entirely encircled by mountains, it appears as if a whole new world lies before you. Admire the strange rock formations to the left, while the mountains in front of you are particularly picturesque. Note the sand pushing right up against the foot of the rocks. Along this face, called 'Wonderwall', there is some reasonable rock climbing, but as usual the climbs can be rather hair-raising as the rock tends to be a little loose. The sandy area at the base of the mountains also makes a comfortable spot to picnic or camp.

Wadi Madbah

Having parked the car, as you wander up the wadi you will come across numerous small pools and rivulets. There is even a falaj-like canal carved out of the bedrock, which effectively channels the water down the wide riverbed. It's an attractive view from here back down the valley.

Madbah Waterfall

The first big pool and its waterfall are reached after 200m. The easiest way around the pool is to scramble up and over the rocks on the right. The riverbed above this point seems dry and stony, but continue around the corner for an even bigger surprise — a large, deep pool and an impressive waterfall (by UAE standards). It's worth the scramble to take a refreshing dip and splash around under the falls with the toads, or just to bask in the sun with your feet in the pool being nibbled by the little fish! There is water here all year round, but obviously more in winter than in summer. Recently Madbah has started to suffer from litter as have other places in the emirates, but not quite on the level of Wadi Wurrayah. Please do your bit by taking everything you bring with you home again!

Plateau Overlooking the Falls

Prepare yourself for a breathtaking view from the plateau above the waterfalls - from here you can peer over the edge of the wadi, with the river and pools surprisingly far below. Be careful of loose ground when approaching the edge. This large, flat area is a wonderful place to camp, as long as you don't have wandering toddlers or sleepwalkers in your group.

Pools above the Falls

Just where the track ends at the 'mini roundabout', there is a path going down into the wadi. It's a quick and easy walk down and at the bottom there is a stream running through the narrow wadi with several pools, some deep enough to swim in. There's plenty of scope for further exploration downstream, towards the top of the waterfall. You'll find the bigger pools and sections where you'll need to climb up or down (the shady side of the wadi has some climbed sports routes with holes drilled, but currently no bolts in place.) Upstream, the stream fades away, sinking underground as the wadi bed gradually rises to the head of the valley.

Further Off-Road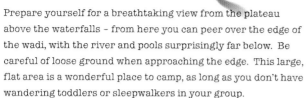

If you want an alternative, quieter area to explore and camp, head south through Madbah village towards the wide gap in the mountains. The track winds its way across a gravelly plateau and a small wadi. There's not much shade, but there are some small clean pools in a canyon cut into the rocks, and plenty of peace and quiet for some remote mountain camping.

Previously, it was possible to keep on going south on a poorly maintained track in and out of the wadi, through the gap in the mountains, and then left onto the graded track heading east up Wadi Ajran in Oman. After a fair distance up the wadi, it was also possible to turn left (north) towards Daqeeq and Kitnah, with their pools which are now beyond the Omani border. With the tightening of the Oman/UAE border, this track is now normally blocked off. If you do manage to sneak your way through, it's an epic drive and one that's well worth doing. However, on your return, make sure you use exactly the same route. If you get it wrong you will end up at the Omani border post, trying to talk your way back into the UAE!

SUN & SAND SPORTS

L.L.C

P.O. Box. 894, Dubai, U.A.E., Phone: +971-4-3599905 Fax: +971-4-3599907, www.sunandsandsports.com

Liwa

Jeep

N

DUBAI

ARABIAN GULF

ABU DHABI

MUSSAFAH

BANI YAS

AL AIN

RUWAIS
← RUWAIS/SAUDI ARABIA

TARIF

UNITED ARAB
EMIRATES

GHAYATHI

MADINAT ZAYED

BU HASA

Route
18

Liwa Oasis
An adventure in
the epic Empty
Quarter - the
biggest sand
desert in the
world!

Page 228

LIWA OASIS

MEZAIRA'A

UMM HISIN

LIWA

ARADA

HAMIM

OMAN

0   Scale 1:1,650,000   75km

SAUDI
ARABIA

These maps are not an authority on international boundaries

UMM AZZIMUL

Liwa Route Overview Table

Route	Name	Page	Total Dist. (km)	Total Unpaved (km)	Terrain			Activity					Route Combinations
					Mtn	Desert	Wadi	Camp	Climb	Hike	Bike	Swim	
	Liwa Road Route	220	322										
route 18	Liwa Oasis 👆	228	150	Endless!		✓		✓					

Liwa Route Combinations

The trip to Liwa is unique, as unlike our other trips in this book, it can't really be combined with other routes. With the length of the drive to Liwa, and the vast area of desert to explore once you get there, this route should really be planned over a few days, preferably with at least two nights spent there or at rest-points on the way down. A three-day stay would allow you to have a good explore around the oasis, and then into the desert for at least two days of real off-road driving. If you can budget even more time to allow for long lunches and early camping stops, you will really get the full benefit of the amazing surroundings. For most people, a trip to Liwa inspires further visits, so don't try cramming too much in – you'll be back!

ARABIAN GULF

DUBAI

P.222

DUBAI - LIWA

E1
311

E1
44

E1
66

ABU DHABI

AL AIN

P.224

RUWAIS

RUWAIS/SAUDI ARABIA

TARIF

E1
11

E1
22

GHAYATHI

UNITED ARAB

EMIRATES

MADINAT ZAYED

BU HASA

OMAN

MEZAIRA'A

LIWA OASIS

UMM HISIN

ARADA

Route
18   LIWA OASIS   R 228

HAMIM

SAUDI
ARABIA

UMM AZZIMUL

0   Scale 1:1,650,000   75km

These maps are not an authority on international boundaries

Liwa

Located way south of Abu Dhabi, further than most people usually venture either on or off-road, Liwa is a destination that will blow you away with it's massive expanses of awesome desert and the biggest dunes this side of the Sahara. The drive down is long, but if you're well prepared with enough music to last the journey, the trip there is well worth it. Prepare for the most adventurous off-road driving the UAE has to offer, and some of its most incredible scenery.

Terrain:	Coastal Plains, Desert, Oasis
Water:	Sea
Driving:	Easy, Long
Activities:	Driving
Culture:	Car Museum

Trip Info

Distances:

Dubai to Abu Dhabi	131km
Abu Dhabi to Liwa (via Tarif)	191km
Liwa to Abu Dhabi (via Hamim)	246km

Jeep

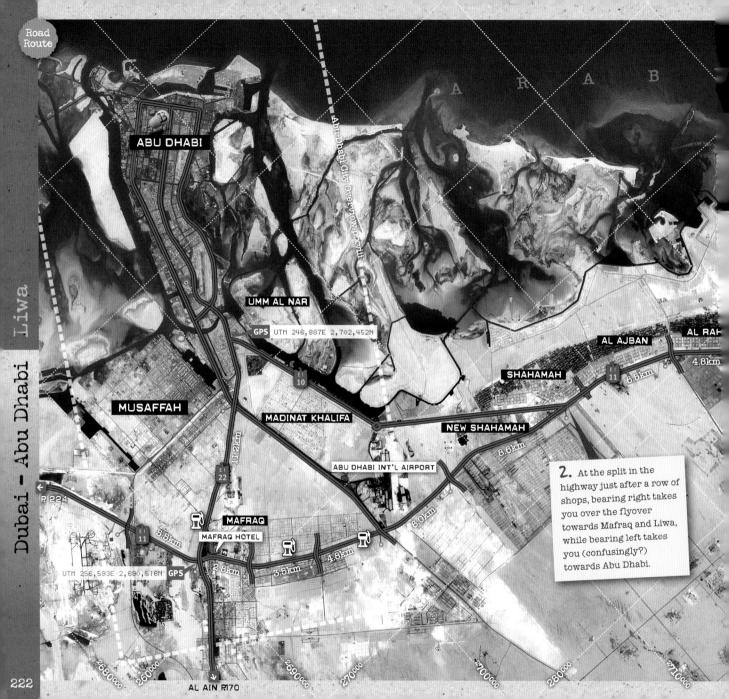

ARAB

ABU DHABI

Abu Dhabi City Overview p.xviii

UMM AL NAR

GPS UTM 246,887E 2,702,452N

E|
10

AL RAH

AL AJBAN

4.8km

SHAHAMAH

E|
11 6.5km

MUSAFFAH

MADINAT KHALIFA

NEW SHAHAMAH

8.6km

E|
22

ABU DHABI INT'L AIRPORT

R 224

←

E|
11 5.5km

MAFRAQ

MAFRAQ HOTEL

6.0km

4.8km

2.8km   3.5km

GPS UTM 256,593E 2,690,516N

2. At the split in the
highway just after a row of
shops, bearing right takes
you over the flyover
towards Mafraq and Liwa,
while bearing left takes
you (confusingly?)
towards Abu Dhabi.

Dubai – Abu Dhabi · Liwa

11.2km

260000   2690000   270000   2700000   280000   2710000

AL AIN R170

N   G   U   L   F

JEBEL ALI BEACH

GOLDEN TULIP AL JAZIRA HOTEL & RESORT

JEBEL ALI GOLF RESORT & SPA

8.0km   4.3km

SAIH AS SIDRAH   E 11

TOURIST INFORMATION   **JEBEL ALI**

2km

AL SAMHA   15.0km   14.3km

8.5km

P XVI

3.0km   5.7km

P XVI

11.4km   E 311   7.4km

1. Head out of Dubai
on Sheikh Zayed Road
past Jebel Ali and
keep going south.

0   Scale 1:250,000   10km

DUBAI-AL AIN ROAD

Warning Grid is in geographic
coordinates as you are crossing
between UTM zones...
Also, if you are using UTM coordinates
for the Liwa road route, as this area
covers zones 39Q, 39R and 40R, make
sure you enter the correct zone
number as well as the coordinate.

ARABIAN GUL

ABU AL ABYADH

Khor Qantar

AR RA

Khor al Bizm

RUWAIS
SAUDI ARABIA

TARIF

UTM 39R 791,119E 2,660,950N GPS

E
11

4.7km   9.0km   6.7km

E
11   19.6km

24.0km

SHAMIS

4. Just after the petrol
station (keep your car
topped up!), take the slip
road signposted Madinat
Zayed and Mezaira'a.

BU HASA

5. Head straight
through Madinat Zayed
then when you arrive in
Liwa at Mezaira'a, (after
108km), see p230.

0   Scale 1:250,000   10km

53°40'   53°50'   54°00'

23°95'

MADINAT ZAYED

FETEISI

BU KESHEISHAH

MUSAFFAH

Khor Qirqishan

P. 223

16.2km

AL MAQATRAH P. 170

E11

UTM 40R 237,410E 2,680,307N GPS

8.0km

14.2km   12.2km

POLICE CHECKPOINT

RUMAITHA

3. Usually used for the
return route, this road
brings you all the way from
the Liwa Crescent to the E11,
where a right turn leads to
Abu Dhabi and Dubai.
Alternatively, it can be used
as a straightforward way to
get down to Liwa.

SHANAYL

6. Errrrmmm.........Go
straight. Then when you
reach Liwa at Hamim,
(after 143km), see p.231.

24°20'

24°15'

24°10'

24°5'

54°20'   24°0'   54°30'   54°40'

HAMIM/LIWA P.231

Dubai - Liwa Highlights

Jebel Ali Beach

With the relentless development along every inch of Dubai's coastline, the search for open, natural stretches of beach brings many people to Jebel Ali. Just south of the Jebel Ali Hotel & Golf Resort, this area of beach is popular for daytrippers and barbcues at the weekend, it is one of the few places near Dubai where you can camp (although 'officially' a permit is required), and is the new home of Dubai's kitesurfers. Its location right next to the trunk of The Palm Jebel Ali means that traffic is increasing, but once you find your spot on the sand it is quiet enough in the afternoons and evenings (apart from the odd rumble from the Palm).

Abu Dhabi

Relatively recently, Abu Dhabi consisted of little more than a fort, surrounded by a modest village of just a few hundred date-palm huts. However, since the discovery of oil in 1958, life has changed beyond recognition. Abu Dhabi is now a modern and lush metropolis, graced with tree lined streets, futuristic skyscrapers, rich shopping malls, luxury hotels and cultural centres, and is surrounded by the sparkling turquoise waters of the Arabian Gulf. The famous 'Manhattan' skyline reflected in the azure waters along the corniche offers a striking contrast to the large gardens and green boulevards that are spread across the island.

The city itself lies on an island, which became home to the Bani Yas Bedouin tribe in 1761 when they left the Liwa oasis in the

↖ Abu Dhabi skyscrapers

Emirates National Auto Museum

Surprisingly located way out of any town, this impressive collection of cars is the work of one dedicated collector: Sheikh Hamad, aka the 'Rainbow Sheikh'. Having recently undergone development after officially opening to the public in 2005, the museum is now home to almost 200 cars including a vast collection of off-road cars and classic American cars, the Sheikh's rainbow collection of Mercedes and the largest truck in the world. Some exhibits may be familiar to visitors from their appearance in the BBC car programme *Top Gear*.

Even if you're not particularly interested in cars, this is a fascinating collection and a great place to stop on the way to or from Liwa. Opening times may change, but last time we checked they were from 09:00 to 18:00, seven days a week. Entry is free. For more information, check out the website (www.enam.ae)

interior. Being an island, it offered security, but the tribe also found excellent grazing, fishing and fresh water supplies. The descendants of this tribe have in fact, in alliance with other important families in the region, governed the emirate ever since. A slower pace is evident when compared to Dubai, and there is much more reliance on oil as the emirate still has so much of it. However, development for tourism and other industries has recently started to increase with the opening of the opulent Emirates Palace hotel and the deluxe, boutique Al Raha Beach Hotel.

Abu Dhabi's Islands

On the maps these islands and flat headlands look like enticing places to explore for remote beaches and clean seas, but they are all unfortunately used by either the Abu Dhabi military or are home to one or other of the sheikh's palaces, and entry is not permitted. If you have your own boat they might be worth exploring from the sea, otherwise they are out of bounds.

↑ Emirates National Auto Museum

ARABIAN GULF

RUWAIS/SAUDI ARABIA

TARIF

→ ABU DHABI

↑ ABU DHABI

AUTO MUSEUM ▶ R 227

E11

MADINAT ZAYED

BU HASA

↑ RUWAIS/SAUDI ARABIA

E11

UNITED ARAB
EMIRATES

DUBAI - LIWA

P.230

MEZAIRA'A

UMM HISIN

ARADA

L I W A   O A S I S

P.232

HAMIM

0   Scale 1:900,000   50km

The maps are not an authority on international boundaries

SAUDI ARABIA

Liwa Oasis

A trip to the Empty Quarter (or Rub Al Khali) is a must for any off-roader during their time in the Middle East. It's the biggest sand desert on the planet, and the sheer scale of the scenery and the size of the dunes has to be seen to be believed. This epic route is more of an expedition than just a spot of dune-bashing, so go prepared... for the experience of a lifetime!

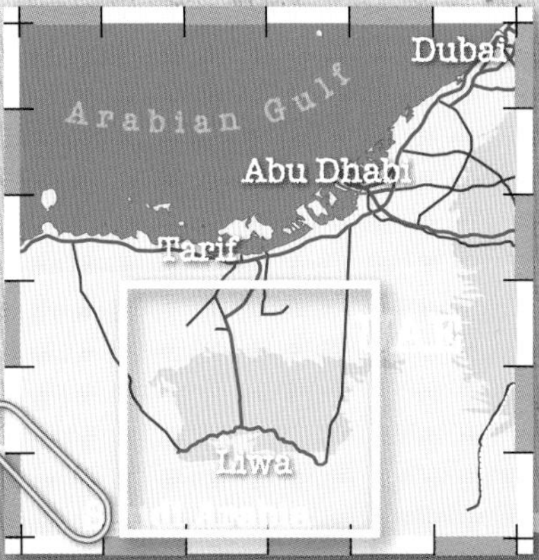

Arabian Gulf

Dubai

Abu Dhabi

Tarif

Liwa

Terrain:	Desert, Oasis, Sabkha	
Driving:	Varied, Spectacular	
Activities:	Camping, Dune Driving, Sand Boarding, Picnics	

Trip Info

Distances:

	Paved	Unpaved
Dubai to start of route	322km	-
Route (Round trip)	150km	Endless!
End of route to Dubai	395km	-

Jeep

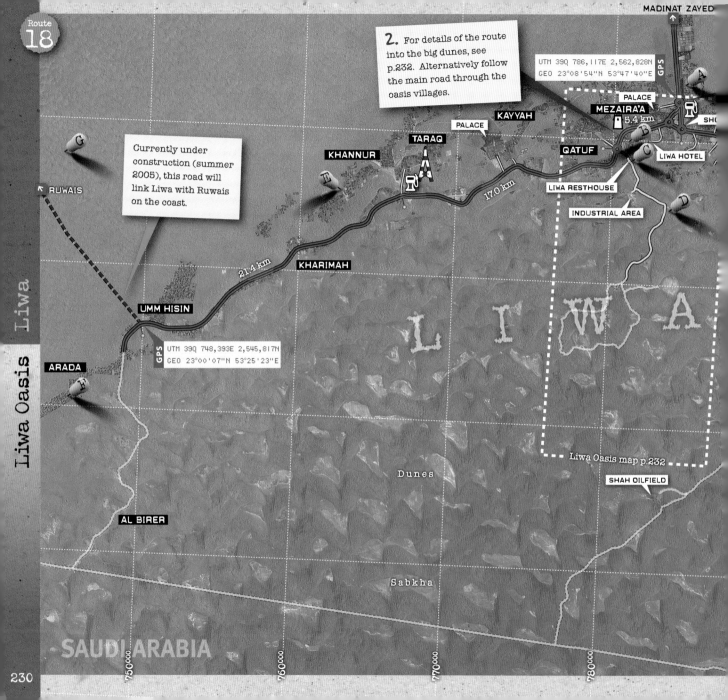

MADINAT ZAYED

2. For details of the route into the big dunes, see p.232. Alternatively follow the main road through the oasis villages.

UTM 39Q 786,117E 2,562,828N
GEO 23°08'54"N 53°47'40"E
GPS

PALACE
MEZAIRA'A
5.4 km
SHC

Currently under construction (summer 2005), this road will link Liwa with Ruwais on the coast.

KAYYAH

PALACE

TARAQ

QATUF

KHANNUR

LIWA HOTEL

RUWAIS

LIWA RESTHOUSE

170 km

INDUSTRIAL AREA

21.4 km

KHARIMAH

UMM HISIN

UTM 39Q 748,393E 2,545,817N
GEO 23°00'07"N 53°25'23"E
GPS

L I W A

ARADA

Liwa Oasis map p.232

Dunes

SHAH OILFIELD

AL BIRER

Sabkha

SAUDI ARABIA

750 000

760 000

770 000

780 000

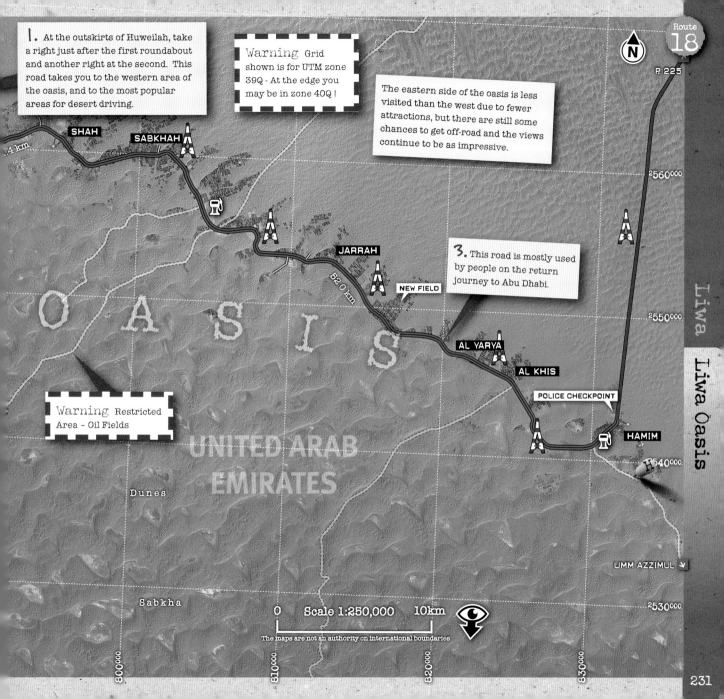

R 225

1. At the outskirts of Huweilah, take a right just after the first roundabout and another right at the second. This road takes you to the western area of the oasis, and to the most popular areas for desert driving.

Warning Grid shown is for UTM zone 39Q - At the edge you may be in zone 40Q !

The eastern side of the oasis is less visited than the west due to fewer attractions, but there are still some chances to get off-road and the views continue to be as impressive.

SHAH

SABKHAH

2560000

JARRAH

52.0 km

NEW FIELD

3. This road is mostly used by people on the return journey to Abu Dhabi.

2550000

AL YARYA

AL KHIS

POLICE CHECKPOINT

Warning Restricted Area - Oil Fields

HAMIM

UNITED ARAB EMIRATES

Dunes

2540000

UMM AZZIMUL

Sabkha

2530000

0   Scale 1:250,000   10km

The maps are not an authority on international boundaries

800000

810000

820000

830000

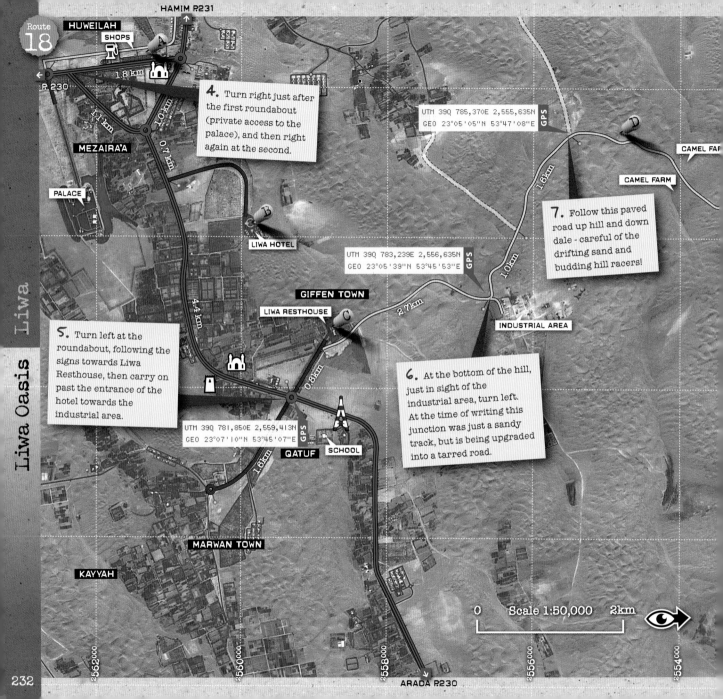

Route 18

HAMIM R231

HUWEILAH

SHOPS

1.8 km

P. 230

1.1 km

1.0 km

0.7 km

MEZAIRA'A

PALACE

UTM 39Q 785,370E 2,555,635N
GEO 23°05'05"N 53°47'08"E   GPS

CAMEL FARM

CAMEL FARM

1.6km

4. Turn right just after the first roundabout (private access to the palace), and then right again at the second.

LIWA HOTEL

UTM 39Q 783,239E 2,556,635N
GEO 23°05'39"N 53°45'53"E   GPS

1.0km

7. Follow this paved road up hill and down dale - careful of the drifting sand and budding hill racers!

4.4 km

GIFFEN TOWN

LIWA RESTHOUSE

2.7km

INDUSTRIAL AREA

5. Turn left at the roundabout, following the signs towards Liwa Resthouse, then carry on past the entrance of the hotel towards the industrial area.

0.8km

6. At the bottom of the hill, just in sight of the industrial area, turn left. At the time of writing this junction was just a sandy track, but is being upgraded into a tarred road.

UTM 39Q 781,850E 2,559,413N
GEO 23°07'10"N 53°45'07"E   GPS

1.6km

QATUF

SCHOOL

MARWAN TOWN

KAYYAH

0   Scale 1:50,000   2km

ARADA R230

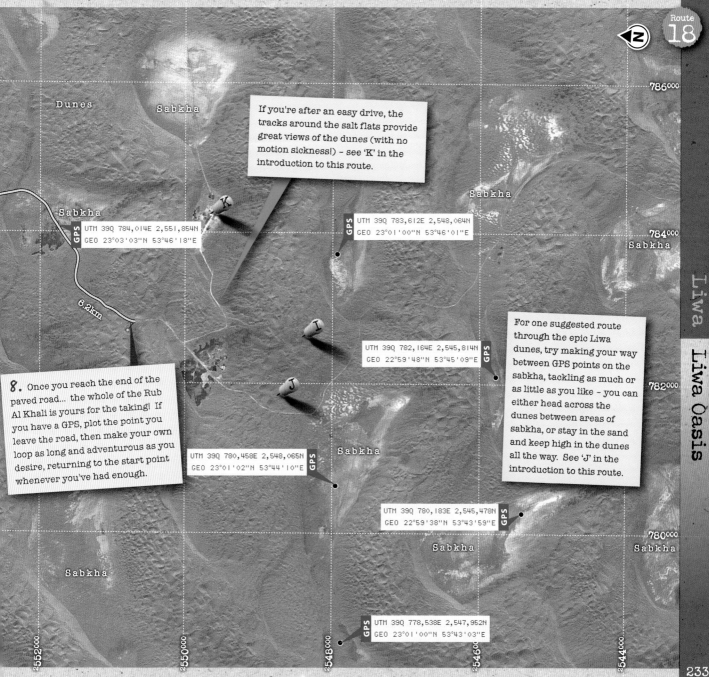

If you're after an easy drive, the tracks around the salt flats provide great views of the dunes (with no motion sickness!) – see 'K' in the introduction to this route.

Dunes

Sabkha

Sabkha

Sabkha

Sabkha

Sabkha

Sabkha

Sabkha

Sabkha

Sabkha

GPS UTM 39Q 784,014E 2,551,854N
GEO 23°03'03"N 53°46'18"E

GPS UTM 39Q 783,612E 2,548,064N
GEO 23°01'00"N 53°46'01"E

6.2km

For one suggested route through the epic Liwa dunes, try making your way between GPS points on the sabkha, tackling as much or as little as you like – you can either head across the dunes between areas of sabkha, or stay in the sand and keep high in the dunes all the way. See 'J' in the introduction to this route.

GPS UTM 39Q 782,164E 2,545,814N
GEO 22°59'48"N 53°45'09"E

8. Once you reach the end of the paved road... the whole of the Rub Al Khali is yours for the taking! If you have a GPS, plot the point you leave the road, then make your own loop as long and adventurous as you desire, returning to the start point whenever you've had enough.

GPS UTM 39Q 780,458E 2,548,065N
GEO 23°01'02"N 53°44'10"E

GPS UTM 39Q 780,183E 2,545,478N
GEO 22°59'38"N 53°43'59"E

GPS UTM 39Q 778,538E 2,547,952N
GEO 23°01'00"N 53°43'03"E

786000

784000

782000

780000

Liwa, Liwa Oasis

233

Liwa Oasis Highlights

Liwa

Covering parts of Oman, Yemen, the southern UAE and almost all of southern Saudi Arabia, the Rub Al Khali (or Empty Quarter) was historically regarded as the edge of civilisation by people living in the region. The Liwa area, situated on the edge of the Rub Al Khali, is one of the largest oases on the Arabian Peninsula. Home to the Bani Yas tribe, ancestors of the current ruling family of Abu Dhabi, the fertile Liwa 'crescent' stretches over 150kms, and is dotted with many small villages. The main feature of this route is of course the desert, with its dramatic dunes rising to heights of over 300m, but there are also several other attractions along the way including a surprising amount of greenery, a fish farm, and a number of palaces visible from the roadside.

The majesty of the red and gold sand dunes and the scale of the vast desert scenery were vividly captured in the writings of adventurer Wilfred Thesiger. Before exploring this region, it's worth getting your hands on a copy of Thesiger's *Arabian Sands*. A reading of this book can enhance your understanding and enjoyment of the area, and make you appreciate the harsh conditions and the fragility of life in the days before air-conditioned 4 WDS.

Mezaira'a

The row of shops and the petrol station at Mezaira'a could be your last chance to buy provisions and fuel if you are planning on heading into the desert, so stock up. If you're going on a long trip, extra jerry cans of petrol may be essential and it's always better to have too much food and water with you than too little.

Liwa Hotel

With its raised location giving spectacular views across the Rub Al Khali (Empty Quarter), and the greenery of the oasis and the palace on the hilltop opposite, Liwa Hotel (02 882 2000) is the best place to stay in the area, if you're not camping. The hotel has good facilities, spacious rooms, and green, landscaped grounds – in keeping with Liwa's reputation as an oasis – with an attractive pool and good leisure facilities. The quality of the facilities and the service in the hotel is also good, and there's a choice of dining options and evening venues.

Liwa Resthouse

One of a number of government-run resthouses in Abu Dhabi, Liwa Resthouse (02 882 2075) is a little past its prime and has been eclipsed by the nearby Liwa Hotel. Its (mainly Arabic) clientele includes visiting business travellers, government officials and families on holiday, and although the

accommodation and facilities are pretty basic, the resthouse is clean and functional. If you are after somewhere cheap as an alternative to camping it might be worth a look, but the Liwa Hotel is recommended as an alternative.

Camping

An essential part of any Liwa adventure, camping in the desert is the most popular way to spend the night, and can be a truly unforgettable experience. Waking up to views of endless waves of sand rolling away into the distance, or the sight of the snaking silvery dunes under the moonlight, are quite magical, looking more like the surface of the moon than normal desert views in the UAE.

You can camp just about anywhere, so take any of the roads and tracks into the desert off the main road through the oasis. Find somewhere near to where you'd like to be for the next

day's driving, but just make sure that you drive far enough from roads, habitation and activity to find a peaceful spot. Try to get settled in your campsite long before the sun goes down, both for safety reasons and to prevent getting stuck in the dark (and of course, to allow you to enjoy the sunset!).

One particularly good area is on the road to Moreeb Hill passing the Liwa Resthouse. This minor, paved road heads into the desert for 11.5km, leading you into some of the best dunes, and crossing plenty of sabkha flats - any one of which allows you to get off-road and into some sheltered areas, far from disturbances, in quite a short time.

Fish Farm

Perhaps the most unusual place to visit in the Liwa area is the fish farm near Khanur with underground sources actually providing water with a salt content almost equals that of the sea, bulti (a species of saltwater fish) is farmed there in several pools. On the road towards Arada, take the right turn after the petrol station on to the road signposted Khanur. At the roundabout turn left, then take another left towards Al Id at the junction near a watchtower and a mosque. Head straight and after several kilometres you'll see a villa with a red roof. When parallel to the villa, turn into its driveway and you should see the fish pools. For a guided tour of the farm and more information on the fish, ask for Ahmed.

Farms

This is a good way to see the cultivation underway in the oasis, enabled by irrigation. The tracks in between the fields lead into an area of dunes, which is great for a play around and some more dramatic views of the expansive desert.

Desert

Although not filled with the dunes of epic proportions that characterise Liwa, this part of desert is an immense area of sand stretching further than the eye can see - offering peace, isolation, the rare absence of any sign of the influence of man. It gives a true sense of the the impressive scale of the Rub Al Khali, the world's largest sand desert. To get there, head up the new road towards Ruwais (currently under construction 2005), then into the desert to the west... and don't get lost!

Hamim to Al Ain (Insha'Allah)

For the most adventurous route back to civilisation, a track starts near Hamim, heading east then north, arriving near Al Ain just south of Jebel Hafeet. However, rules change all the time and differ according to who you ask, so a certain amount of luck is needed to get past the police posts and border patrols, and all the way to Al Ain.

Moreeb Hill

Moreeb Hill is a huge dune which tops out at nearly 300m, and is the site of several hill-climb races for high-powered four-wheel drives every year, including the annual international championship (usually in January). The competition is hot and heavy, with a new course record of just under 12 seconds being set in 2004, but the emphasis is on opening the event up for anyone. Spectators are a particularly important and welcome part of the whole event. This area has also appeared in stages of the UAE Desert Challenge, with Moreeb being the spot for the bivouac. Keep your eyes on the press for details of these events throughout the year, or simply get yourself down there and try out your driving on the dune.

Dune Drive

Once you're out here you can blaze your own trail, making your route as adventurous and exciting as you want. The dunes between the areas of sabkha provide fun and challenge enough for any level of dune-basher. As a GPS is essential equipment for any Liwa desert trip, we've listed some points on the map to enable you to pick your own way through the desert with regular checkpoints, so you can do as much or as little as you'd

like, and you can change the route however you like at any point. All GPS points are on the flat plains, so how to link them up is your choice.

Easy Riders

If you have elderly passengers with you, or young children, or if you just prefer sedate over severe, the tracks across and around the salt flats provide easy routes through the dunes and plenty of spectacular desert views without having to leave the horizontal... so no motion sickness! Just be careful when crossing the sabkha after rains as the surface can look hard but can get dangerously soft and very difficult to get out of if your car gets stuck. If in doubt, keep to the edges where the ground should be firmest.

**With AXA
Be Life Confident**

Norwich Union Gulf is now AXA

Better insurance solutions. Better future for you.

Go ahead with any project you have in mind at any   advice to help you and your family choose the best
moment in your life. Everyday, AXA offers care, support and   solution for Motor, Housing, Travel and Health insurance.

AXA
INSURANCE

Call 800 4845
www.axa-gulf.com

Be Life Confident

Natural World

Jeep

Natural World

As there is far more diversity of life in the desert than you would expect, this guide can only offer a tantalising glimpse of what you may find when you are out exploring. Far from being an exhaustive authority, we have simply attempted to whet your appetite by highlighting some of the most common trees, plants, insects and animals that you are likely to come across. Note that the common Arabic and Latin names have been included where appropriate.

Depending on where your interests lie, we hope that you will delve into the reference books suggested in the Further Reading section for more detailed information.

Mammals

To many residents and visitors of the UAE the desert may seem devoid of animal life, but in this case appearances do deceive! Most mammals have adapted to the hot, dry climate by leading a nocturnal life and are therefore seldom seen. Only the herbivores are out at dawn and dusk, browsing the sparse vegetation. Many cope with the lack of available water by recycling fluids, or make do with the dew on plants or the body fluids of prey.

Over recent years, the number of wild animals has reduced considerably due mainly to hunting and loss of habitat. The rarest two species, the Arabian Leopard and the Arabian Tahr (a small mountain half-goat), can be counted on the fingers of two hands. For predators (and raptors, ie. birds of prey), the loss of prey animals poses the greatest problem, since they have to resort to killing goats and then become the target of irate farmers. If habitats are protected and herbivores reintroduced, these carnivores could possibly make a comeback on their own, although certain species, like the wolf and the hyena, may need more of a helping hand.

Arabian Leopard
Panthera pardus nimr

It is highly unlikely that you will ever get a glimpse of this rare predator, as it is active at night and very shy. You may come across its droppings and even its prints on mountain hikes, and campers have reported hearing a leopard roar from time to time.

The cat is not dangerous to people as it avoids human contact, but it is often hunted when it kills feral goats. Only half a dozen remain within the UAE borders, but a breeding programme at the Sharjah Desert Park has been successful with four offspring born by mid-2000. The Arabic name is actually the word for tiger.

Arabic Name 'nimr'

Arabian Red Fox
Vulpes vulpes arabicus

Smaller and more slender than its European cousin, the Arabian Red Fox varies in colour from pale sand to a darker russet and light brown. It is active both day and night and is the most commonly seen predator in all habitats (including city dumps) – a great ability to adapt to all circumstances has ensured its survival.

Since rabies has entered the country in the last decade, be very wary of friendly foxes! Healthy foxes are shy and will not approach you.

The other two species of fox in the UAE are much smaller (cat-sized) and entirely nocturnal in their activities. The Rueppell's or Sand Fox lives in the great sand dunes, while the recently discovered Blanford's Fox is especially well adapted to life on steep mountain slopes.

Arabic Name 'theeb'

Caracal
Caracal caracal schmidti

This large, russet-coloured wild cat is active at dusk and dawn and therefore it is possible to come across one on camping trips. It is not dangerous to man and lives mostly on small prey like birds and rodents.

Because it occasionally takes young goats and chickens, it is regarded as vermin and unfortunately mercilessly hunted by local farmers.

Arabic Name 'al washaq, anaq al ardh'

Mountain Gazelle
Gazella gazella cora

This dainty ungulate inhabits the mountains, lower hills and dunes. Living in groups of up to six, it feeds at dusk and dawn and can live without access to water. The young are born in the cooler spring months, usually one per season. Since the hunting of gazelles has been banned, their numbers are on the rise. However, in the deep sands of Liwa the larger and paler 'rheem', or Sand Gazelle, has become very rare, most likely due to hunting in the past (it is now forbidden and there are game wardens who patrol the desert in the hopes of catching offenders).

Arabic Name   'idhmi' or 'dhabi'

Camel
Camelus dromedarius

Although there are two types of camel, in the Emirates we only see the Dromedary (one-humped) camel, as Bactrians (two-humped) mostly live in the colder climates of China, Russia and Asia. Nowadays camels in the UAE are mainly bred for racing, although in other parts of the world they are raised for meat, milk and transport.

All the camels you see wandering around here belong to someone (there are no feral camels left in the UAE), and are marked with their owners brand; many have numerous brand marks from changing hands several times. These camels are usually female, as the males are kept in pens to prevent random breeding and fighting with other males. The unconfined camels browse on grasses and scrubby bushes (but do not eat the Desert Squash), until the end of the day when they are rounded up and taken back to their breeding farm to be fed hay, maybe some alfalfa and water.

Camels are generally very placid animals, although they may bite or kick if antagonised, especially males. They are fully grown after about four years, but may not reach puberty until they are five and they can live for as long as 30 or 40 years. The gestation period is a long 13 months and they only give birth to one calf, very rarely to twins. The calf is left with its mother for about a year before starting training for its racing career. If they show potential, they begin competing at around three years and will continue for as long as they keep doing well. Younger camels race over about 5km and build up to about 10km. While they are not as fast as horses, they have better endurance. Everyone prefers to race female camels as they are less temperamental and faster. The good ones have a numbered microchip placed just under their skin and their details, race wins and family history are recorded on computer.

Successful racing camels are worth a lot of money – often thousands of dollars change hands for them and the prizes for the big races are often luxury cars for the owner, trainer and jockey!

A trip to a camel racetrack can be one of the most memorable highlights of any visit to the UAE. There are tracks all over the Emirates, but probably the best places to go to are Nad Al Sheba Racetrack (see Directory) in Dubai, or the tracks at Dhaid and Digdagga. Races take place during the winter months, usually on Wednesdays, Thursdays and Fridays, with additional races on National Day and other public holidays.

Arabic Name   'jamal'

Mouse-tailed Bat
Rhinopoma muscatellum

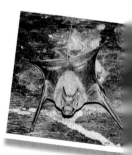

The Mouse-tailed Bat spends its days in buildings and caves, then hunts around streetlights at night. It is only a few centimetres in length with a wingspan of about 15 - 20cm, and is easily recognised by the fact that its tail is free of the hind feet membrane. While most species of bats in the UAE are insectivores, there is also one fruit-eating bat, the Egyptian Fruit Bat.

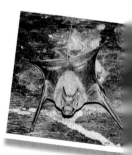

Brandt's Hedgehog
Paraechinus hypomelas

Of the three species of hedgehog that occur in the region, the all-black Brandt's Hedgehog is the most numerous. It's found in all habitats, including the high mountains, and at one location in Wadi Bih, a local farmer feeds between 40 and 200 hedgehogs every night! The other two species are the Ethiopian Hedgehog, which has a white band around its face, and the Long-eared Hedgehog, whose ears are even larger than those of the other two species.

Arabic Name 'quoonfodh'

Gordon's Wildcat
Felis sylvestris gordoni

This forerunner of the domestic tabby cat is a very shy and fierce inhabitant of all areas, except the great sand dunes. It spends the days in burrows or ghaf trees and hunts at night, but its existence is threatened by loss of habitat and cross-breeding with domestic cats. However, a breeding programme initiated in the UAE by the Arabian Leopard Trust has placed pairs of these cats in more than a dozen European and American zoos, and should ensure its survival as a species.

The other smaller wildcat of the region is the Sand Cat, which is especially adapted to life in the deep soft sands. The soles of its feet are covered with wiry hair to prevent it from sinking into the sand or burning its feet.

Arabic Name 'gatt al barra'

Arabian Tahr
Hemitragus jayakari

This small half-goat lives on steep mountain cliffs, to which it clings as if its hooves were made of Velcro. It was thought to be extinct in the UAE, but was rediscovered in 1995 in a wildlife survey conducted by the Arabian Leopard Trust. Only a handful remain, often consorting with herds of feral goats. Unfortunately, this rare animal is still being hunted for its meat.

Arabic Name 'wa'al al qurm sagheer'

Cape Hare
Lepus capensis

The desert hare is still fairly common in all habitats but the high mountains, and it is important as a prey animal for many predators and raptors. Its activities are mostly nocturnal and during the hot hours of the day it's generally found lying in a small hollow in  the sand in the shade of a bush. It can give birth to litters of over 20 babies, which are scattered in various places (to increase their survival rate) and become independent in a matter of days.

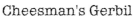

Arabic Name 'arnab'

Cheesman's Gerbil
Gerbillus cheesmani

Many small rodents, like the ubiquitous Cheesman's Gerbil, are active at night, foraging for seeds and other vegetable matter, then spend the hot days in underground burrows. Most live in sandy areas where their prints can be found in the early morning before the wind wipes them away. Only Wagner's Gerbil and the Egyptian Spiny Mouse are known to occur in the mountainous regions.

Donkey

The very shy donkeys that are often encountered in the mountains are introduced domestic animals that have become feral. Used in the past as a reliable means of travelling through rocky wadis and across mountain passes, their role has been usurped by the ubiquitous 4 WD.

While donkeys are a pleasing feature of the landscape, their increasing numbers are unfortunately doing great damage to the mountain vegetation.

Goat

Most goats are the property of farmers, although it is suspected that not everyone keeps track of their animals and many of the goats that roam the dunes and mountains are in fact feral. Goats need daily access to water and where they occur in large numbers both the vegetation and the rare water sources are under great pressure. More than any other factor, the unhampered roaming of goats has contributed to the near extinction of original wild species like gazelles, and in turn their predators.

Birds

The UAE has a wonderful diversity of bird species. Over 400 different species have been discovered, spread across the country's varied landscape of desert, mountain and shoreline. Apart from special indigenous species, such as Chestnut-bellied Sandgrouse, White-collared Kingfisher, Hume's Wheatear and Purple Sunbird, the typical Arabian landscape supports over 320 migrants from Siberia and Central Asia. These birds pass through during the spring and autumn on their north-south migration routes, or spend the cooler months wintering in the country. The UAE's prime position on a migratory crossroads helps to explain the presence of such a varied selection of birds not found anywhere in Europe or the Middle East.

Dubai is a good place to start looking for birds – it's quite normal to find 80 species during a morning's planned birding in the Dubai area. For the more adventurous, a visit to the east coast or the numerous lagoons on the Gulf coast on the way to Ras Al Khaimah will prove interesting. Wetland species form a large proportion of the country's birdlife and it's not unusual to see thousands of Arctic shorebirds feeding on the mudflats. The Shell Birdwatching Guide to the UAE is essential for finding the best birdwatching places, while binoculars are a must to fully enjoy this increasingly popular pastime. The following descriptions of individual species includes information on how common the bird is in the UAE and where it is most often seen.

Black-crowned Finch Lark
Eremopterix nigriceps

A desert nomad, the male Black-crowned Finch Lark is highly distinctive, with

its black head, belly and underwing pattern, which it uses to attract the rather dull-coloured brown female. A bird of coastal sand dunes and flat gravel plains, it can be heard high above you, singing its squeaky gate-like song. It is indigenous to the deserts of Arabia, where it is completely at home, but it also undertakes local migratory movements, for reasons that are not yet understood, and forms sizeable flocks inland in winter.

Fairly common   From February to July it is common in coastal dune scrub between Abu Dhabi and Ras Al Khaimah and at Kalba. It is particularly prevalent in the Jebel Ali area. In winter, it can be seen on the plain around Madam and the scrubby area between the beach and mangroves at Khor Kalba.

Common Mynah
Acridotheres tristis

An abundant bird of urban areas, parks and gardens, this cheeky and obtrusive resident first arrived in the country in the early 1970s from the Indian subcontinent and has found conditions in the UAE ideal for feeding and nesting. Identified by its dark brown plumage, with a yellow eye patch and bill; it shows a white wing patch in flight and is usually in small parties in the day, before flocking to huge, noisy communal roosts in the evening.

Very common   Seen along landscaped streets and in urban gardens of all towns, plus inland cultivations and other irrigated areas.

Hoopoe
Upupa epops

Probably one of the country's most recognisable species; its numbers are increasing rapidly in response to the abundance of newly landscaped areas and the availability of insect food. The resident population is swollen in spring and autumn by thousands of birds passing through on migration between Asia and Africa. Identification is made easy by its black and white wings, long down-curved bill and hammer-headed crest.

Common   Several pairs are resident at Kalba corniche, in Dubai at Emirates Golf Club and Safa Park, Ras Al Khaimah and city parks in the Northern Emirates, but it can also be found anywhere older trees occur and around cultivated areas inland. Scarce in Abu Dhabi, except on migration.

Greater Flamingo
Phoenicopterus ruber

This common migrant is sometimes found in large numbers in lagoons and shallow mudflats on the Gulf coast. It's a 'flagship' species for the Dubai Wildlife & Waterbird Sanctuary at Khor Dubai where several thousand winter annually, though nesting attempts have yet to bear fruit in Dubai. It is the only species of pink flamingo to occur regularly in Arabia and most birds come from vast colonies in north-west Iran.

Common   Besides Khor Dubai, it can be seen in most shallow coastal lagoons between Dubai and Ras Al Khaimah, particularly Umm Al Quwain, Al Jazeerah Khor and Rams. It is also scattered throughout the shallow inshore lagoons along the Abu Dhabi coast.

Hume's Wheatear
Oenanthe alboniger

Hume's Wheatear is one of the country's most attractive mountain residents. It is identified by its striking black and white plumage, which sometimes makes it difficult to find in the contrasting, stony landscape where it lives. Confined almost entirely to eastern Arabia, this species is more common in the UAE than anywhere else and attracts birdwatchers from all over the world. It nests from February and can often be located in wadis by its bright song.

Common Most likely to be seen perched on rocks by the roadside during a drive up Jebel Hafit. It occurs more thinly in the Masafi region and all mountain areas, but never away from the mountains.

Little Green Bee-eater
Merops orientalis

This very attractive and brightly coloured resident is usually found in pairs or small groups. Its bee diet is supplemented by crickets, butterflies and wasps, and the abundance of food means that this bird is becoming increasingly common throughout the northern and eastern Emirates. It's often seen perched prominently on bushes, wires or even television aerials and it nests in holes in sandbanks. Identification is simple – look for its bright blue throat and emerald green body, plus a long tail and curved black bill.

Localised Semi-desert areas on the outskirts of northern mirate towns, adjacent to cultivated areas and water sources. Not found in Abu Dhabi.

Indian Roller
Coracias benghalensis

Quietly sitting high on a wire or branch, this bird will suddenly explode into noise and colour as it takes flight. Its bright blue wings and rolling flight are its trademark around fields, parks, large gardens and cultivations. The northern emirates possibly hold the world's greatest concentration of the species and it is expanding its range. It nests in holes, lampposts and among the old fronds of date palms.

Locally common Most commonly seen on telegraph wires between Kalba and Dibba on the east coast, and on high perches in fields near the Ras Al Khaimah airport. About 30 pairs are resident in the Dubai area, including at the Emirates Golf Club and other large irrigated public gardens and palaces. Rarely found south of Jebel Ali.

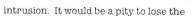

Socotra Cormorant
Phalacrocorax nigricollis

Arabia's only nesting cormorant, endemic to Arabia and once present in large numbers offshore in the Arabian Gulf, is now under serious pressure from man as its nest sites become disturbed by development and human intrusion. It would be a pity to lose the impressive spectacle of thousands of birds flying in close formation – the sheer numbers sometimes taking hours to pass.

Locally common Large numbers are most likely to be seen flying just offshore between Umm Al Quwain and Ras Al Khaimah between July and November. Otherwise small numbers can be seen anywhere off the UAE's coast at any time of the year.

White-cheeked Bulbul
Pycnonotus leucogenys

Approachable and jaunty, and a favourite garden resident, this bird is becoming more common as irrigation and cover increases. Its very vocal, two-syllable call is heard around all the parks and gardens of Dubai, Abu Dhabi and most desert cultivations. This bird is easily recognisable by its black head, bright white cheeks and yellow undertail colouring. It eats mostly insects and fruit, but will take bread from bird tables.

Common Prefers irrigated gardens and cultivated areas, mostly in Abu Dhabi and Dubai, but is spreading rapidly along tree-lined highways to inland gardens and plantations.

White-collared Kingfisher
Halcyon chloris kalbaensis

This is the country's only resident kingfisher and a very important species. Only 55 pairs have ever been counted of this endemic bird, which is resident only in an area of ancient mangroves at Khor Kalba on the east coast. Once found, this large, noisy bird can be quite approachable, giving fabulous views of its striking turquoise-blue plumage. It feeds on several small crab species and is best seen at low tide, when the mudflats are exposed and its prey is active on the surface.

Rare Only found among the mangroves at Khor Kalba.

Reptiles

Deserts all over the world abound with reptiles which, by nature, can adapt readily to hot and dry conditions. The UAE has over 50 species of terrestrial reptiles, while nine sea snakes and five sea turtles have been recorded in the surrounding seas.

Lizards are the most often encountered. The common house geckos and small geckos in the sandy dunes or the rocky hills are mostly active at night, while others, like Skinks, Agames and Lacertids, are often seen foraging or sunning themselves in the daytime.

There are no venomous lizards in the UAE, but a few of the snakes can be dangerous. An easy way to distinguish between a very poisonous viper and a rear-fanged snake that poses little or no danger is by looking at the head – a large triangular head with an obviously smaller neck belongs to a viper, while a bullet-shaped narrow head belongs to a less dangerous snake. Many snakes are beneficial to man since they help control the number of rodents.

Desert or Grey Monitor
Varanus griseus

This is the largest of the lizards of this region, growing up to 1.2 metres long, two-thirds of which is a thin whip-like tail. It is a scavenger and because it eats carrion, its bite can cause severe infections, although it is not poisonous. It lives in burrows and can cover large areas in search of prey.

Arabic Name 'wirral'

Arabian Toad
Bufo orientalis

There are no frogs in the UAE and of the two species of toad, this one is the most common. It lives in or near water and can survive long periods of drought by digging deep into the wadi gravel and staying in a state of torpor for many months or even years. Its small eardrum, situated away from the corner of the eye, differentiates it from the rarer Dhofar Toad, which has a large eardrum that touches the corner of its eye.

Tadpoles are a tasty titbit for many wild animals and after spring rains wadi pools can hold thousands of them.

Sand Skink or Sand Fish
Scincus mitranus

You have to be an early bird to catch a Sand Skink hunting in the morning. The Skink emerges from the steep soft side of sand dunes, warming up to its optimum temperature before daring to move to the more compact windward side of the dune. There it dips its head or whole body into the sand to catch insects. They are well adapted to their mainly underground existence, having smooth skin, a shovel-shaped jaw and protected ears and eyes. Skinks used to be a gourmet item on the Bedu menu, but it takes an expert to catch one!

Jayakar's Oman Lizard
Lacerta jayakari

This is one of the two endemic lizards of the Hajar Mountains, and grows to a total length of 60cm, two-thirds of which consist of its tapering tail. They live near water, often among the rocks that line the walls of a well in an oasis. Since they are mainly active in the hot season and very well camouflaged, they are not easily noticed.

Rock Semaphore Gecko
Pristurus rupestris

Active during the day, this small gecko is easily recognised by the horizontal white strip that runs through each eye. It sits on rock faces and walls of deserted buildings to catch its prey, often signalling with its tail to other geckos. A whole range of messages can be conveyed by the posture of its tail and body. Most of the 18 species of geckos recorded in the region so far are nocturnal and therefore have big eyes.

Yellow-spotted Agame
Trapelus flavi maculatus

Coming across a Yellow-spotted Agame in its breeding colours can be a mind-blowing experience. The males can 'turn on' brilliant colours to attract a female or to warn off a competitor. With their indigo throats, lapis lazuli bodies and bright orange tails they have been called psychedelic dragons!

Sawscale Viper
Echis carinatus

Of the four species of viper in the UAE, the Sawscale is the most commonly encountered, even though it has a nocturnal lifestyle and spends the day in hiding. It inhabits the sandy desert as well as the low hills, while the similar looking Carpet Viper is mostly restricted to mountainous areas.

Its bite is dangerous if it is not treated properly. The best prevention against snakebites is to be careful where you put your hands and feet and to wear closed shoes when out in the desert at night.

Spiny Tailed Agame
Uromastyx aegyptiacus

This gentle dragon of the desert grows to a length of over half a metre and spends most of its life in deep underground burrows, foraging only for a couple of hours in the early morning or late afternoon. As a species they have been around for 25 million years! The adult Agame eats only plants. Its main enemies are the Desert Monitor and humans; the former competes with it for burrows, while the latter believes its fat spiny tail has aphrodisiac properties.

Arabic Name 'dhub'

Wadi Racer
Coluber rhodorhachis

For people who regularly hike in the wadis, this is the most commonly encountered snake. It is long and thin with a narrow head, and is not venomous. Appropriately for its name, it moves quite fast and can scale steep wadi banks, living on fish, toads and small rodents.

Other long and thin innocuous snakes in the UAE are the Leaf-nosed Snake, the Hooded Malpolon and the Hissing Sand Snake.

Insects

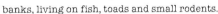

Anyone who has camped or picnicked in the desert will have experienced the nuisance of the many insects that occur here. The Yellow Hornets that plague us at times are only one of over 200 species of bees and wasps that have been recorded. Some insects we rarely see - over 300 night flying moths have been identified. There are also over 20 species of butterfly, while the identification of beetles and spiders has barely been tackled. When the water flows in the wadis, colourful dragonflies can be seen hunting and the water itself is home to many interesting creatures. Of the 14 species of ants recorded so far, the very small black ant has a bite that can be fatal to those who are allergic to its poison (see First Aid p.306).

Camelspider
Solifugidae spp.

Camelspiders have an undeserved bad reputation. Wild stories circulate about people sleeping in the desert and having half their faces eaten away by these creatures, while adult camels are said to die from their bite! Nothing is further from the truth. The Camelspider is nocturnal and quite shy. During the day it hides in dark places and when it is accidentally exposed to sunlight, looks frantically for shade (its Latin name means 'flees from the sun'). Unfortunately that shade is usually thrown by the person who uncovered it, so it runs quickly towards you, an action that has been wrongly interpreted as an attack. Its bite is probably only mildly venomous, if at all, but its fierce appearance will never win it any brownie points!

Domino Beetle
Anthia duodecimguttata

This large, predatory beetle is commonly seen after rains and can sometimes be found in large numbers congregating at the entrance of rodent burrows. Its striking white spots gave it the local name 'mother of yoghurt'.

Other interesting beetles are the Dung Beetle, which rolls perfect round balls of dung into which it lays its eggs; the Rhinoceros Beetle, which has a single curved horn on its head and the brightly coloured Oil Beetle, which is venomous and will cause blisters on your skin if you touch it.

Arabic Name   'umm al roob'

Honey Bee
Apis mellifera

The small Honey Bee's product is much sought after by the residents of the UAE. Wild honey gathered by jebalis can fetch several hundred dirhams per kilo. However, not all honey sold in bottles along the roadside is the genuine article! Bee-combs are usually found in trees and caves and the bees are not at all aggressive.

Black Scorpion
Andractonus crassicauda

Of the various species of scorpion, this is the most commonly encountered. Scorpions are nocturnal and hide during the day in dark, cool places. If you are careful not to put your hand or foot where you cannot see (take care when rolling up your sleeping bag or tent in the morning), you have nothing to fear from scorpions. The smaller greenish-white scorpion also has strong poison and could be dangerous to children (see First Aid p.306).

Oriental Wasp
Vespa orientalis

This large, conspicuous red and yellow wasp occurs wherever there is vegetation. They often congregate at the water's edge to drink and collect water to carry back to their larvae. Both this and the slightly smaller all-yellow Arabian Paper Wasp or Hornet, are very aggressive and it is advisable to avoid disturbing their nests.

Globe Skimmer
Pantala flavescens

Both dragonflies and damselflies (like a dragonfly, but its wings fold over its body when resting), are common wherever there is water. Many spectacular species, like this skimmer and the Large Blue Skimmer, have been recorded in the UAE and new species are still being discovered. Dragonfly larvae live underwater, where they are fierce predators. For their metamorphosis into the adult insect, they climb out of the water onto rocks or plants – if you look carefully, you can find the skins that they shed.

Common Swallowtail
Papilio machaon

The two species of Swallowtails are the largest of the 20 or more species of butterfly that occur in the UAE. They are mostly encountered in plantations, although they can also be observed in wadis, laying eggs on the wild food plants of their larvae. The colourful caterpillar has a unique defence mechanism; when touched, it pops out two 'horns' from an area behind its head and ejects a strong smell of either carrot or lemon, having absorbed the juices from the food plants. This is enough to frighten off most predators!

Crimson Speckled Footman
Utetheisa pulchella

Most of the 300 plus moth species recorded in the UAE are nocturnal and seldom seen by people. The day-flying Crimson Speckled Footman (also known as the Polka-dot Moth), can be seen feeding on Heliotropium flowers. Its bright colours seem conspicuous, but when it sits on the sand with its wings folded, they provide the perfect camouflage. The caterpillar is spectacular with a silver body striped in black and red.

Orb or Signature Spider
Argiope spp.

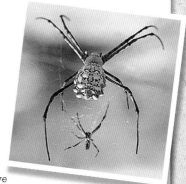

The many species of spiders that occur here have not yet been studied. The most commonly encountered is the Orb Spider, which weaves webs that are suspended from extremely strong horizontal threads – people have reported walking up against such threads and not breaking them! The male is a fraction of the size of the female, which grows to body size of five centimetres.

Other interesting spiders are Crab Spiders, which are the colour of the flowers on which they prey for insects; Wolf Spiders, which do not weave webs but hunt among the vegetation; and the only spider harmful to humans, the Australian Redback, which is easily recognised by the bright red spot on its black body (see First Aid on p.306).

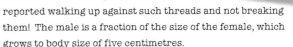

Water Scorpion
Laceotrephes fabricii

This interesting insect is becoming increasingly rare in the wadis. The rear appendix that gives the insect its name is not a sting, but a snorkel through which the animal breathes when underwater (you can see the tip of the filament just above the water level). Other water beetles include the Giant Water Bug, the Diving Beetle and smaller insects like the Whirligigs and Backswimmers.

Marine Life

Marine life in UAE waters is varied and bountiful. The shallow warm waters allow corals that teem with colourful species of fish to grow , sea cows graze on sea grass beds and sea turtles come ashore to lay their eggs. The deeper water offshore is home to whales and dolphins, as well as Hammerhead Sharks and sea snakes, while the wide sand beaches are ideal for shell collecting (at least in those places where they have not been destroyed by the indiscriminate use of 4 WDs).

Clown Fish

Several species of this lovely patterned fish are common residents of coral reefs, where they live among the arms of the Sea Anemone. While the Sea Anemone's sting kills other fish, the Clown Fish is immune to the poison and feeds on the leftovers of its host's dinner.

Bottle-nosed Dolphin
Tursiops truncatus

This is the largest of the eight species of dolphin that have been recorded in UAE waters. They are often encountered on east coast boat trips, when they come to play around the boat and show off their incredible acrobatic skills. Other dolphins that live here are the Common Dolphin, the Spinner Dolphin and the Humpback Dolphin. Whales are also represented in this region by four species of toothed whales, as well as the enormous Sperm Whale.

Shark

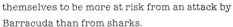

There are at least 10 species of sharks in UAE waters, including Reef Sharks, Blacktip Sharks, Hammerheads and Tiger Sharks. Very few of the potentially dangerous sharks come in close enough to present a problem to swimmers. Pearl divers considered themselves to be more at risk from an attack by Barracuda than from sharks.

Paper Nautilus
Argonauta hians

This extraordinary shell can be found on the beaches of the Arabian Gulf during February and March. The beautiful feather-light structure is made by the Argonaut Octopus and held underneath her belly after she has deposited her eggs in it. Baby octopuses have a protected environment until the mother lets them go and their cradle washes up on the beach.

Sundial Shell
Architectonica perspectiva

The east coast beaches have different shells to those of the Arabian Gulf coast. The Sundial Shell can be found on Kalba beach, while further north is a good place to find opercula (plate-like structures that close the opening of a shell when the organism is retracted) of gastropods (molluscs, like snails or slugs).

Stingray

Hopefully you will never have too close an encounter with a stingray, because this invariably turns out to be a very painful experience. Stingrays are flat fish of about 25cm diameter, with a long whip-like tail that is fortified with a mucus-covered bony sting at its base. During the months in which the hot season turns into the cooler season and vice versa, they come close in to the shore and lie buried in the sand. Often bathers step on them inadvertently and the ray retaliates by using its sting. The pain is said to be excruciating and lasts for seven to nine hours. The only immediate treatment is to keep the affected area immersed in very hot water (see First Aid p.306). Later treatment includes antibiotics, as the wound can give a nasty infection.

Sea Cow or Dugong
Dugong dugon

Although it is highly unlikely that you will ever see this marine mammal, it deserves a mention because of its history and future. It is the animal that gave rise to the legend of the mermaid. Related to elephants and rock hyrax, it has breasts between its front legs, nails instead of claws and lives in herds led by a female. There are probably less than a thousand of these gentle creatures left in the Gulf, where they face the continual hazards of shipping, oil pollution and degradation of the sea grasses that they feed on. The Arabic name means 'bride of the sea'.

Arabic Name   'arus al bahr'

Green Turtle
Chelonia mydas

A few decades ago Green Turtles used to haul themselves up onto Dubai beaches by the dozens to lay their eggs. Now their nesting grounds are covered by harbours, hotels and high rises and their breeding sites are restricted to some of the offshore islands. Although five species of sea turtle have been recorded in the region, only the Green Turtle and the Hawksbill Turtle breed here. The breeding season is in the early summer (May – August).

The existence of turtles is threatened, not only by destruction of habitat, but also by the predation of their nests by humans and feral dogs.

Yellow-bellied Sea Snake
Pelamis platurus

Of the nine species of sea snake that occur in the Arabian Gulf, the Yellow-bellied Sea Snake is the one that is most encountered on beaches. It is wise to remember that all sea snakes carry deadly poisons and that a washed-up sea snake may not be dead. Like most wild creatures, sea snakes are not usually aggressive. The exception is the Beaked Sea Snake, which does not take kindly to being handled and may attack without provocation.

Trees

For such an arid country, the UAE has an amazing number of trees. These are mainly scattered over large areas, but sometimes they grow close together forming small forests. Palm trees are obviously one of the most important, as not only the fruit, but the fronds and bark have been indispensable materials in the daily lives of the local people for centuries. The three largest trees of the region are the salam, the ghaf and the sidr which are all detailed below.

Christ Thorn-tree
Ziziphus spina-christi

This is a common tree in wadis and plantations, growing where the underground water level is close to the surface. Its tangy fruits, called 'nabaq', are a favourite with both man and beast, while goats also eat the fallen blossoms. The cultivated fruits are sold in the local markets.

Arabic Name   'sidr'
Height   To about 10m

Date Palm
Phoenix dactylifera

The date palm plays an important role in the culture of the desert Arabs. It is reported that there are a hundred different recipes based on dates. Besides the fruit, many other parts of the tree are used: leaves for thatching and making walls and boats, trunks for roof beams, bark for making rope, etc. The date palm is unable to survive in the wild without a continuous supply of water, and so must have been introduced by man at some point in the distant past. An interesting story is told in Wendell Philips' book *Enchanting Oman*. An Omani man received a letter one day, but it was already too dark to read it, so he took some dates and kneaded them into a paste from which he shaped a small bowl. He filled it with some vegetable oil and made a wick from some date palm fibres. By the light of his improvised lamp he read his letter, then he threw out the wick, drank the oil and ate the lamp!

Arabic Name   'nakhl'
Height   To about 10m, occasionally higher

Arabian Almond
Prunus arabica

Notable for its beautiful white blossoms in the spring, this shrubby tree is a high-mountain plant. The long branches have small leaves that fall soon after spring and the little nuts are edible. Mountain dwellers use the hard wood of the tree to make strong handles for their small axe-head, the 'yir' – a handy tool for decapitating snakes!

Arabic Name   'mizzi'
Height   To 2½m

Acacia
Acacia tortilis

Of the half-dozen Acacia species that are found in the UAE, the umbrella-shaped salam tree is the most common, occurring on gravel as well as on sandy plains. Its flowers are pale yellow and all parts of the tree are browsed by camels, in spite of the vicious thorns. Sometimes you can see 'double-storey' acacias – this happens when browsing camels cannot reach the central branches of the tree, which then get a chance to form shoots and grow a second bush on top of the lower one that is being continuously cropped.

Arabic Name   'salam' or 'samr'
Height   4 - 6m

'Ghaf'
Prosopis cineraria

The ghaf tree grows in both sandy and rocky habitats. It can survive periods of drought because its tap root penetrates to depths of up to 65 metres to reach water reservoirs under the dunes and hills. The leaves, branches and fruits are favourite fodder for wild and domestic ungulates (hoofed mammals). Camels browse the lower branches as high as they can reach, giving the tree a shorn-off appearance, while unbrowsed trees resemble weeping willows.

Height   10 - 15m

Black Mangrove
Avicenna marina

The mangrove occurs in many coastal areas of the country, with the largest and oldest trees growing at Khor Kalba on the east coast. Mangroves have a special root system with 'breathing roots', the so-called pneumatophores, that stick up out of the mud. They can also excrete excess salt through their leaves, enabling them to live in very saline conditions. Mangrove forests are important for both bird and marine life. Their roots give protection to young marine life, which in turn is a rich source of food for the birds that nest and breed in the trees or visit on migration.

Arabic Name   'qurm'
Height   3 - 6m

Sodom's Apple
Calotropis procera

Growing in sandy desert, this shrub occasionally reaches tree height and is common in overgrazed areas because goats and camels do not like eating the white latex that it produces. The large leaves are covered with fine white hairs that create a moisture-retaining microclimate close to the surface of the leaf. The fruits resemble squat bananas (not apple-shaped like those of the similar plant in North Africa) and contain thousands of seeds that are attached to long silken threads, enabling them to be carried far and wide by the wind when ripe. The wood was once used to make charcoal for the production of gunpowder.

Arabic Name   'ashar'
Height   To 5m

Tecomella
Tecomella undulata

During the flowering season this tree is adorned with large yellow flowers. It may originally have been an introduced species, but it is now well established along the edge of several wadis and plantations. The fruits are 20cm long curved pods and the seeds are winged.

Arabic Name 'farfar'
Height 4 - 6m

Toothbrush Tree
Salvadora persica

This plant is most commonly found as a shrub, but it can grow into a tall, rather straggly tree. It is a food source for the caterpillars of the Blue-spotted Arab butterfly. Small branches of the tree are chewed by local people to clean the teeth and massage the gums. It has tiny flowers and small red berries, as well as a strong smell reminiscent of fox urine!

Arabic Name 'arakh'
Height To 10m

Wild Drumstick Tree
Moringa peregrina

This is the most common tree of higher elevations, and is beautiful in spring when in full flower. The pink blossoms have a sweet fragrance, while the pods are 20cm long, dark brown and woody.

Arabic Name 'yasar'
Height To 10m

Shrubs

Perennials are found all year round, although in the UAE they can become insignificant during the hot, dry season. There may be a reduction in the number of leaves and some plants withdraw underground. Even in the cooler months, most desert wild flowers are rarely spectacular and in some cases the seed wings of the fruits are more colourful and eye-catching than the flowers themselves.

Arta
Calligonum comosum

Most of the year the straggly arta bushes look barely alive. However, after rains fresh green shoots appear on the branches – a much-liked vegetable green for the desert Bedu. The tiny white flowers with their bright red stamens develop into lantern-like hairy seedpods, turning the bush into a red flame of fire. The plant occurs in areas of loose sand and helps to stabilise sand dunes. The thick wooden branches used to be a major source of firewood.

Height To 2m

Ra
Aerva javanica

This common plant of sandy areas has tiny white flowers that appear in plume-like clusters at the end of the stems. The fluffy hairs surrounding the seeds were used in the past to stuff saddles and cushions.

Height To 1.2m

Gahlqah
Pergularia tomentosa

You can see this member of the milkweed family in both sand and gravel habitats. The flowers are fragile brown and white bells, the seedpods are paired curved 'horns' and the seeds have silk 'parachutes'.

This plant hosts the caterpillars of the Plain Tiger Butterfly (Danaus chrysippi), its latex providing this insect with the poison that protects it from birds. Birds have learnt that eating a butterfly with the colours of Danaus chrysippi makes them sick, and so they avoid catching it. Another butterfly, the Diadem, also profits from this scheme. In a tactic called mimicry, the female of the species looks almost the same as the Plain Tiger, although the male is entirely different.

Height   **Vine stems can be over 100m long**

Firemaker Bush
Leptadenia pyrotechnica

The dunes between Al Awir and Fossil Rock are full of a broom-like bush. It is seldom browsed and provides shade and protection for gazelles and hares during the hottest hours of the day. When in bloom, it has clusters of tiny star-shaped flowers. It also has very long seedpods containing seeds attached to long silken hairs, which enable them to float far away on the wind. The Bedu once used wads of these hairs as tinder, hence the name 'firemaker' (pyrotechnica).

Arabic Name   **'markh'**
Height   **To 2m**

Eyelash Plant
Blepharis edulis

This spiny plant owes its name to the shape of its flower, which consists of one blue petal upturned like an eyelash. It grows in rocky habitats and has an ingenious method of seed dispersal. The seeds are contained in a two-valve capsule that opens very suddenly after the plant has been immersed in water for ten minutes or more. The sudden action throws the seeds distances of up to one metre away from the mother plant. This 'explosion' is not triggered during a short rain shower and in this way the seeds are only dispersed if conditions are right for them to germinate.

Arabic Name   **'neqeil'**
Height   **To 20cm**

Oleander
Nerium mascatense

After good rains many wadis are bordered with lush stands of Oleander, the dark leaves offsetting the bunches of bright pink flowers. All parts of this plant are poisonous. Another member of the Oleander family, Rhazya stricta, grows on gravel plains and is a small, 30 cm high shrub with dark green pointed leaves. It has tiny sweet-smelling white flowers (not easily spotted from a car), and long seedpods. The plant used to be considered such a powerful medicine for skin ailments, that dried wild Rhazya was exported from Oman during the early 1900's.

Arabic Name   **'haban'**
Height   **To 3m**

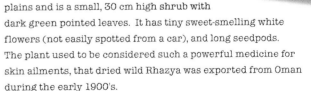

Dafra
Tephrosia apollinea

A common plant of sandy and gravel plains and mountain slopes is the Tephrosia, with its red pea flowers and flat-backed seedpods. It can be found flowering throughout the year, but in spring the flowers are larger and more profuse. This woody shrub is not grazed by animals and can survive extreme conditions.

Height   80 - 100cm

Zahra
Tribulus omanense

Of the various different Tribulus species in the region, this one has the largest flowers. It occurs in areas of loose sand and high dunes. The bright yellow flower has been suggested as the UAE's national flower. The feathered foliage is favourite fodder for gazelles and oryx, as well as for domestic livestock.

Height   **To 80cm, stems often half-trailing**

Reeds
Arundo donax

Of the various types of reeds that can be found along wet wadis, this is the tallest - its majestic plumes waving high against the blue skies. Although the stems can become very large, it has never been used by the local people as extensively as, for instance, bamboo has been in the Far East.

Height   **To 4m**

Desert Squash
Citrullus colocynthis

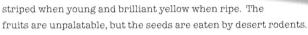

Any recently disturbed sandy soil makes the perfect habitat for this ground-covering vine. The long vines carry beautifully shaped leaves and the tennis ball-sized fruits are also attractive - green striped when young and brilliant yellow when ripe. The fruits are unpalatable, but the seeds are eaten by desert rodents.

Arabic Name   **'handal'**
Height   **Ground level (Ground-covering vine)**

Isbaq
Euphorbia larica

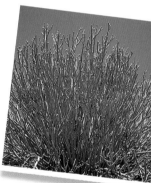

These light green shrubs can be seen everywhere on the gravel plains and mountain slopes. The plant has leafless stems, which point straight towards the sky. This is an adaptation to the hot climate - the plant exposes only the smallest surface to the rays of the sun. When the plant dies, the stems fall outwards and these dried stems are used for thatching the roofs of animal shelters and houses. The plant produces white latex and is not grazed by animals.

Height   **To 1m**

Senna Plant
Cassia italica

With long trailing stems, this bushy plant grows on sandy plains and recently disturbed soil. Its blooms are large yellow flowers. The black, curved seeds are a natural laxative and have been used all around the world as a herbal remedy for constipation (locally available as the brand medicine 'Senokot').

Arabic Name	'ishriq'
Height	To 30cm

Flowers

Over 800 species of wild flowers have been recorded in the UAE and the neighbouring parts of Oman accessible to UAE residents. Most of these are seen only in the springtime (March/April) after rains.

Desert plants are mostly pollinated by the wind or by night flying moths and as a consequence the flowers are small, with muted colours, but at times with a strong scent. Many of the plants in the UAE have been used in the past as food supplements, or for medicinal purposes to treat both humans and domestic animals. For example, Reichardia tingitana, a small spring daisy, was used to treat abdominal pain (colic) and eye infections, while tea made from the leaves of Sonchus olereacus (the local dandelion) was used as a diuretic, a laxative and as a general tonic.

Arabian Primrose
Arnebia hispidissima

After spring rains, the sandy plains turn into meadows covered in all sorts of annuals. Very common is the Arabian Primrose, which belongs to the borage family, and has a woody base with stiff stems covered in bristly hairs and bright yellow flowers. Its roots and branches contain a crimson dye that was once used by Bedu women as rouge make-up.

Arabic Name	'al hamra'
Height	To 20cm

Blue Pimpernel
Anagallis arvensis

The blue version of the Scarlet Pimpernel grows in wet wadis and plantations. Its striking colours are a joy to behold, and possibly triggered the belief in bygone days that the flower could dispel depression. The Arabic name, which means 'cat's or camel's eyes', is rather strange, as cats or camels with blue eyes are not exactly prevalent in the UAE!

Arabic Name	'ayn al gatt' or 'ayn al jamal'
Height	Slender trailing herb, with stems reaching a length of 40cm

Desert Hyacinth

Cistanche tubulosa

Found on the salty plains, this member of the broomrape family is a parasite which gets its nutrients via a fine thread that runs from the thickened lower end of its stem to the roots of nearby salt bushes. Local belief is that the plant is poisonous – it is certainly never eaten by animals.

The other parasitic plant of the sabkha is the Red Thumb, the roots of which can be cooked and eaten like asparagus.

Arabic Name **'thanoon'**
Height **15 - 40cm**

Maidenhair Fern

Adiantum capillus-veneris

The Maidenhair Fern and the only UAE orchid (*Epipactis veratrifolius*) often grow together at the edge of wet wadis. They have no other function than to cheer our days with their fragile beauty, which is even more striking in such a harsh landscape. The fern can be found all year around, but the orchid only emerges in the winter months to flower in February and March.

Arabic Name **'khuwaysat mai'**
Height **fronds reaching 30cm**

Little Star

Asteriscus pygmaeus

This tiny woody plant with its central yellow daisy flower grows in the limestone hills. When the plant dies down at the end of the season the seeds are enclosed in a tight woody bud, which opens if doused with water (you can try it if you find one). In heavy rain the seeds are catapulted over a considerable distance so that new plants grow in a circle around the old one.

Arabic Name **'qahwayan'**
Height **To 5cm**

Sorrel

Rumex vesicarius

After spring rains, many local people search the rocky mountain slopes for their favourite salad green, the local Sorrel. Though the flowers of this plant are barely noticeable, the seeds are covered with large, bright red wings that make the plant conspicuous against the dark rocks. The leaves are full of vitamin C and can be chewed raw as a thirst quencher and mouth freshener.

Arabic Name **'hummad'**
Height **To 20cm**

Popcorn Plant
Pseudogaillonia hymenostephana

This plant grows in abundance on the rocky slopes of the Hajar Mountains. The flowers are tiny white trumpets, emerging from the middle of a velvety pink calyx. When the seeds are ripening this calyx becomes larger, lighter in colour and increasingly transparent. Eventually the little balloons that are created are carried off by the wind to deposit the seeds wherever they may land.

Height   To 20cm

Asphodel Lily
Asphodelus tenuifolius

Growing on gravel and sandy/gravel plains, this common lily can either be a small single-stemmed plant or a little, much-branched bush, depending on the frequency of rains. The leaves look very similar to those of chives and the flowers are tiny and white, striped with maroon. The seeds are held in little capsules that rattle in the wind.

Arabic Name   'barwag' or 'kufer'
Height   20 - 60cm

Desert Campion
Silene villosa

The Desert Campion opens its lovely large flowers at dusk and is pollinated by night flying moths. In years of little rain, only small seedlings with two or three flowers appear, but if there are frequent rains, the plant develops into a large round bouquet of white flowers.

Arabic Name   'gharera'
Height   To 20cm

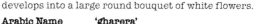

Rocks

Geologists around the world dream of visiting a country like the UAE because the lack of plant cover allows them to observe geological phenomena without any barriers. In addition, within a small surface area many interesting features can be observed, from the great barchan sand dunes at Liwa in the south or the flat sabkha (salt-flats) of the south-west to the various types of mountains in the eastern ranges. The jagged Hajar Mountains, which form a backbone down the east of the country and into Oman, are composed of ophiolite rocks that rose from the ocean bed under the influence of volcanic eruptions in the former Sea of Tethys. The beaches of this prehistoric sea were pushed into folds, a phenomenon that is easily visible in many places. These limestone mountains contain marine fossils, like corals and sea urchins.

Acteonellids

Some types of fossils are unique, like the hand-grenade-like acteonellids (shown) of Jebel Fayah and the one-celled nummulites (disc-shaped fossil shell of a foraminiferous protozoan) of Jebel Hafeet. You can find cross-cuts through these fossils that show their rolled-up structure.

Ammonites

Ammonites (any extinct cephalopod mollusc of the order Ammonoidea, with a flat, coiled spiral shell found as a fossil) are important in the study of fossils as the age of the strata where they were found can be deduced from the species of ammonite. So far, only two proper ammonites have been found in the UAE, although Fossil Valley near Al Ain has plenty of small pieces of straightened ammonites. A large plate-sized ammonite found near Jebel Fayah has been added to the collection at the Natural History Museum in London.

Chlorite

Chlorite is a soft rock that was used in ancient times to make beakers and bowls; examples of these can be seen at several of the local museums. The rock looks greenish and feels soft and slippery like soap.

Echinoderms

Over 30 different species of echinoderms (sea urchins) have been recorded in the UAE and several of those discovered within the last decade are new to science. If you are interested in searching for fossils, the Dubai Natural History Group (DNHG) organises fossil hunting trips on a regular basis, (contact 04 349 4816, or go to the free meetings at the Jumeirah English Speaking school every first Sunday of the month at 19:30pm). One sea urchin fossil was named after the DNHG member who discovered it!

Hatta Rocks

Among the most spectacular geological features in the area are the layered rocks at Hatta, best seen in the late afternoon when the sunlight brings out the red strata to perfection. The layers were formed as sediments and then twisted and uplifted by the forces in the earth's crust.

Fossil Shells

Along the west side of the volcanic Hajar Mountains runs a series of lighter coloured limestone mountains that are often fossil bearing. So far, no vertebrate fossils have been found in the area, however, the marine invertebrates are well represented. Many species of ordinary bi-valves (compressed bodies enclosed within two hinged shells, e.g. oysters and mussels) and gastropods (a mollusc that moves along by means of a large muscular foot, eg. sea snail or slug) can be found.

Quartz

The Hajar and Mussandam mountains abound in many different types of rock, both loose (and collectible), and embedded as strata in other rocks. Seams of marble, mica or the quartz shown can easily be seen on vertical rock faces. Quartz is a mineral defined by its chemical composition and crystal structure.

Magnesite

Magnesite is a soft white mineral ($MgCO_3$) that occurs as veins in ophiolite (black lava) rocks. When it weathers it looks a bit like Styrofoam. It is formed when magnesium leaches out from the ophiolites and precipitates along rock fissures, combining with the CO_2 in the air, to form $MgCO_3$. It is most common along the west flank of the Hajar Mountains.

Sands

In the souks you can find a tourist item for sale that has some geological interest – a small display of the seven different types of sand in the Emirates. The white sands of Dubai consist of shell and coral remnants, while the black sand of the east coast is of volcanic origin and the red sands of Al Ain contain a great deal of iron.

Driving

Jeep

Driving Overview

Off-road driving is exciting and adventurous, but it requires skill. To ensure that most of your off-roading memories are good, we've listed a few pointers in this section to help you get on your way. The key elements are simple – be prepared and use your common sense. Leave your macho fantasies of invincibility at home – the good off-roader is careful and cautious, and has a high regard for safety and the environment (this goes beyond taking your rubbish home: for more information on the environmental considerations of off-roading, see p.280 in the Activities section).

In this section you'll find out what essentials you should pack before you hop in your 4 WD, as well as learn how to tackle the challenges of the varying terrain that you will encounter.

Driving Overview

The Basics

The basic items of essential equipment (right) can be sourced through the directory at the back of the book.

If your trip takes you into Oman territory, including any of the Omani enclaves, make sure your vehicle is insured for both the UAE and Oman. If not, you should be able to extend your cover to include Oman for the duration of your trip, although this will probably involve an extra charge. You'll need to collect a certificate from your provider to prove that your insurance covers you for driving in Oman.

When hiring a 4 WD, ensure that the insurance specifically covers off-road driving. Bizarrely, not all companies will provide off-road cover automatically, even though you are hiring an off-road vehicle!

Essential Equipment

- ☐ Jack – conventional or air bag (for serious off-roading, a highlift jack is best, as it can also serve as a winch if required)
- ☐ Plank or block of wood (for supporting the jack on soft ground)
- ☐ Tow-rope and shackles
- ☐ Basic tool kit (including tools to change a wheel)
- ☐ Mobile phone (fully charged)
- ☐ Shovel
- ☐ Fire extinguisher
- ☐ Tyre pressure gauge
- ☐ First-aid kit
- ☐ Spare tyre in good condition, fully inflated
- ☐ Well-maintained, fully serviced vehicle
- ☐ Fluid levels checked (water, oil, clutch, steering, coolants, radiator, battery)

Accidents Will Happen...

If you are involved in an accident off-road, you are required to get a police report at the scene (even if it is a minor mishap or if only your car is involved). In some cases this may mean driving out to find the police and leading them back to where the accident took place, but without the report you will not be able to make your insurance claim or get repairs carried out on your car.

When accidents happen in remote areas, where there are no hard-and-fast rules of the road, it may be difficult for the police to assign blame. In such cases, both parties may have to bear joint responsibility for the accident and each driver must submit insurance claims only for the damages to their car.

Safety

Off-road driving is fun, but safety should be your top priority. Always be sensible and patient, and practise your off-road skills whenever you can. The following safety guidelines will help you get out of a mishap with as little drama as possible.

- Take your mobile phone – even if network services are poor in some remote areas, in an emergency someone can try to reach a high point to get a signal. Make sure your phone is fully charged, and for longer trips take your charger – don't let it be the battery that lets you down.
- Travel with a buddy – if you are going more than a kilometre or two off the beaten track, always go with an experienced off-road driver. That second vehicle or extra pair of hands could literally be a lifesaver. You are never too experienced to take a second vehicle.

Optional Equipment

- ☐ Foot pump or compressor
- ☐ Tyre repair kit (tubeless)
- ☐ Sand mats or trays
- ☐ Jump leads
- ☐ Spare fuses
- ☐ Heavy-duty gloves
- ☐ GPS receiver
- ☐ Multi-purpose pocket knife
- ☐ Torch (and spare batteries)
- ☐ Camera (and spare film)
- ☐ Binoculars

Paperwork

Carry the following documents with you:

- ☐ Insurance papers (copies are fine)
- ☐ Vehicle registration card
- ☐ UAE driving licence
- ☐ Accident report (if you have existing damage to your car, however minor)
- ☐ Ensure your passengers have personal ID

- Pack a first-aid kit – fortunately the UAE has very few nasty plants and animals, but you need to be prepared if they do come into contact with humans (see First Aid on p.306). Know the medical histories of your passengers or companions – if they are on medication or have any chronic conditions, make sure before you leave that they are fully equipped and fit to go.
- Keep the water handy – always take plenty of water; at least three litres of drinking water per person per day.
- Wear your seatbelt – it might not be comfortable while bumping over dunes, but the benefits far outweigh the inconvenience. ALWAYS wear your seatbelt, and ensure that your passengers, both front and back seat, do the same.

- Spread the word – even though you might not be getting that far away from 'civilisation', try to let someone know where you're going and when you'll be back. If nothing else, in a mishap it may be comforting to know that there is someone who will raise the alarm if you don't return.

Tyres

Ensure that your tyres are in good condition and that you select the correct tyre pressure for a particular terrain (this is discussed in greater detail on the next page). The following guidelines are general considerations for your tyres:

- Inspect the tyres carefully before you leave and in between periods of driving. Check each tyre for worn tread, damaged side walls and for any wear in or around the valves. Check for cuts and gashes caused by sharp stones (usually after wadi driving).
- The difference between inner-tube tyres and tubeless tyres is not critical. In general, tubeless tyres are less likely to puncture abruptly, and punctures in a tubeless tyre can be 'quick-fixed' until a more reliable repair is possible. However, inner-tube tyres are usually more reliable at low pressures.
  - Don't neglect your spare tyre – check its condition regularly to make sure it is sufficiently inflated. Make sure you have the key if your spare tyre is fitted with a locking wheel nut. And if it is bolted to the underside of your vehicle, make sure you have the correct tools for its removal.

Gears

4 WD High Range

This is what you will use for most of your off-road driving. The torque of the engine is distributed between all wheels, front and back.

4 WD Low Range

Low range is engaged only when driving challenging terrain, or when stuck or bogged down. It allows for controlled and steady movement. Engine revs are much higher and progress is slow.

Diff-lock

Power from the engine is usually distributed through a number of differentials to all four wheels. These differentials are located on the front axle, the rear axle and on the drive shaft between the two axles. This means that if one of more of the wheels gets stuck, the differentials transfer power to the free wheels, causing them to spin aimlessly, doing nothing to get the car unstuck.

If your car is fitted with diff-lock, engaging the locks forces the wheels to move at the same speed, which cuts down on spinning and allows the wheels with the best traction to pull you out of trouble.

For wadis and mountains, you should be able to drive mostly in high range without diff-lock, while in the desert, engaging central diff-lock assists in providing even power and traction between the front and rear wheels.

As a rule, rear diff-lock is for when you get stuck – it can get you out of trouble in the desert, or help you over uneven, rocky ground if one or more wheels lose contact with the ground. Don't forget to disengage diff-lock once you are out of trouble, otherwise you can seriously damage your vehicle. It should only be used for driving in a straight line, and not for going uphill or turning. Most importantly, diff-lock will not stop you from sliding in wet or slippery conditions, and will only worsen your predicament.

Driving in Convoy

The first rule of driving in convoy is that each driver is responsible for the car behind. This ensures that the convoy travels at the speed of the slowest car, and everyone returns to civilisation together. The second rule is to leave sufficient space between you and the car ahead. This obviously depends on the speed you are travelling and the terrain, but should be 20 to 40 metres. Not only does this prevent pile-ups if the lead car stops suddenly, but it also stops you from getting bombarded by clouds of dust and flying stones.

Don't worry if you can't always see the car ahead, especially in confined areas where it's impossible to tailgate a car to the top of a dune. But it can be useful to watch how the driver in front of you handles tricky situations, such as ridges and dunes, before you follow them. Don't attempt to negotiate tricky parts of your route before the car ahead of you has cleared it – if they fail and you are in hot pursuit, both vehicles can come to an abrupt stop and get stuck. If your lead car does get stuck, keep your hand on the horn to warn oncoming cars before they come flying over the dune. If you are last in the convoy and you get stuck, turn your headlights on so that those ahead of you can see you're in trouble.

Sand Driving

The key to driving on sand is maintaining controlled momentum by using higher than normal revs. Make sure that you are in 4 WD mode and stick to the lower gears (not low range yet). Selecting the correct gear and engine revs will

come with experience, but try not to over or under accelerate when tackling soft sand. The more you practise, the more you'll be able to anticipate where your vehicle is going to struggle, and change down a gear before you hit the tricky patches. It is all too easy to grind to a halt in sand, so practise flipping the clutch down and changing gear with lightning speed.

Sand driving should be seen as 'surfing' the dunes, not ploughing through them. Look at the shape and form of the dune. It is usually better to travel with the direction of the dunes (ie. the direction of the wind). But be careful, because while you may find it easy going with the flow on the way up, it gets a bit tricky if you find yourself going back against it when you turn around.

Existing tracks normally define the best route to take. If there are no tracks, plan a route that seems the easiest and limits damage to flora and fauna. You should only be using the accelerator, and barely touching the brakes or clutch. The general aim is to gain enough momentum going down to allow you to coast over the top of the next dune smoothly.

The sand's consistency changes during the day and also seasonally. When it is very hot, dry conditions render the surface soft and loose. Blowing sand collects in hidden hollows and can catch out an unwary driver. Driving at around midday, especially in the summer, is particularly tricky as there are few shadows and little contrast to show the bumps and hollows before it's too late.

If you are unsure of the best way to proceed, then stop in a safe spot (as defined below) and get out to have a look. In addition to keeping your momentum going at crucial points and learning to 'read' the sand, the following are key elements for driving successfully.

Tyres

Reduction of tyre pressure to between a half and two-thirds of road pressure (normally between 15 and 22 psi) is generally recommended. This increases the surface area of the tyre that is in contact with the sand and spreads the weight of the vehicle, providing added traction in soft conditions.

Instead of fiddling about with a tyre pressure gauge, an easier approach is to simply let the air out of each tyre evenly for 40 to 60 seconds. Check the pressure and take it down more if needed, but remember it's better to let out too little air than too much! In very soft sand a minimum of 12 psi can be attempted, but with caution.

Don't forget to re-inflate your tyres as soon as possible after leaving the desert. Finding the nearest petrol station is usually the easiest solution.

Gears

Always use 4 WD. If you have a diff-lock or low range, engage it to get through the tricky bits. When you are in low range, you don't need to use first gear - you can pull away in second or even third.

Automatics

The performance of an automatic transmission in the desert differs from a manual in a number of ways. Automatics are smoother and faster at gear changes than a manual, which can make it easier to keep your momentum, and easier to drive. However, you may find that automatics can change gears at inopportune moments. But as you get used to your car's performance, you will probably be able to predict when this might happen, and know how to stop it. With a little practice, you can get the engine to stay in a particular gear, or to change gear up or down, just by use of the accelerator. Additionally, the gear selector can be used to limit the gear so that it doesn't change to a higher gear when you don't want it to.

Another major difference involves engine braking. An automatic does not offer the same engine-braking ability as a manual, especially if the car is kept in the 'drive' gear all the time. There will be some circumstances where you will need to use the other gears - when descending dunes, for example, you will have to change down gears to control your speed with engine braking. Staying in 'drive' gear will result in you freewheeling down the dune - only by selecting a lower gear will your engine control the speed of the car.

Also, if you are cruising over undulating terrain in 'drive' gear, you can't slow the car down simply by taking your foot off the accelerator as you would in a manual. If you want to slow down you will need to use the brake lightly, but remember that when you do accelerate again you should do it gently to keep the car moving smoothly.

Stopping Safely

- Always stop at an angle that allows you to move on, preferably forwards. If the sand is hard, you can stop on level ground. If not, stop on a downward slope.
- Small dunes - stop at the top of the dune, just over the top, to evaluate your route. The car following you should stop on the top of the dune behind you.

- Large dunes - stop towards the bottom of the dune on the downward slope, with enough space to pick up momentum before tackling the next dune. The cars following you can either stop behind or next to you, depending on space. If you stop on the ridge of a large dune, you risk getting stuck with no wheels touching the sand. Always try to stop just after you clear the ridge and are on the downward slope.
- Never brake abruptly, as you will force the tyres into the sand. Before you stop completely, release the brake and roll gently to a halt.

- Keep your eyes peeled for those little dry bushes and never park over one - your engine will be hot after the vigours of dune driving and the risk of starting a bonfire under your car is enormous!

Getting Unstuck

- When you get stuck (and believe us you will!) don't slam your foot hard on the accelerator and hope that this will move the vehicle - it will only sink you deeper into the sand.
- Remove any sand or obstacles that have built up around the front, back or sides of the wheels.
- Unload any excess weight, starting with your passengers and even your baggage if you are well and truly stuck.
- Check your tyre pressure and, if necessary, reduce it. This may give you the extra traction you need to get you moving.

Going up a Dune

DO
- Select the route of least resistance - get out of the car and have a look if necessary.
- Give yourself a good run up and the momentum will carry you to the top, but remember - not too much, not too little!
- Stick to lower gears to keep your revs high.
- If you start losing traction move your steering wheel quickly from side to side to help the wheels find extra traction as you tackle a slope.
- Allow your 'buddy' vehicle to safely negotiate the slope before trying it yourself.
- Make sure that no one is barrelling up the opposite side of the same dune.

DON'T
- Drive diagonally across the slope, especially in very soft sand (this predicament sometimes arises as a result of doing a U-turn). If this happens, make sure you keep your momentum going to stop the car from rolling - if you are going too slow, gravity will win and pull the car over whichever way is down. Make sure you have just enough forward motion to fight it.
- Tailgate another vehicle whilst going up.

Going down a Dune

DO
- Stay in a low gear.
- Let the engine do the braking.
- Point the car straight down the dune (not at an angle).
- If the run out is smooth, accelerate slightly as you exit the bottom of the dune to gain momentum for the next climb.

DON'T
- Brake sharply - this may cause the car to slur, roll or even flip over.
- Do not deviate from your straight line, however scary the descent!
- Freewheel.
- Close your eyes - this is slightly unnerving for your passengers!

- Switch off the air conditioning to direct 100% of the available power to the wheels.
- Change into low range if the situation requires it (and use second gear), or engage the diff-lock.
- Wiggle the steering wheel from side to side as you begin to move – this sometimes gives that crucial bit of extra traction.
- Inch forwards and backwards, slowly clearing an area to give you a better chance of picking up momentum.
- Release the clutch slowly (assuming your vehicle is not an automatic), ensuring minimum wheel spin. Never let your wheels spin too much – you will only sink further and once you are buried up to your axles in sand, it is pretty much only a rescue company that can get you out (see Directory – Recovery Services).

If you have done all of the above and are still stuck, you need to evaluate your predicament carefully. Will you be able to free yourself or do you need assistance? Consider the following suggestions and whether any of them are relevant to your situation:

Pushing

If you are simply bogged down in the sand, try to clear the sand away from the tyres that are stuck. If you have some willing passengers, they can assist with a push – it is surprising how much help even just a couple of people pushing can be. Put something underneath the wheels to give you the traction you need. Mats, dead twigs or logs will help and sand trays are ideal, if you have them.

Jacking

Jack the car up and place something under the wheels that will give better traction, such as your picnic blanket, firewood or sand trays. Release the jack and repeat for each wheel until the car is raised beyond the obstruction. If you are using a regular jack, you'll need a block of wood to prevent it sinking into the sand. It's easier to use a high-lift jack or an airbag jack (which is like a large inflatable cushion).

Rocking

In some situations, it may be possible to repeatedly rock the car forwards and backwards or from side to side. Rocking will allow the hollows formed by the tyres to gradually fill with sand, and when combined with some gentle use of low gears, this can be enough to free the car.

If your car is completely stuck, and you have no other car with you for towing, try rocking the vehicle much more vigorously from side to side, until the wheels lift up. This allows sand to fill the space beneath the tyres, as described above. The idea is to get the car to rise up gradually out of the sand, until it is possible to drive it out.

Towing

If you are travelling with a second car, the least sweaty solution is probably for them to tow you out. Obviously the second vehicle should be in a solid position to tow, otherwise you'll end up with two stuck vehicles. 'Solid' is defined as having good traction (on sand this usually means on a downhill slope) and a smooth run out in front of the towing car. It is preferable to have a straight line between the towing car and the stuck car. You can join two tow ropes together to give you more help finding a solid towing spot (but remember it's better to use shackles rather than tie two ropes together).

A smaller 4 WD is not going to be much help pulling out a heavier vehicle if it is stuck fast. A winch (if fitted) is a bonus – a high-lift jack can also serve as a winch. Ensure that both ends of the winch cable are well-anchored, and make sure everyone stands well clear of a cable or tow rope when under strain.

General Rules of Towing

- Attach the rope according to the manufacturer's instructions. It is not usually recommended to use the bumper.
- Avoid tying ropes together or onto your car if possible. Shackles won't tighten and you'll be able to get them undone much easier. If you do have to use a knot, make sure that it is strong but can be easily undone.

- Take the slack up slowly, unless executing a 'jerk-tow' manoeuvre. Jerking should be the very last resort, because something can easily come flying off with all the strain, risking injury to bystanders or damage to vehicles.
- Coordinate efforts between cars. Uncoordinated attempts often have little effect and can worsen the situation. Agree on a code between helpers and drivers for 'start' and 'stop', and have both cars move at the same time.
- Get all bystanders well out of the way of the cars in case the towrope snaps.

Golden Rule

If none of these tactics helps, think twice before leaving your car, especially if you have no mobile coverage. If you can follow a clear road through the desert to the main road, you have water and know exactly where you are going, then you may choose to go for help. If you don't know where you are, or how far it is to the nearest road, or even which direction it is in, STAY WITH YOUR CAR. The desert is harsh and unforgiving, but at least your car can provide some shade and protection from the elements. And if someone comes looking for you, it is much easier to spot a car than a solitary soul wandering aimlessly through the desert. Even though it seems passive, your chances of survival are much greater if you stay with your vehicle than if you decide to try and find your way through sand dunes that all look the same.

Mountain and Wadi Driving

Driving in the mountains and wadis of the UAE is less demanding than the rigours of sand driving. Most tracks are graded and in good condition, so there is less chance of getting stuck. The main things to consider are speed control on loose surfaces (it is possible to skid off the road or roll your car on graded roads), and to exercise caution on steep gradients and near steep drops. You should also watch out for sudden appearances by wild animals and crazy drivers!

When driving along rocky wadi beds, negotiate large rocks carefully so that you don't leave your undercarriage or exhaust behind, or end up perched on a rock with your tyres spinning in the air. When driving over rough sections of track, try to keep your wheels on the highest points so nothing will catch underneath.

Remember that wadis are just empty riverbeds, so although they are dry for most of the year, they can suddenly fill up with water. Rainfall many kilometres away will find the quickest way out of the catchment area, so even if there are clear skies and bright sunshine above the wadi you are in, it can start filling up with water. Any sign of rain in the area, however slight, should be seen as a warning not to venture into the wadis. If you are caught in a flash flood, head for the highest ground you can reach – be prepared to abandon your vehicle if necessary.

Tyres

Maintain normal to slightly higher tyre pressure to prevent side-wall damage and punctures from sharp rocks. Try to pick lines through rocks which will minimise damage to your tyres, and maintain steady speeds on rough tracks – not only will this prevent unnecessary damage to your tyres, but your comfort will be greater as well.

Gears

Drive in 4 WD using normal gears and always check ahead to avoid large boulders or holes that can cause damage to your vehicle. Know your ground clearance and negotiate your route accordingly. Engage low range for rocky, challenging spots and steep ups and downs. In bumpy, rocky areas, this means that you are not constantly using the clutch to change up or down a gear, so your progress is much smoother and more controlled. For a steep downhill you should let the engine do the braking, and for a very steep uphill, low range gives you the increased traction and power to reach the top.
(The difference between low range, high range and the diff-lock is explained under The Basics – Gears on p.269)

Wadi Crossing

If you need to cross a water-filled wadi, the depth and strength of the flow needs to be tested by wading in carefully. If it is okay to cross, use a low gear at a steady 5-10 km/h (this depends on the width of the wadi – if you have a long way to go, you may want to engage the diff-lock or low range). If you drive steadily into the water you can create a wave, behind which it is then possible to drive through the water, pushing the water out of your way all the way to the other side. Maintain slightly higher than normal revs as this keeps the engine hot and prevents it from stalling easily. If the water is deep, remove the fan belt to prevent it drawing in water. Vehicle manufacturers generally have a stated maximum depth that their vehicle can safely accommodate. If in convoy, wait for the first vehicle to cross safely before following.

Getting Unstuck

If you become lodged on rocks, any attempt to move backwards or forwards may cause damage to the underside of the vehicle.

In these situations follow a similar technique to that used in the sand. Use a jack to raise the vehicle and then slowly fill the gaps underneath the tyres with stones, until the car is raised above the obstruction. Remove the obstruction if possible, or otherwise build gradual 'ramps' for the wheels to grip and drive up.

Sabkha Driving

The UAE has many flat areas characterised by a crusty, salty layer where the water table is close to the surface. These are known locally as sabkha, and are typically found around Liwa and in some coastal areas. In summer these dried salt-flats are usually stable, but in the wetter months of winter their ability to support a vehicle is severely compromised. In coastal areas the water level is also influenced by the tides, so an area you crossed relatively easily just an hour previously can suddenly be unstable on your return journey.

It is not advisable to drive across sabkha unless you absolutely have to. If you do, keep to existing tracks to avoid finding yourself in a sticky mess, and never stop on sabkha – keep driving until you hit firmer ground. If you stop and then try to restart, your tyres can break through the thin surface layer to the water below (and then your day has just taken a turn for the worse!).

Accidents and Breakdowns
Accidents
If you have an accident, having a second vehicle may be a lifesaver. In some emirates you have to leave your car at the scene so that the police can inspect it - unless you have a second car or you are extremely close to civilisation, this may be impossible. If you are using GPS, mark the coordinates of your abandoned car. If not, try to remember the location as meticulously as possible (especially in the desert, where everything looks the same).

Common sense should prevail, so if driving out in the damaged

car is the only sensible solution, then you should do it. Go straight to the police for an accident report and explain the situation. If you have a camera with you, take some pictures of the accident scene.

If there are any injuries, apply basic first aid where appropriate (see the First Aid section on p.306).

It Could Happen To You
These are the 10 most common reasons, listed in order of frequency, for off-road rescues in the UAE (courtesy of the AAA Service Centre):
1. Getting stuck in the sand or mud
2. Burnt-out clutch
3. Engine failure
4. Electrical failure
5. Gearbox failure
6. Rolled vehicle
7. Multiple punctures
8. Completely burnt-out vehicle
9. Washed away (in a wadi or sabkha)
10. Car losing control over a cliff or into a ravine

Breakdowns
Don't despair if your car breaks down. It is advisable to know a few basics of car maintenance, such as how to change a tyre or check the oil. And make sure you have enough petrol for your journey, to avoid the embarrassment of having to call out a recovery service because you have an empty tank!

There are certain common problems caused by off-road driving. Excessive desert driving at high revs can cause your vehicle to overheat. If this happens, do not turn off the engine – just stop the car and allow the engine to cool down while it is still running. Turning it off will stop the flow of coolant and lead to a temporary increase in temperature that may make things worse. Switch on the car heating – this will redirect the engine heat.

A burning smell (when you are driving in sand) usually means that you are riding the clutch. Stop the vehicle to cool the clutch, that you are riding the clutch. Stop the vehicle to cool the clutch, and when you set off again use your gears to control the speed of the car – don't slip the clutch in an effort to get more traction. If your car breaks down while you are in convoy, get someone to tow you to the nearest road. In the busier areas you'll usually find small garages that may be able to do temporary repairs, or you can call your local garage for help. There are some recovery companies that specialise in getting off-road vehicles back to 'civilisation' and the nearest garage. This could be your only option in more difficult situations (see Directory – Recovery Services on p.318).

Navigation

Finding your way to where you want to go, finding your way back home and having fun while doing it, are important elements of successful off-roading. Below are some guidelines to navigating your way from A to B and back again.

Finding North

Compass

A compass makes navigating open terrain easy, especially when used with a good map. A prismatic compass is recommended, as it has a sight for taking more accurate bearings. Bearings are taken clockwise with magnetic north as 0° and south as 180° opposite north.

Wristwatch

If you do not have a compass, true north can be determined with an analogue wristwatch (or clock). Point the hour hand towards the sun, then divide the angle between this direction and the direction of 12 o'clock on the watch dial – this is south.

Sun

The sun rises in the east and sets in the west.

Sundial

During the course of the day, the passage of the sun across the sky can be recorded by placing a stick upright in the sand and tracing the shadow at regular intervals. If you join the end of the shadow made at two different times, then the line will be in a west to east direction, with west being the first shadow and east the second. Drawing a line at 90° to this line forms the north-south line.

Stars

You can impress everyone with your knowledge of the night sky, and figure out which way is north, by looking up at the stars. In the UAE, north is located by the Pole Star. The two lowest stars of the Plough or Great Bear point towards the Pole Star, which is about four times the distance between the two stars away.

GPS

Global Positioning Systems (GPS) have been in operation since the 1980s and are now the primary navigation aids for terrestrial, aeronautical and marine transport applications. A handheld, stand-alone GPS receiver, costing from around Dhs.550, can provide users with a position on the earth's surface to within approximately ten metres. Not bad, considering the results come from a satellite 16,000km away! The receivers can plot positions as you are moving, record waypoints, plot a continuous route and allow you to track back along that route.

Most receivers can display your position in various coordinates, for example in latitude and longitude or in UTM. Most countries have their own unique coordinate system applied to their mapping, so when using a GPS receiver, make sure that the coordinates shown on the screen match the map system.

Plotting your position on a map or image is therefore a piece of cake. In our case, we use the Universal Transverse Mercator (UTM) projection, with a WGS-84 spheroid. Each digit on the grid represents one metre. The Northern Emirates is in grid zone 40R.

INSPIRED BY NATURE

LANTERNS

STOVES

JUGS

CHEST COOLERS

THERMOELECTRIC COOLE

OUTDOOR FURNITUR

SLEEPING BAGS

TENTS

Activities

Jeep

Activities Overview

Contrary to many people's impression of the country, the UAE has a surprising amount of wilderness and natural beauty, and a lot to offer outdoor enthusiasts. The Hajar Mountains running up the east side of the country into Mussandam offer some awesome hiking and rock-climbing, while the foothills of these mountains and the adjacent rocky plains are great to explore for mountain bikers. As well as being enjoyed by off-road drivers, the desert is equally popular with off-road motorcyclists and quad-bikers, while the waters off the coast offer spectacular diving and snorkelling, especially in the Gulf of Oman.

For more leisurely pursuits, camping can be enjoyed almost anywhere in the countryside, birdwatching turns up an unexpected amount of birdlife on the coasts and in the oases in the interior of the country, and history buffs can unearth interesting finds dating from as far back as 5000BC. Whatever your hobby is, or if you fancy taking up something completely different, the UAE will have something for you.

Archaeology Overview

The UAE may be a young country, but if you look closely you will find evidence of a strong heritage. Although today modern technology is taking the country into the future at alarming speed, the government is actively promoting the preservation of traditional ways of life.

Over the past 20 years, archaeological digs have uncovered a great deal of interesting information about the people who inhabited this area from the 5th millennium BC and onwards. This information is recorded and carefully preserved, and some is on display in national museums (such as the museums in Al Ain, Ras Al Khaimah and Sharjah).

You can visit the sites of these archaeological digs, if you enquire at the various museums or government departments. Archaeological teams are usually more than willing to share information about their finds.

Apart from official archaeological sites, there are also records of people from past ages in rock carvings ('petroglyphs') and on headstones of ancient graves throughout the eastern mountains. In some villages you can find relics of everyday life, such as large earthen storage jars (used for grains and water), goatskins (which were used to swirl milk into butter) and clay pots (metal pots were rare and expensive, and if a family was fortunate enough to own a metal pot it would be melted down and remodelled when it got old).

Archaeological Sites

The earliest evidence of man's presence in the UAE can be dated back to the Late Stone Age, about 7,000 years ago. Recent finds include Luluiyah Fort, which is believed to date back to the 13th century. Excavated in late 2000, this is the first Islamic site on the east coast to be investigated. Finds include pottery, beads and bracelets, while the structure includes a mosque, a tower, fireplaces and courtyards.

The following two archaeological sites in Ras Al Khaimah date from much later. They are included here because they are easily accessible from the main road, and both have undergone extensive restoration work.

Falayah

Falayah consists of three complexes of buildings, erected near a palm garden to the south and a major wadi to the north. It was built by the Quwasim family in the 18th century, and used as a summer home until the end of the 19th century. The buildings have a historical significance, being the site where the peace treaty of 1820 (considered as the foundation of the UAE) was signed between the sheikhs of the coastal Gulf states.

The westernmost building is a mosque, which was used by the family and possibly served as the main Friday mosque for the area. An interesting feature is a small Minbar (place for the Friday prayer), which was built with two steps into the eastern wall in order to leave maximum room for people praying inside.

Part of the courtyard is covered to provide shade to people praying outside. The elevated, walled corner to the north-east was used as a minaret (in the UAE only modern mosques have tall minarets).

The other two buildings formed part of a single complex. The large tower in the middle was once connected with a wall to the eastern portion, and the courtyard and tower formed the public area of the complex. The tower was built with a majlis on the first floor, which may have been the state majlis (and the room where the treaty was signed).

The eastern complex houses the private family rooms, which are built in a row and divided down the middle by a mud-brick tower. The complex was connected with a second, private courtyard to the east – the Harim. The northern room of this complex is a private majlis connecting both courtyards. From the Harim, the other rooms of the complex could be accessed. The second room is a typical living room with a secondary wall in one corner to

hide the bathroom. The end of the room towards the tower has a hollow used for storage jars.

The room south of the tower may have been used as a stable or for storage. A secondary building, built from mudbricks, stood at the eastern side of the courtyard and was possibly used as a kitchen and servants' quarters.

Shimal

The area of Shimal is one of the most fertile plains in the UAE. It became inhabited in the 3rd millennium BC when the high water table could support a dense population. It is now the site of many archaeological remains of the last 5,000 years. Some of these have been excavated and are worth a visit – the National Museum at Ras Al Khaimah has more information.

To reach Shimal, turn left at Lantern Roundabout in Ras Al Khaimah, go past Nakheel and towards Rams. About three kilometres after Nakheel, the buildings end and there is a turning to the right. Take this right turn and follow the tarmac road for about 500 metres, stopping immediately after it turns to the right. Here you can see a fenced area protecting a large tomb excavated in 1998.

Built about 5,000 years ago, this round tomb belongs to the Umm An Nar period. It was built as a communal burial place and the remains of more than 400 bodies have been found here. The tomb is over 120 metres in diameter and was once about three metres high. The outer face was lined with smoothed limestone slabs, some of which are still in place. The tomb is divided into several chambers, accessible by at least three entrances.

Follow the road for another 300 metres and then turn left onto a track running to the left of a small white building inside a fenced area. After 20 metres you will reach an excavated structure near an old tree – this is another tomb, which was excavated in 1986 and dates back to the Wadi Suq period (200 - 1600BC). The original tomb consisted of a long inner chamber with an entrance to the north. Later a ring chamber was added around the structure and both chambers were roofed with corbelled stones. About 60 bodies were buried in this tomb.

ther areas of archaeological interest that you might
want to visit are:

Abu Dhabi

Umm An Nar Tomb (you'll need an entry permit from
the Department of Protection of Oil Installations to visit
this site).

Al Ain

Hili Tomb, Hili Archaeological Garden and Bini bin Saud
Graves (north of Dolphin Roundabout).

Bidiyah

Here you can see the oldest mosque in the UAE (refer to
the Dubai to East Coast road route for further details).
The site of the Portuguese Fort at Bidiyah has recently
been excavated.

Bitnah

Bitnah Fort. The main archaeological site is the Long
Chambered Tomb (also known as the T-shaped tomb),
12km north-west of Fujairah (you can find a detailed
display of the tomb at Fujairah Museum). See 'Dubai to
East Coast' for more details.

Fujairah

Qidfa site – 18km north of Fujairah; Hayl Castle – in Wadi
Hayl just outside Fujairah.

Maleihah

Various sites in the area (about 50km east of Sharjah).

RAK

Falayah, Shimal, Qasr az-Zubba (Sheba's Palace). Various
burial sites from the Umm An Nar period.

UAQ

Ad Door site (on the coast near Umm Al Quwain town), Tell
Abraq site (between Sharjah and Umm Al Quwain). To visit,
obtain permission from the Department of Antiquities or
from the archaeologists working at the sites.

If you continue through this wadi you will find several more
tombs of various sizes. If you proceed a further 50 metres
(towards a triangular mountain), another fenced area protects
the remains of a settlement from the late 2nd millennium BC.
Unfortunately there is not much to see other than the remains of
foundations of houses and walls.

One kilometre to the south is a large, flat plateau just above the
modern village of Shimal. You can find the remains of a medieval
palace on top of the plateau. It is likely that it was here where the
ruler of Julfar (a large medieval trading town) enjoyed a view
over the palm gardens. To reach the plateau, enter the village and
leave your car where the road borders the mountains. Enter the
fenced area and walk up the ravine near the fence.

Further Reading

If you want to explore the Abu Dhabi or Dubai emirates in
greater depth, get your hands on a copy of the *Abu Dhabi &
Al Ain Explorer* and the *Dubai Explorer*. Both books contain
detailed information on heritage sites and museums in the UAE.

Birdwatching Overview

There are currently over a hundred bird species that breed in the UAE, a number that has risen gradually over the last few years as a result of greening programmes. During spring and autumn, over 300 additional species have been spotted on their migration route from Africa to Central Asia. You can usually expect to see species such as Hume's Wheatear, Bonelli's Eagle, Crab Plover, White-collared Kingfisher, Hypocolius, Great Knot, Grey Francolin, Lappet-faced Vulture, Purple Sunbird, Red-wattled Lapwing, Socotra Cormorant or Saunders' Little Tern. The continuous agricultural developments in the UAE, using natural oases and underground water, have created new habitats that are attractive to birds because of the fruits, flowers and insects available in these areas.

Thanks to the increasing greenery in cities, in the form of parks and gardens, a wider variety of birdlife can be seen in urban areas than ever before.

At the end of Dubai Creek, just a short distance from one of the city's main business district, is the Ras Al Khor Wildlife Sanctuary – it is the only nature reserve within the city and is a superb place to see Greater Flamingos, as well as many other shore birds and waders. On an average day in winter you can find up to 15,000 birds, including up to 1,500 flamingos. Dubai Municipality is increasingly concerned about the protection of these birds and their ecosystem, and you'll see police patrolling the area around the clock. There are three recently built hides from where you can watch the birds with the provided telescopes or binoculars supplied, view information on the types of birds it is possible to see there and pick up their guide to the sanctuary. One of these hides is situated beside Ras Al Khor Road, the other two off Oud Metha Road. All three are manned, have their own car parks and are free to visit for small numbers at a time. Groups of more than 10 may need to contact the Environment Department at Dubai Municipality in advance (04 206 4240). You can also usually spot the flamingos from the Ras Al Khor road, as you drive from the Bu Kidra roundabout towards Hatta or on Oud Metha Road going towards the junction at Wafi City. Other birdwatching sites include the many parks and golf clubs, where Parakeets, Indian Rollers, Little Green Bee-eaters and Hoopoe can be spotted and heard.

One of the UAE's prime birding spots is the mangrove swamps at Khor Kalba – the only place in the world where you can see the rare White-collared Kingfisher. This bird is so rare that it is thought there are only around 50 pairs still in existence, but it is usually possible to catch a glimpse of one

or two on a visit to Khor Kalba. It's a common destination for birdwatching tours, as well as canoe tours on which you can also see plenty of marine life (see 'Birdwatching' and 'Canoeing' in the Directory, p.315).

At the mangrove swamps in Umm Al Quwain you can see Crab Plovers and Socotra Cormorants, while around Hatta and the fields near Ras Al Khaimah there are opportunities for spotting Indian Rollers and Bee-eaters.

Twitcher Locations

Abu Dhabi
Abu Dhabi Golf and Equestrian Club, Mushref Palace Gardens, Al Wathba camel track, Eastern Lagoon, Khalidiyah

Al Ain
Jebel Hafeet, Hanging Gardens, Ain al Faydah reed beds, Al Ain camel track, Khutwa oasis

Dubai
Khor Dubai Wildlife Sanctuary, Emirates Golf Course, Safa Park, Creekside Park, Al Mamzar Park, Mushrif Park

East Coast and Khor Kalba
Khor Kalba mangroves, beach, gravel plains and seasonal pools, Kalba corniche, Fujairah Port beach (for seabird roosts), Ras Dibba

Ras Al Khaimah
Al Jazirah Khor, Rams and Dhaya mangroves and mudflats, Hamraniyah fields and Digdagga area, Wadi Bih

Sharjah
Sharjah Natural History Museum and Desert Park

Umm Al Quwain
Umm Al Quwain corniche, beach and breakwater, Khor Al Umm Al Quwain and Khor Beidah, Dreamland beach, Al Rifaa coastal scrub

Further Reading
See the 'top ten' birds of the UAE under the Natural World section of the book. The Further Reading section is also an excellent source for more detailed information. Refer to the Directory for a tour operator running professional birdwatching tours.

Check out *The Shell Birdwatching Guide to the UAE* for the best birdwatching places, and don't forget your binoculars – a must to fully enjoy this increasingly popular pastime.

Camping Overview

One of the best ways to appreciate living in the UAE is to escape the cities and experience the natural wonders that The Arabian countryside has to offer. Geographically, this is a relatively small country, so even after only a short drive you can leave the stresses of city life far behind.

Although no official campsites exist there are very few problems with camping anywhere in the 'outback'. The weather is rarely bad and basic camping equipment is usually sufficient. The more temperate months between October and April are preferable, but it is still possible to camp during the summer if you choose your campsite carefully. Camping at elevation in the mountains (top of Wadi Bih and Mussandam routes, or Jebel Shams, Oman) will usually mean the temperature being up to five degrees lower than near sea level and you will have a more tolerable night's sleep. At the beginning and end of summer camping near the coast can give a cooling breeze off the sea which makes things more comfortable, although in the middle of summer it gets too humid for this.

For tranquility and solitude there's little that beats a night under the stars. If however, you prefer the idea of a soft bed and satellite TV over a well-inflated Thermarest, check out the hotel list in the Directory section of the book.

Locations

There are numerous areas to camp and few hazards in the UAE, so camping here can be the perfect introduction for first timers or families with children of any age. Safe and comfortable campsites can be found only short distances from tarmac roads, so a 4 WD is not necessarily required.

Choose from the stillness of the desert, the tranquility of a wadi in the mountains or the peacefulness of a site next to a trickling stream in a lush oasis. There are no restrictions on where you can camp, but obviously people's privacy and property (farms and plantations) needs to be respected. While the people you encounter in the countryside are generally friendly and helpful, this doesn't that mean they want you sleeping on their crops or in their grazing area. This is especially true after rains.

If you do end up camping near habitation, or even near other campers if you have no other choice, try to be considerate with the amount of noise you make.

Remember – caution should be taken in or near wadis, especially during the winter months. While the UAE has low rainfall, flash floods are powerful and dangerous. At the first sign of inclement weather, even far off in the distance, pack up and move your campsite if you are anywhere in or near a wadi – it may only be raining in the mountains miles from where you are, but the runoff may flood the wadi you are in.

Camping icons have only been used on the maps to mark the most popular areas for campsites, as you can really camp just about anywhere.

Camping

In general, warm temperatures and very little rain mean you can camp with less equipment and preparation than in other countries. However, during the winter months it can get cold at night, so it is important to pack more rather than less, especially if you are in a 4 WD and have no space issues. Tents aren't always necessary, and sleeping out under the stars has to be tried, especially in the desert. When camping near water, or if you suspect a cold or wet night, a tent is advisable to keep you safe from the elements.

For campfires, try to take firewood from a building site (do ask) or rubbish tip beforehand. Alternatively purchase some from roadside stalls (Dhs.5 -10 per bundle). Wood can sometimes be found in the wild, but never chop down trees unless they are definitely dead. Some trees and plants in this arid climate look as if they are dead or dying due to the low levels of water they get. But they are actually alive, and live trees don't burn well.

The following is a basic list of personal gear that you may want to take with you:

- Tent (to avoid creepy crawlies/heavy dew/rare rain shower/wind/goats)
- Lightweight sleeping bag (or light blankets and sheets)
- Mattress (or air bed)
- Torches and spare batteries (a head torch is a useful investment)
- Cool box
- Water (for drinking and washing)
- Food and drink
- Camping stove, firewood or BBQ and charcoal
- Newspaper to light the fire
- Matches or lighter
- Insect repellent and antihistamine cream
- First aid kit (including any personal medication)
- Sun protection (hats, sunglasses, suncream)
- Warm clothing for cooler evenings
- Toilet roll
- Rubbish bags
- Shisha pipe

Further Information

See the Directory for essentials and various 'toys' to buy. In addition, refer to the Driving section of the book for details on off-road equipment to load into the car. The Directory section of the book details the main shops for buying outdoor supplies in the UAE.

Diving Overview

The waters off the UAE coast are home to a rich variety of marine and coral life, as well as a surprising number of shipwrecks. Not only does this make diving here fascinating, but the warmth of the water and the lack of pollution (relatively speaking) make it possible to dive all year round. You can expect to see some exotic fish (such as clownfish and scorpionfish), and also spotted eagle rays, parrot fish, moray eels, small sharks, barracuda, sea snakes and stingrays. The UAE has two distinctive coastlines: the west coast, covering Abu Dhabi, Dubai and Sharjah, is home to most of the shipwrecks. And the east coast, covering Fujairah, Khorfakkan and Dibba, is where you can some of the most beautiful reef flora and fauna. A third possible dive area is the Mussandam Peninsula, the Oman enclave to the north of the UAE.

Dive Companies

With such interesting diving waters, the UAE has plenty of diving schools and adventure-tourism companies that cater to beginners, intermediates and experienced divers. Various courses are available under the usual international organisations (CMAS, PADI, NAUI, IANTD and HAS).

Abu Dhabi

Many good dive sites are easily accessible from Abu Dhabi. Apart from shallower dives for the less experienced, there are some wreck dives, reef dives and deep-water dives. A good shallow dive (up to a maximum of 12m) is Cement Barge; and deeper dives (over 18m) can be found at MV Hannan, Jasim and Lion City. On most dives you'll see various marine species and coral, and occasionally turtles and sharks. The breakwater off Abu Dhabi island is a good training dive, with plenty of coral and marine life.

Dubai

There are some great dive sites off the coast near Dubai, all easily accessible from the city. Visibility usually ranges from 5-20m, but the construction of The World and The Palm islands has affected some sites close to the coast. However, there are plenty of old favourites that are still highly recommended such as Energy Determination, Turtle Barge and Zainab, as well as new sites like Mariam Express. This wreck only went down in 2006, but has already gained quite a following among Dubai's divers and boasts a variety of fish life. Large barracuda, snappers, pennant fish, jacks and blennies can all be found in the wreck and exploring the contents of the hold.

East Coast

With many different species of coral and marine life, a dive off the UAE's east coast is generally more interesting than a dive in the waters of the sandy Arabian Gulf. Popular dive sites are Martini Rock (a small underwater mountain covered with colourful, soft coral – depth ranges from 3 - 19m) and Car Cemetery (a reef that thrives around a number of old cars sunk into 16m of water). Visibility off the east coast ranges from 5 - 20m.

Mussandam

This area is actually part of the Sultanate of Oman, and is often described as the 'Norway of the Middle East' because of its numerous inlets and sheer cliff faces. It offers some of the most spectacular dive sites in the region. Sheer wall dives with strong currents and clear waters are challenging for advanced divers, while huge bays, calm waters and shallow reefs offer slightly easier dives for intermediates. Visibility ranges from 35-10m.

Whether you're learning to dive or you're a seasoned old salt, the revised and updated 3rd edition of UAE Underwater Explorer is brimful with detailed descriptions of over 60 spectacular dives, stunning photography, maps and all the other practical stuff you need to get you out there.

Written by avid divers who want to share their knowledge with others, the *Underwater Explorer* includes all the crucial information diving enthusiasts need to know about diving in the UAE.

Environmental Action Overview

We all share responsibility for caring for the environment. The basic steps to making a difference are simple. In the UAE, off-roaders currently have the freedom to travel almost anywhere in the countryside – but this level of access depends on off-road enthusiasts being cautious, respectful and responsible.

• Wherever possible, travel on existing tracks. It's not just the visible flora and fauna that needs protection, but also the sensitive seeds, bulbs and wildlife that lie on or just below the surface. This delicate ecosystem lies dormant for long periods, springing into life after sufficient rain and providing much-needed food for inhabitants of harsh environments.

• In the desert, avoid what little plant life there is (this is better for your car too – desert plants often have roots that extend extremely deep into the ground in search of water, and as a result they are fixed very firmly in place). There is lots of sand but only a few plants, so you should have no trouble picking a route that avoids any damage to ground vegetation.

• Never throw litter from your vehicle or leave rubbish behind – when you are packing up after a picnic or a camping trip make sure you pack your rubbish as well. Apart from the harm it can do to wildlife, nobody wants to arrive at their favourite spot to find it covered with litter left by the previous inhabitants.

• Respect private property and the rights of others to enjoy their activities undisturbed. In remote areas keep your distance from people's homes and private land, remembering that what might look like an abandoned home could be a summer home or store house. When camping in the mountains, if you stumble upon a perfect, flat area for setting up tent, it is possibly cultivated fields for animal crops. It is difficult enough to grow viable crops in this harsh climate without having campers trample over or pitch tents on arable land.

People in rural areas tend to be more conservative, so adapt your dress and behaviour appropriately.

• Remember that excessive noise is offensive and it scares wildlife, so keep it down!

• Graded tracks should be used with caution and at slow speeds. Bumpy, gravel surfaces and unexpected twists and turns make it dangerous to drive at high speeds. Slow down for oncoming vehicles to minimise the risk of loose stones flying up and shattering windscreens. Slow down for hikers and cyclists, who won't be too pleased when they are showered with stones and dust as you race past. And to avoid surprises, always assume that a wayward goat is standing in the middle of the road around the next corner!

Take Action

Awareness of environmental issues in the UAE is growing slowly but surely. But there is always more that could be done by all sections of the community. Today's schools incorporate environmental awareness into their education programmes, but many adults continue to set bad examples by dropping litter and being wasteful. There are increasing numbers of recycling points around the UAE, and so there is little excuse for not recycling your paper, plastic and glass.

Environmental Groups

In addition to action on a personal level, there are also various groups in the UAE that exist to protect the environment and the natural world, and educate and inform the public. Most environmental groups are run by volunteers, and operate on a non-profit basis without government support. Organisations such as the Emirates Environmental Group always need more support in the form of helpers, funds and new members.

Go on, do your bit!

Emirates Bird Records Committee

They keep records of all sightings, as well as monitor numbers and breeding programmes.

(www.uaeinteract.com/nature)

Emirates Diving Association (EDA)

The EDA runs dynamic education programmes that promote protection of the environment.

(www.emiratesdiving.com)

Emirates Environmental Group (EEG)

This active group provides education on general environmental awareness and recycling, and they organise various environmental drives and clean-up operations.

(www.eeg-uae.org)

Environment Friends Society

A society that promotes protection of the environment through research and education programmes.

Environment Agency - Abu Dhabi

Previously known as Environmental Research and Wildlife Development Agency (ERWDA), the Environment Agency assists the Abu Dhabi Government with conservation and management of the UAE's natural environment, resources, wildlife and biological diversity.

(www.erwda.gov.ae)

Natural History Group

This group holds regular talks on topics relating to fauna, flora and archaeology. They keep a record of sightings of rare plants and animals.

Environmentl Action

Hiking Overview

While the area around the west coast is mostly flat with sandy desert and sabkha (salt-flats), there are areas inland that are a paradise for the adventurous hiker. To the north, the Ru'us Al Jibal Mountains contain the highest peaks in the area at around 2,000 metres. To the east, the impressive Hajar Mountains form the border between the UAE and Oman, stretching from the Mussandam Peninsula north of Ras Al Khaimah to the Empty Quarter desert, several hundred kilometres to the south.

WARNING

No mountain rescue services exist, therefore anyone venturing into the mountains should be reasonably experienced or be with someone who knows the area. Tragedies have occurred in the past. Consider yourself forewarned.

Terrain

Hiking in the UAE is completely different to what most people expect or are used to. There are hardly any established tracks, apart from either goat trails or rough paths between settlements, and there is often little shade or relief from the constant sun. Rocks and boulders are sharp and often unstable, the general terrain often heavily eroded and shattered due to the harsh climate, so much of the time is spent watching where you are walking. In addition, no signposts, combined with a lack of distinguishable features, can make it difficult to orientate yourself. However, having said this, once you become more

Hikes Covered

	Route	
Northern Emirates		
Jebel Qihwi (1792m)	Wadi Bih	(p.52)
Jebel Bil 'Aysh (1930m)	Stairway to Heaven	(p.42)
Jungle Book/Wadi Luwayb	Wadi Bih	(p.52)
Stairway to Heaven	Stairway to Heaven	(p.42)
Ainee Village Hike	Wadi Bih	(p.52)
Hibs Village Hike	Wadi Bih	(p.52)
Quick Hike to Plateau	Wadi Bih	(p.52)
East Coast Hike	Wadi Bih	(p.52)
Hatta Area		
Jebel Hatta (1311m)	Hatta Road Route	(p.128)
Jebel Rawdah (845m)	Hatta Road Route	(p.128)
Jebel Sumayni (1073m)	Ray	(p.152)
Al Ain Area		
Hanging Gardens	Hanging Gardens	(p.180)
Jebel Qatar Ridge Hike	Hanging Gardens	(p.180)
East Coast Area		
Hike from Wadi Madhah	Wadi Madhah & Shis	(p.102)
Hike along wadi	Wadi Wurrayah	(p.110)
Hike above falls	Wadi Wurrayah	(p.110)

experienced and accustomed to the local environment, your perceptions change, and you will find it easier to recognise different rocks and trees, and simpler to navigate.

Hikes can range from short, easy walks leading to spectacular viewpoints to difficult, exposed, all-day treks. Many of the routes follow centuries-old Bedouin and Shihuh trails through the mountains. Some of these are still used for access to a few of the more remote settlements that are still inhabited. Some of the terrain is incredible and you can only wonder at the skills of the hardy mountain people who pioneered the trails.

We strongly advise that you purchase, and learn how to use, a simple GPS (Global Positioning System) receiver. You can then confidently plot the position of your car (or your starting point) every time you are out. You should then have no difficulty wandering all day and then finding a route back to your car.

REMEMBER...

- Be prepared and be sensible - let someone know where you are going.
- Don't underestimate the strength of the sun — take sunblock, hats, glasses and wear long sleeves and trousers if you're particularly vulnerable or you'll be out for particularly long periods.
- Take far more water than you think you'll need. You'll probably end up using it all!
- Personal hydration systems are excellent for allowing you to keep drinking on the go.
- Take a compass and preferably a GPS and if possible, someone who is familiar with the area.
- Take some food for energy. Salt can sometimes be needed to replace body salts lost by sweating.
- Be especially careful in wadis during the wet season; dangerous flash floods can flood a wadi in seconds.
- Basic first aid kit and fully charged mobile!
- Stout walking boots or shoes (necessary for the uneven terrain and loose rock).
- Have FUN ...

Routes

For the nearest hiking to the cities, you should explore the Hajar Mountains. Just turn off the road onto any track you like the look of, and start climbing! For specific routes described in more detail within this guide, see the list of 'Hikes Covered' on the opposite page. The mountains will certainly not disappoint, and the further off the beaten track you go the more likely you are to find interesting villages where people live much as they have for centuries.

Further Information

For further information on hiking in the UAE, contact Hiking@Explorer-Publishing.com

The Directory section of the book details the main shops for buying outdoor supplies in the UAE, as well as online from international retailers.

Mountain Biking Overview

Opportunities for mountain biking in the UAE are plentiful and extremely varied; from straightforward terrain for beginners to highly technical, bone jarring gnarly for the experts. The beauty of mountain biking is that it's possible to see, and really feel, some of the most remote places that are inaccessible even by 4 WD. Areas for rides include the Hajar mountains, their passes, and the foothills extending all the way from Ras Al Khaimah in the north to Hatta and further south, with some possibilities near Al Ain.

Heat and humidity mean that less committed mountain bikers prefer to ride during the cooler months between November and April, but the hardcore few ride all through the summer. If you time your ride for the last few hours of daylight, while not exactly 'pleasant', it can be cooler and easier to ride in than the middle of the day.

Warning – No off-road rescue services exist. Consider yourself forewarned.

Terrain

For hardcore mountain bikers there is a good range of terrain, from super technical rocky trails in areas like Fili and Siji to mountain routes like Wadi Bih, which climb to over 1,000m and can be descended in minutes. The riding is mainly all rocky, technical and challenging, but rides purely on 4 WD tracks can be found for less experienced riders. There are many tracks to follow and, if you look hard, some interesting singletrack can be found.

REMEMBER...

- Be prepared and be sensible – if you're planning an epic, let someone know where you are going.
- Carry far more water than you think you'll need. You'll probably end up using it all!
- Personal hydration systems are excellent for allowing you to keep drinking on the go.
- Take a GPS if possible, or someone who is familiar with the area.
- Take some snacks for energy. Salt can sometimes be needed to replace body salts lost by sweating.
- Be especially careful in wadis during the wet season; dangerous flash floods can flood a wadi in seconds.
- Basic first aid kit and fully charged mobile!
- Falling off on rocky terrain can be very painful.
- Helmets and proper gear are essential.
- Puncture repair kit — save yourself a long walk!
- Basic tool kit.

Mountain Biking Areas

Jebel Ali
A great place for training rides, with reasonable climbs and some good technical sections. Close to town. Start at the entrance to Etisalat satellite station.

Fili
For easy loops, technical singletrack, and good scenery, turn east off the Madam-Dhaid Road into the low mountains, and saddle up at the Fili dam car park.

Hatta
Either an easy out and back route to the pools (Route 12 p.144), or head for the Hatta-Kalba road into the mountains (p.134), off of which there are numerous options for off-road loops.

Siji
A good place to explore, with countless options of snaking trails across rolling hills. Start near Siji crusher, just south of the E88 near Siji Eppco.

Masafi Plantations
One of the best areas in the Emirates with technical singletrack, rolling 4 WD tracks, great scenery and an excellent finish through the leafy plantations. Start at Masafi.

Wadi Sana
A steep, very demanding climb of 500m takes you to the plateau, where you can rest before the five-minute descent back down – the best downhill in the country.

Wadi Bih
A long demanding point-to-point ride with an 800m climb in the middle and a long fast descent out to the east coast.

Masafi-Fujairah Road to Wadi Madhah
A great point-to-point route over the mountains to the east coast, with a side trip to the pools at the end of Wadi Shis Start near Dafta.

Jebel Hafeet
A tough, tarmac climb of 800m rewards you with stunning 360 degree views and an exciting race back down.

Routes
Basically, you can hop onto your mountain bike anywhere, or follow any of the wadi routes covered in this guide. Depending on your technical ability and fitness, you can follow existing trails or go cross-country through wadis or along goat tracks... the possibilities are endless. See the list of areas worth checking out to the left for descriptions of the kind of riding that can be found.

Further Information
For more information on mountain biking in the Emirates, contact Pete@Explorer-Publishing.com

The Directory section of the book details the main shops for buying outdoor supplies and biking gear as well as online international retailers.

Rock Climbing Overview

Despite the shattered appearance of most of the mountains in the UAE, excellent rock climbing can be found in a number of locations, particularly near Ras Al Khaimah and the Al Ain/Buraimi areas. By choosing your crags carefully, it's possible to climb all year round — even in summer when daytime air temperatures approach 50°C (120°F).

Routes

To date more than 200 routes have been climbed and named. These vary from short 'juggy' routes to heart-pumping, finger jamming delights, guaranteed to separate the men from the boys! New routes are generally climbed on sight with traditional protection. There is also a profusion of boulder problems to exhaust yourself on.

WARNING

No mountain rescue services exist, so anyone venturing into the mountains should be basically competent, even if they do not climb to a high standard.

Routes range from (British) Very Severe, up to extreme grades (E5). Due to the nature of the rock, some climbs can feel more difficult than their technical grade would suggest, with loose rock and poor belays making them unsuitable for total novices. However, there are some excellent easier routes for new climbers, especially in Wadi Bih and Wadi Khab Al Shamis. A few areas have been developed a little for sport climbing with a number of routes bolted where protection would otherwise be a problem.

Clubs

No formal climbing or mountaineering clubs exist in the UAE, but an effective grapevine means that new or visiting climbers can generally be pointed in the right direction. If you wish to meet like-minded people, there always seems to be someone doing something in Wadi Bih each weekend. Or the Pharaohs Club at the Pyramids, Wafi City in Dubai has the only indoor climbing wall in the country and is a good place to hook up with other climbers. You can either train at public sessions or new climbers can register for an introductory course with a professional instructor.

To get crimping and slapping, contact the Pharaohs Club in Dubai, or the 'Lord of Ras Al Khaimah', John Gregory (see Directory).

The Directory section of the book also details the options for buying outdoor supplies, however, climbing gear available is very limited, with just a small amount on sale at the climbing wall in the Pyramids and Picnico in Jumeira. Most climbers bring equipment from there home countries or source it online. If you plan on heading further afield, the guidebook *Rock Climbing in Oman* by RA McDonald (Apex Publishing 1993, London/Oman), covers routes in Oman, most within an easy drive of the UAE, and check out the **Oman Off-Road Explorer**, for help on how to get there. This guide, the sister publication to the **UAE Off-Road Explorer**, has 26 adventurous routes into the huge and magnificent scenery of Oman, and information on all the activities which can be enjoyed there.

REMEMBER...

• Take all your own gear. And bring it all back with you!

• With all the loose rock around, a helmet is advisable, particularly if you are climbing an unfamiliar area.

• Some food and water for energy (you can normally park your car at the base of the crag you are climbing, so don't worry about packing everything into a rucksack).

• Sunblock.

• There is no mountain rescue service, so be prudent.

Further Reading
For detailed information on climbing in the UAE, a guide is available on CD-ROM format called *United Arab Emirates – A Climbers Guide*, featuring over 500 routes on 50 separate crags, with over 100 maps and photo-diagrams. First released in 2003, it was updated in early 2005. It is currently only available by mail order from the UK for £13.50, including postage to the UAE. Contact Alan Stark at alstark@blueyonder.co.uk for more details.

Off-Road Biking Overview

Introduction

While it is no doubt a potentially dangerous sport, off-road biking is exciting and enjoyable, and many of the routes will take you places not easily accessible in a 4 WD. Riding in desert sand is a lot different to riding on a conventional motocross track, and it will be a long time before you can 'read' the desert and become familiar with the reaction of your bike in various sand types. Your first experience of riding in the sand is a little scary as the sand grabs the tyres, which makes you feel very unstable, especially at low speeds. If you do come to a stop, don't pull away when sitting otherwise the bike can bog down.

Not all sand will give the same ride, but you will learn to know the difference between hard sand and

soft, powdery sand, which is sometimes hard to spot and can be quite dangerous if you are not expecting it. You'll be able to identify hard-packed sand by ridges or grooves on either side of the dunes. Another clue to the texture of the sand is the colour. One of the most important rules to remember when riding in the desert is never to ride hell-for-leather over a dune without knowing what is on the other side. There may be something unexpected, like a sudden drop, a quarry or a happy family enjoying a nice Friday picnic, and by the time you've shot over the top of the dune, there's little you can do about it. If you don't like hospital food, dunes should always be approached by going up at an angle, so that you can check what lies ahead and choose your

descent based on any obstacles in your path. Another hazard to watch out for is 'camel grass' – these are hard mounds of sand with bunches of grass growing through them – and while they should be dodged by inexperienced riders they are good fun to jump over once mastered.

Routes

There are many different routes to choose from when riding through the desert. Off-road biking is quite a social sport and there are large groups of riders who usually depart from fixed points and follow set routes, especially on weekends. When planning your route, you need to ensure that you will have access to fuel and water at regular intervals. Common rides are from the Al Awir army camp (GPS coordinates 25° 11.658N 055° 36.105E) to Fossil Rock (GPS coordinates 25° 08.192N 055° 40.630E), which is around 30km; or from the army camp to cattle grid (GPS coordinates 25° 01.427N 055° 40.630E), which is about the same distance. You can ride the triangle and cover all three points in one ride, and this works out to be about 100km depending on what route you take and how many times you get lost!

A popular spot to stop for a play-around is at a huge dune known as the Nosebleed: the drop from the top will take your breath away, but the views are amazing especially in the morning or late evening. It is very close to Fossil Rock and is a good chance to practise your skills on some really challenging dunes. There are lots of 'bowls' that you can whizz around, as if you were riding around the inside of a glass.

On any of these routes you can choose between taking the sand tracks, which are used by 4 WDs, or riding over the camel grass or through the dunes. It is not recommended to ride out alone, and you can easily get lost even if you are only a couple of kilometres away from the nearest road. If you lose your group, try not to create any fresh tracks, but just get to the top of the nearest, tallest dune.

Kit

The basic kit needed for off-road biking really varies on the safety needs of each rider and the amount of money he is prepared to spend to avoid a spell in hospital should he lose his concentration. However the following items are highly recommended, and should be seen as necessary items for beginners: A good helmet, goggles, a chest protector (preferably with built-in elbow protection and back support), a Camelbak, a pair of boots, and as you usually land on your knees, a pair of knee guards. A note about Camelbaks: these are backpacks containing a 'bladder' which you fill with water, connected to a pipe long enough to reach your mouth. They are very popular with cyclists, hikers and bikers, as you don't need to stop to have a drink of water. Since most off-road biking is done between set points, and you are never more than one hour away from your next rest point where you can get more fuel and water, the smaller your Camelbak the better. You shouldn't carry additional weight (particularly to over 45C) if you can avoid it, and an extra litre or two of water strapped to your back is going to drain extra energy. Therefore a one-litre Camelbak is recommended for most off-road biking; if you have a specially modified bike and are doing longer distances between fuel stops, then obviously you will need to take more water with you.

Riding pants and a shirt can be bought later, although as they usually allow for better air circulation and can keep you cool in hot climates, they are worth the investment. Kit can be purchased from a few outlets, but Sandstorm Motorcycles in Al Quoz (04 339 5608) is a good one-stop shop. It is a good idea to have a GPS into which you can enter the coordinates of the destinations available. You can buy your GPS unit from the bike shops, but Carrefour, Plug-Inns and other electronics shops generally have a wider range.

Second-hand bikes can be bought at Motorcycle City and KTM on the Hatta Road Highway or Sandstorm Motorcycles on Sheikh Zayed Road. If you are looking to buy a new bike, you'll find Honda, Yamaha, KTM and Suzuki all have dealerships here, stocking the most recent models. Second-hand dealers will also take care of maintenance for you at reasonable prices. Unless you want to ride around your neighbourhood forever, you will need to get a trailer at some stage. A bike trailer does not need lights or registration plates, and can be custom-made to suit your needs (ie one bike, two bikes, bike + quad, etc). You can order your trailer from Al Bawaba Al Zahabiya in Rashidiya (tel 285 2111 or mob 050 456 4205), and it usually takes a few days to make.

The UAE Desert Challenge

This rally is a professional event, and as it is near the end of the annual rally schedule, it is an important fixture for top riders competing for the championship. It is one of the only rallies in the world where amateurs are allowed to compete in the same event as professionals. However, not just anybody can do it: it is a gruelling challenge of 1,900km over some of the region's

harshest terrain. As an amateur competitor, you will need a lot of preparation and hard training to be able to complete the race, as well as an experienced back-up team of seconds and mechanics. The five-day event attracts participants from around the world, and usually happens in November every year. For more information on the Challenge, visit www.uaedesertchallenge.com.

SAFETY

There are several non-negotiable safety rules that you should follow when riding:

- Never ride alone. Riding out in a group is not only more sociable, it is essential for your safety.
- If you lose your group, head for the nearest, tallest dune. Make as few new tracks as possible, so that if your riding buddies try to find you they don't embark on a wild goose chase along dead-end tracks.
- Never speed up a dune and over the top unless you have checked what's on the other side. Many a rider has landed in a ditch, or some other hazard, with numerous broken bones.
- Don't try and do too much too soon: it takes time to learn how your bike will cope with different types of sand, so wait until you can 'read' the sand before you go racing across the desert.
- Wear the correct kit. At the very least you will need a good quality helmet, chest protection, elbow and knee protection, and boots.
- If you get lost, a GPS can mean the difference between being home in time for Friday brunch or spending a long, hot, miserable day (and night) in the desert. If you're a regular rider, get one.
- Keep your eyes peeled at all times for camels, goats, and of course, 4 WDs.

Discover new lands…

Navigate the seas…

Explore the skies…

Let **GARMIN** lead the way.

The world is your playground with Garmin GPS. With revolutionary satellite technology, you'll feel at home in places you've never visited before. For the latest Aviation, Marine and Land GPS technology, visit us at Adcom. It's where, every GPS comes with guaranteed after sales service, extensive product knowledge and a friendly face always ready to answer your queries. So to find your way around the world, find your way to us.

 **GARMIN** ® Visit us at: Lafzaeyya Towers, New Souq, Opposite Omeir Travel Agency, Khalifa Street, Abu Dhabi. Tel: +971 2 6224467 E-mail: adcomshr@emirates.net.ae GPS Location: N 24° 29.348' E 054° 21.420'

ADCOM *Advanced Communication Systems*

First Aid

Jeep

First Aid Overview

With some planning and common sense, you should hopefully never have any serious problems while outdoors. However, accidents DO happen. The following are some basic pointers on how to cope under the most unfortunate of circumstances (whether governed by accidents or by the laws of nature). However, for the fuller picture, refer to an approved first aid book, since the wrong approach can create further injury.

In many cases treatment will simply involve reassuring the victim and taking basic measures to prevent any further trauma while getting to the nearest hospital. For less dramatic incidents it may be advisable for the casualty to visit a doctor on their return to 'civilisation'.

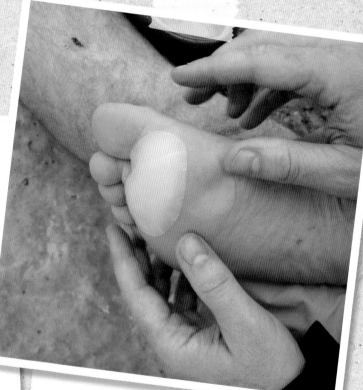

First Aid

Hospitals

In less critical circumstances, you may find treatment at one of Dubai's private hospitals more reassuring. If time is of the essence aim for the nearest hospital. (See Directory - Hospitals on p.320). In the meantime, uninjured parties can create a beneficial atmosphere of confidence and reassurance by:

- Being in control of both yourself and the problem.
- Acting calmly and logically.
- Being gentle but firm, both with your hands and by speaking to the casualty kindly, but purposefully.

Abrasions, Cuts and Wounds

Cause Trauma leading to a break in the skin. (see three types of symptoms below)

Symptom-1 Minor bleeding.

Action

- First wash your hands thoroughly.
- Rinse the wound under clean running water.
- Pat dry with a sterile swab or clean tissue.
- Clean the skin around the wound by wiping away from the wound, using a clean swab for each stroke.
- Pat dry and cover with a plaster or adhesive dressing.

Symptom-2 Severe bleeding.

Action

- Remove clothing to expose the wound.
- Apply direct pressure to the wound with your fingers or hand, preferably over something sterile, for at least 10 minutes.
- If there is an object protruding, apply pressure either side of it.
- Lay the person down and raise the injured area to decrease blood flow to the wound.
- Leave any sterile dressing you may have been pressing on in place and bandage the wound firmly. Make sure that the bandage is not too tight as to impede circulation.

Survival Hamper

- **Aches & Pains** Paracetamol (such as Panadol) Avoid aspirin or Ibuprofen.
- **Sprains** Ace bandage, ice-pack.
- **Insect bites** Aspivenin vacuum pump. After-bite stick or xylocaine ointment. Antihistamine tablets in case of allergic reaction.
- **Other bites** One roll of strong, wide bandage to apply splint.
- **Cuts & Wounds** Adhesive dressing & tape, plasters, antiseptic cream.
- **Dehydration** Salt sachet (e.g. Dioralyte), isotonic drinks, water.
- **Eyes** Sterile eye pad.
- **Marine stings** Vinegar, sodium bicarbonate, powdered meat tenderiser or any powder.
- **General** Scissors, sterile or saline water, tweezers.
- **Personal medication**
- An up-to-date tetanus vaccination.

- If the bleeding seeps through, bandage another layer firmly over the last.
- Get to a doctor as soon as possible.

Symptom-3 An object protruding from a wound.

Action

- Small pieces of grit or glass can be either rinsed or picked out of the wound.
- Do not remove larger embedded objects; you can easily cause further tissue damage and bleeding.
- Control bleeding by applying pressure on either side of the protruding object and by raising the wounded area.

- Bandage the wound by either padding or working around the object. This will minimise the risk of infection.

Breaks and Fractures

Cause   A sudden blow usually incurred while slipping or falling.

Symptoms   Pain and tenderness.

Action

Arms:
- Support the injured arm across the chest.
- If necessary, expose and treat any wound.
- Make a sling to support the arm.
- Take the patient to hospital in a sitting position.

Legs:
- Help the casualty to lie down - gently steady and support the injured leg.
- If necessary, expose and treat any wound.
- Gently straighten the leg by pulling in the line of the shin.
- Splint the injured leg to the good leg by bandaging at the knees and ankles and either side of the fracture. Insert padding, such as a blanket, in between the legs. Bandage firmly, avoiding any jerky movements.

Burns and Sun Related Casualties

Burns

Cause   Dancing too close to the campfire!

Symptoms   Searing pain, redness, inflammation and possible blistering.

Action
- Cool the burnt area with cold water for about ten minutes to stop the burning and relieve the pain. If you have no cold water, any other cold liquid like milk or canned drinks will do the job.
- Remove any clothing or jewellery from the area before it starts to swell.
- Cover with a sterile dressing (even a polythene bag or kitchen film makes a good temporary dressing).
- Never break a blister - you are likely to encourage infection.

Dehydration

Cause   Not drinking enough (your body is already mildly dehydrated by the time you feel thirsty - you need to drink before you even feel the need).

Symptoms   Dizziness, headache, tingling sensation on the skin, goose bumps.

Action
- Rest the affected person in a cool place and replenish lost fluids and salts.
- Isotonic glucose drinks are good, as are the special replacement fluids available in powder form.
- A good substitute is a teaspoon of salt and five teaspoons of sugar mixed with a litre of water or diluted orange juice.

Heat Exhaustion

Cause   Loss of water and salt from the body as a result of excessive sweating. It usually develops gradually, and generally affects those unused to a hot and humid environment.

Symptoms   Headache, dizziness, nausea and confusion. Pale, clammy and sweaty skin. Cramps. Accelerated, weakening pulse and breathing.

Action
- Move the afflicted person to the coolest place available. Lie them down with their legs raised and supported.
- Replace lost fluid by offering small sips of a weak salt solution. Use either the specialised solutions or one teaspoon of salt per litre of water.

Heatstroke

Cause   Prolonged exposure to very hot conditions, or illness involving a high fever. The body no longer regulates its temperature normally.

Symptoms   Headache, dizziness, restlessness, confusion. Hot, flushed and dry skin. A hammering pulse and deterioration in the level of response. Body temperature of 40°C (104°F), or more. This can lead to unconsciousness in minutes.

Action
- Move the afflicted person to the coolest place available and remove all outer clothing.
- Wrap them in a cold, wet sheet, keeping it constantly damp.
- Once their temperature has dropped to 38°C (100.4°F) replace the wet sheet with a dry one and observe constantly. Be prepared to repeat the process if their temperature begins to rise again.
- Get to a doctor as soon as possible.

Sunburn

Cause   Over-exposure to the sun.

Symptoms   Redness, itching and tenderness. Blisters in extreme cases.

Action
- Move the afflicted person to the coolest place available.
- Sponge with cold water.
- Give frequent sips of cold drinks.
- Apply after-sun lotion, calamine aloe vera or yoghurt to soothe mild burns.
- For extensive blistering or skin damage, go to a doctor.

Obstruction in the Eye

Cause   A foreign body lodged in the eye.

Symptoms   Blurred vision, discomfort, redness, watering of the eye.

Action
- Do not rub the eye!
- Separate the lids and examine the eye thoroughly.
- If you can see a foreign body, wash it out with clean water.
- If this does not work, lift it off the eye using a damp swab or tissue.
- Do not touch anything sticking to or embedded in the eyeball. Cover the injured eye with an eye pad and then bandage both eyes firmly to prevent movement.
- Get to hospital as soon as possible.

Bites, Stings and Poisons

The UAE's flora and fauna does not hold many nasty surprises, and only a few plants and animals need to be treated or approached with special care.

Poisonous creatures need their poison to kill their prey and since humans are too large a prey for them, they will try to avoid using it needlessly. Some plants can cause problems through ingestion or as a skin irritant. If you are out and about with children it is useful to learn which plants to keep them away from.

Strangely enough, the small black ant has caused the largest number of fatalities in the UAE over the last 15 years.

Black Ants

While for most people a bite by a black ant may cause redness and itching, for those who are allergic to its poison, anaphylactic shock or Quincke's edema (swelling of the throat) can be rapidly fatal.

While you are unlikely to develop these serious reactions from a first bite, allergic people usually have a much stronger reaction than non-allergic people do. In these cases, it's advisable to carry an allergy kit consisting of an adrenaline injection and antihistamine tablets. It has been suggested that those who are allergic to poison ivy are definitely at risk of a severe allergic reaction to a bite from this ant.

Plants

Cause	Ingestion of poisonous plants.

Iphiona aucheri; a yellow composite with thick succulent leaves that grows along the track that leads from the Dubai-Hatta road to Mahdah. It only arrived in this area in the 1980s and during the first two years many camels died after eating it. Now the camels have learned to avoid it.

Nerium oleander and *Rhazya stricta* are both from the same family. They are very common, the former in wadis and the latter on gravel plains. All parts of the plants are poisonous. This fact is obviously known by domestic and wild animals as the plants are never grazed.

Ricinus communis, the castor oil plant, is more rare. The pretty seeds of this plant are very poisonous (only one would prove fatal if eaten by a child). Oil that is pressed from these seeds is used as a laxative; its poison obviously weakened in the extraction process, but still enough of an irritant to get lazy bowels to move!

Symptoms	Vomiting, loss of consciousness, impaired breathing.

Action
- Make sure that the airway is clear.
- Try to identify the plant and which part of it has been eaten. Keep pieces of the plant and any vomited material to show the doctor.
- Get to a doctor as soon as possible (they can contact an international poison centre if necessary).
- Do not try to induce vomiting as this may harm the person even further.

Puncture Wounds – Marine Life

Cause	Puncture wounds by a sea urchin or spiny fish.
Symptoms	Redness, swelling and a painful local reaction.

Action
- Soak the area in water as hot as the person can stand for at least 30 minutes. But be careful not to add a scalding to their injuries!
- Do not pull out any spines that may still be protruding. Go to hospital to have these removed.

Scorpions

Cause	The large black scorpion of the sands and the small yellow scorpion of rocky habitats and plantations are the most common. Both can inject strong poison and cause nasty symptoms, but fatalities are rare.
Symptoms	Pain and numbness at the site of the sting. Drowsiness and disturbances of salivation in mild cases, haemorrhages and convulsions in severe cases.

Action
- Place a firm bandage over the affected limb (a splint will help prevent movement).
- Do not apply a tourniquet, cut or suction the bite wound. This does not help and can make things worse.
- Do not apply ice. The reactive dilation of the blood vessels when the ice is removed causes the venom to spread more rapidly around the body.
- There is no anti-venom and treatment is symptomatic. Symptoms subside within three hours. Go to hospital for more severe cases.

Snakes

Cause	Poisonous vipers can be distinguished by their thicker bodies and triangular head, which is separated from the body by a clearly visible neck. They move more slowly than other snakes. They

leave a characteristic track in sand - a series of slanted parallel lines. Their poison is dangerous, but not every bite injects poison.

Symptoms   A pair of puncture marks and severe pain at the site of the bite, redness, swelling, nausea, vomiting, laboured breathing, disturbed vision, increased salivation and sweating.

Action
- Lay the victim down and keep them calm and still.
- Bandage the affected limb firmly (a splint will help prevent movement).
- Until treatment is given, nothing should be ingested because of the risk of vomiting.
- Do not apply a tourniquet, cut or suction the bite wound. This does not help and can make things worse.
- Do not apply ice. The reactive dilation of the blood vessels when the ice is removed causes the venom to spread more rapidly around the body.
- Try to identify the snake. In the UAE there are only four species of dangerous vipers so the location of the accident, the colour of the snake and a description of its head and markings will help to ensure that the correct anti-venom is used.
- Do not try to catch or kill the snake - further bites might be incurred.
- Go to the nearest hospital.

Spiders

Cause   All spiders are poisonous, but few can inflict harm to humans. In the UAE, the only spider to stay away from is the Australian Redback or Black Widow spider (*Latrodectus sp.*), which occurs in urban gardens and the desert. It is easily recognisable by the bright red mark on its abdomen.

Camel spiders are not dangerous, despite their aggressive appearance!

Symptoms   Swelling, pain spreading over large parts of the body, shock, fever, nausea, headache,

sweating and a rise in blood pressure. Breathing can become difficult. The greatest risk is for small children.

Action
- The bite is not felt, but noticed later when the wound starts to swell.
- All symptoms disappear within 48 hours and are treated as they appear.

Stings - Bee, Wasp, Hornet

Cause   Bee, wasp or hornet sting.

Symptoms   Stinging and swelling.

Action
- Remove the sting with tweezers or scrape it out with the edge of a knife. Be careful not to apply pressure to the poison sac.
- Apply ice or something cold to relieve pain and swelling.
- For a sting in the mouth, give the victim ice to suck while you get to the nearest hospital. This is a very dangerous situation, as the swelling can rapidly obstruct the airway.

Stings - Marine Life

Cause   Stings by jellyfish, stingrays, coral, anemones, etc.

Symptoms   Redness, swelling and great discomfort.

Action
- Pour vinegar over the sting for a few minutes to prevent stinging cells from firing.
- Apply a paste of sodium bicarbonate (baking soda), mixed with equal parts of water, to the sting.
- Dust the area with meat tenderiser (this contains papain, which can inactivate venom) or any dry powder.
- If you don't carry vinegar, baking powder or meat tenderiser to the beach, apply fresh urine to the area.
- If the injuries are severe or there are signs of a possible allergic reaction (such as difficulty in breathing), get to a hospital as soon as possible.

Extra Info

Jeep

Extra Info

Directory

Activities

Amusement Parks
Al Ain	Hili Fun City	03 784 5542
Dubai	Fruit & Garden Luna Park	04 337 1234
	WonderLand Theme & Water Park	04 324 3222
UAQ	Dreamland Aqua Park	06 768 1888

Aviation
Fujairah	Fujairah Aviation Centre	09 222 4747
UAQ	Umm Al Quwain Aeroclub	06 768 1447

Birdwatching Groups
Dubai	Birdwatching Tours	050 650 3398

Camel Riding
Al Ain	Al Ain Camel Safaris	03 768 8006
Dubai	Mushrif Park	04 288 3624
	WonderLand Theme & Water Park	04 324 1222
	Orient Tours	04 282 8238

Canoeing
Dubai	Desert Rangers	04 340 2408
	Jebel Ali Sailing Club	04 399 5444
Fujairah	Beach Hut, The	09 244 5050
RAK	Al Hamra Fort Hotel	07 244 6666

Climbing
Dubai	Desert Rangers	04 340 2408
	Pharaohs Club	04 324 0000
RAK	John Gregory (Active Climber)	050 647 7120

Cycling
Dubai	Dubai Roadsters	04 339 4453

Desert Driving Courses
Dubai	Al Futtaim Training Centre	04 285 0455
	Desert Rangers	04 340 2408
	Emirates Driving Institute	04 263 1100
	Off-Road Adventures	04 343 2288
	Voyagers Xtreme	04 345 4504

Diving
Abu Dhabi	Abu Dhabi Sub Aqua Club	02 673 1111
	Blue Dolphin Company LLC	02 666 9392
	Golden Boats	02 665 9119
	Sirenia	02 645 4512
	Sun & Sand Sports	02 674 6299
Ajman	Ajman Kempinski Hotel & Resort	02 745 1555
Dubai	Al Boom Diving	02 342 2993
	Emirates Diving Association	04 393 9390
	Pavilion Dive Centre, The	04 406 8827
	Scuba Dubai	04 331 7433
	Scubatec	04 334 8988
Fujairah	Sandy Beach Diving Centre	09 244 5050
	Scuba 2000	09 238 8477
	Scuba International	09 222 0060
	East Coast Outdoor Activities	050 649 9858
Sharjah	7 Seas Divers	06 238 7400
	Divers Down	06 237 0299
	Sharjah Wanderers Dive Club	06 566 2105

Dune Buggy Riding
Dubai	Desert Rangers	04 340 2408
	Orient Tours	04 282 8238

Flying
Dubai	Dubai Flying Association	04 351 9691
	Emirates Flying School	04 299 5155

Fujairah	Fujairah Aviation Centre	09 222 4747		RAK	Ras Al Khaimah Shooting Club	07 236 3622
UAQ	Umm Al Quwain Aeroclub	06 768 1447				

Hashing

Abu Dhabi	Abu Dhabi Island HHH	02 404 8325
	Mainland Hash House Harriers	02 665 5893
Al Ain	Al Ain Hash House Harriers	050 663 1745
Dubai	Barbie Hash House	04 348 4210
	Creek Hash House Harriers	050 451 5847
	Desert Hash House Harriers	050 454 2635
	Moonshine Hash House Harriers	050 452 3094

Hiking

Dubai	Desert Rangers	04 340 2408
	Explorer	Hiking@Explorer-Publishing.com

Horse Riding

Abu Dhabi	Abu Dhabi Equestrian Club	02 445 5500
Al Ain	Inter-Con Al Ain Riding Stables	03 768 6686
Dubai	Club Joumana	04 883 6000
	Emirates Riding Centre	04 336 1394
	Jebel Ali Equestrian Club	04 884 5485
Hatta	Hatta Fort Hotel	04 852 3211
Jebel Ali	Club Joumana	04 883 6000
Sharjah	Sharjah Equestrian & Racing Club	06 531 1155

Hot Air Ballooning

Dubai	Voyagers Xtreme	04 345 4504

Moto-Cross

Dubai	Dubai Youth Moto-Cross Club	050 452 7844

Motor Sports

Dubai	Emirates Motor Sports Federation	04 282 7111

Shooting

Dubai	Hatta Fort Hotel	04 852 3211
	Jebel Ali Shooting Club	04 883 6555

Snorkelling

Dubai	Al Boom Diving	04 342 2993
	Scuba Dubai	04 331 7433
Fujairah	Beach Hut, The	09 244 5050
	Scuba 2000	09 238 8477
Sharjah	Oceanic Hotel	06 238 5111

Water Parks

Dubai	SplashLand	04 324 1222
	Wild Wadi Water Park	04 348 4444
UAQ	Dreamland Aqua Park	06 768 1888

General Supplies

Bookshops

Abu Dhabi	Al Mutanabbi	02 634 0319
	All Prints	02 633 5853
	Book Corner	02 681 7662
	Books Gallery	02 644 3869
	House of Prose	02 632 9679
	Jarir Bookstore	02 673 3999
	Spinneys	02 681 2897
Al Ain	Book Corner	03 763 0911
	University Book House	03 755 9480
Dubai	Al Jabre Al El Miah Book Shop	04 351 6740
	Book Corner	04 345 5490
	Books Plus	04 336 6362
	Magrudy's (City Centre)	04 295 7744
	Titan Book Shop	04 331 8671

Camera Equipment

Abu Dhabi	Grand Stores	02 645 1115
	Salam Studio	02 645 6999
	Plug-Ins	02 681 5509
Dubai	Grand Stores	04 282 3700
	Jacky's Electronics	04 881 9933

	M.K. Trading Co. L.L.C.	04 222 5745
	National Stores	04 353 6074
	Salam Studio	04 324 5252
	UCF	04 336 9399

Hotels & Accommodation

Abu Dhabi	See Abu Dhabi Explorer	
Ajman	Ajman Kempinski Hotel & Resort	06 745 1555
Dubai	See Dubai Explorer	
Fujairah	Al Diar Siji Hotel	09 223 2000
	Fujairah Hilton	09 222 2411
	Fujairah Youth Hostel	09 222 2347
	Hilton Fujairah	09 222 2411
	Le Meridien Al Aqah Beach Resort	09 244 9000
	Sandy Beach Motel	09 244 5555
Liwa	Liwa Hotel	02 288 2000
	Liwa Resthouse	02 882 2075
RAK	Al Hamra Fort Hotel	07 244 6666
	Hilton Ras Al Khaimah	07 228 8888
	Ras Al Khaimah Hotel	07 236 2999
Sharjah	Dar al Dhyafa al Arabia	06 569 6111
	Khor Fakkan Youth Hostel	06 237 0886
	Millennium Hotel	06 556 6666
	Oceanic Hotel	06 238 5111
	Sharjah Youth Hostel	06 522 5070
UAQ	Flamingo Beach Resort	06 765 1185
	Palm Beach Resort	06 766 7090

Motoring

Car Rental Agencies

Abu Dhabi	Abu Dhabi Rent a Car	02 644 3770
	Al Ghazal Transport Co.	02 634 2200
	Avis Rent a Car	02 621 8400
	(24 hour airport branch)	02 575 7180
	Budget Rent a Car	02 633 4200
	Diamond Lease	02 622 2028
	Emco	02 633 8933
	Europcar	02 626 1441
	Hertz Rent A Car	02 672 0060
	Inter Emirates Rent a Car	02 645 5855
	Thrifty Car Rental	02 634 5663
	(24 hour airport branch)	02 575 7400
	Tourist Rent a Car	02 641 8700
	United Car Rentals	02 642 2203
Dubai	Autolease Rent-a-Car	04 282 6565
	Avis Rent a Car	04 224 5219
	Budget Rent-A-Car	04 282 3030
	Diamond Lease	04 331 3172
	Hertz Rent a Car	04 282 4422
	Thrifty Car Rental	04 224 5404
	United Car Rentals	04 266 6286

New Car Dealers

Abu Dhabi	Abu Dhabi Motors	02 558 2400
	Al Otaiba Group	02 444 3333
	Trading Enterprises	02 633 3408
	Al Jallaf Trading	02 677 3030
	Al Futtaim Motors	02 419 9888
	Galadari Automoblies	02 677 3030
	Emirates Motor Company	02 444 4000
	Elite Motors	02 642 3686
	Al Masaood Automobiles	02 677 2000
	Ali & Sons	02 681 7770
Dubai	AGMC	04 339 1555
	Al Futtaim Motors	04 228 2261
	Al Ghandi Automotive	04 266 6511
	Al Habtoor Motors	04 269 1110
	Al Majed Motors	04 269 5600
	Al Naboodah Automobiles	04 338 6999
	Al Naboodah Automobiles	04 347 5111
	Al Rostamani Trading	04 347 0008
	Al Tayer Motors	04 201 1001
	Al Tayer Motors	04 266 6489
	Arabian Automobiles	04 295 1234
	Autostar Trading	04 269 7100

Galadari Automobiles	04 299 4848
Gargash Enterprises LLC	04 269 9777
Gargash Motors	04 266 4669
General Navigation & Commerce Co.	04 396 1000
Juma Al Majid Est	04 269 0893
Liberty Automobiles Co.	04 282 4440
National Auto	04 266 4848
Swaidan Trading Co.	04 266 7111
Trading Enterprises	04 295 4246

Off-Road Motor Equipment

Abu Dhabi	Ace Hardware	02 673 3174
Ajman	Ace Hardware	06 743 4448
Dubai	Ace Hardware	04 338 1416
	Trading Enterprises	04 295 4246
Sharjah	Ace Hardware	06 532 2600

Recovery Services

Abu Dhabi	Ghazal Al Wadi	02 554 0000
	IATC Recovery	02 632 4400
Dubai	Arabian Automobile Association	04 800 4900

Used Car Dealers

Abu Dhabi	Abu Dhabi 4X4 Motors	02 664 9942
	Ali & Sons	02 665 8000
	Automall	02 699 3215
	Reem Automobile	02 446 3343
Dubai	4x4 Motors	04 282 3050
	Al Futtaim Automall	04 347 2212
	Auto Plus	04 339 5400
	Boston Cars	04 333 1010
	Car Store, The	04 343 5245
	House of Cars	04 343 5060
	Motor World	04 333 2206
	Off Road Motors	04 338 4866
	Quality Cars	04 295 4246
	Used Car Complex (Al Awir)	04 333 3800

Museums & Heritage Sites

Abu Dhabi	Cultural Foundation	02 621 5300
	Handicrafts Centre	02 447 6645
	Petroleum Exhibition	02 626 0817
	Women's Handicraft Centre	02 447 6645
Ajman	Ajman Museum	06 742 3824
Al Ain	Al Ain Museum	03 764 1595
	Al Ain University Nat. Hist. Museum	03 767 7280
Dubai	Al Ahmadiya Sch. & Heritage House	04 226 0286
	Children's City	04 334 0808
	Dubai Museum	04 353 1862
	Godolphin Gallery	04 336 3031
	Gold & Diamond Museum	04 347 7788
	Hatta Heritage Village	04 852 1374
	Hatta Heritage Village	04 852 1374
	Heritage & Diving Village	04 393 7151
	Juma Al Majid Cultural & Heritage	04 262 4999
	Majlis Ghorfat Um Al Sheef	04 394 6343
	Sheikh Saeed Al Maktoum's House	04 393 7139
	Sheikh Mohammed Centre for Cultural Understanding	04 353 6666
Fujairah	Fujairah Heritage Village	09 222 6662
	Fujairah Museum	09 222 9085
RAK	National Museum of Ras Al Khaimah	07 233 3411
Sharjah	Al Hisn Fort/Heritage Museum	06 568 5500
	Al Hisn Kalba	06 277 4442
	Arabian Wildlife Centre	06 531 1411
	Discovery Centre	06 558 6577
	Sharjah Archaeological Museum	06 566 5466
	Sharjah Art Museum	06 568 8222
	Sharjah Desert park	06 531 1999
	Sharjah Heritage Museum	06 569 3999
	Sharjah Islamic Museum	06 568 3334
	Sharjah Natural History Museum	06 531 1411
	Sharjah Science Museum	06 566 8777

Outdoor Equipment

GPS Suppliers

Abu Dhabi	ADCOM	02 622 4467
Dubai	Picnico General Trading	04 394 1653
	Ramy Trading	04 269 8138
	Sandstorm Motorcycles	04 339 5608

Outdoor Goods

Abu Dhabi	Ace Hardware	02 673 3174
	Carrefour (Airport Rd)	02 449 4300
	Carrefour (Marina Mall)	02 681 7100
Dubai	Ace Hardware (Burjuman)	04 355 0698
	Ace Hardware (Shk. Zayed Rd)	04 338 1416
	Carrefour (Al Shindagha)	04 393 9395
	Carrefour (Deira City Centre)	04 295 1600
	Harley-Davidson	04 339 1909
	Picnico General Trading	04 394 1653
Sharjah	ULO Systems Ltd	06 531 4036

Sporting Goods

Dubai	360 Sports	04 352 0106
	ACE Hardware (Shk. Zayed Rd)	04 338 1416
	Adidas	04 295 4151
	Al Boom Marine	04 289 4858
	Al Boom Marine	04 394 1258
	Al Hamur Marine	04 344 4468
	Alpha Sports	04 295 4087
	Body Glove	04 339 0511
	Carrefour (Al Shindagha)	04 393 9395
	Carrefour (Deira City Centre)	04 295 1600
	Dubike	04 343 4741
	Emirates Sports Stores	04 324 2208
	Emirates Sports Stores	04 344 7456
	Emirta Horse Requirements	04 343 7475
	Golf House	04 295 0501
	Golf House	04 334 5945
	Golf House	04 351 4801
	Heat Waves	04 399 3161
	Horse World Trading	04 339 3183
	Magrudy Shopping Mall	04 344 4193
	Picnico General Trading	04 394 1653
	Royal Sporting House	04 295 0261
	Sandstorm Motorcycles	04 339 5608
	Scuba Dubai	04 331 7433
	Skechers	04 352 0106
	Sport One Trading	04 351 6033
	Studio R	04 295 0261
	Sun & Sand Sports	
	Al Ghurair City	04 222 7107
	BurJuman	04 351 5376
	City Centre	04 295 5551
	Jumeira	04 344 3799
	Souk Madinat Jumeirah	04 368 6120
	Trek	04 394 6505
	Wheels Trading	04 331 7119
	Wolfi's Bike Shop	04 339 4453
Sharjah	ULO Systems Ltd	06 531 4036

Services & Groups

Embassies/Consulates

Abu Dhabi	Oman Embassy	02 446 3333
Dubai	Oman Consulate	04 397 1000

Environmental Groups

Abu Dhabi	Emirates Natural History Group	050 611 8846
	Feline Friends	02 673 2696
Al Ain	Al Ain Emirates Nat. Hist. Group	050 533 0579
Dubai	Dubai Natural History Group	04 349 4816
	Emirates Environmental Group	04 331 8100
	Feline Friends	050 451 0058
	K9 Friends	04 347 4611

Hospitals

Abu Dhabi	Al Noor Hospital	02 626 5265
	Corniche Hospital (maternity only)	02 672 4900
	Golden Sands Medical Hospital	02 642 7171
	Mafraq Hospital	02 582 3100
	National Hospital	02 671 1000
	New Medical Centre Hospital	02 633 2255
Al Ain	Al Ain Hospital (Al Jimi)	03 763 5888
	Emirates International Hospital	03 763 7777
	Oasis Hospital	03 722 1251
	Tawam Hospital	03 767 7444
Dubai	Al Amal Hospital	04 344 4010
	Al Baraha Hospital	04 271 0000
	Al Maktoum Hospital	04 222 1211
	Al Wasl Hospital	04 324 1111
	Al Zahra Hospital	04 331 5000
	American Hospital	04 336 7777
	Belhoul European Hospital	04 345 4000
	Dubai Hospital	04 271 4444
	Emirates Hospital	04 349 6666
	International Private Hospital	04 221 2484
	Iranian Hospital	04 344 0250
	Rashid Hospital	04 337 4000
	Welcare Hospital	04 282 7788
Sharjah	Al Zahra Hospital	04 561 9999

Tour Operators

Abu Dhabi	Al Ain Golden Sands Camel Safaris	02 768 8006
	Al Mahboob Travel	02 751 5944
	Al Rumaithy Travel & Tourism	02 765 6493
	Arabian Adventures	02 691 1711
	Emirates Holidays	800 5252
	Emirates Travel Express	02 765 0777
	Gulf Travel Express	02 766 6737
	Middle East Travel	02 764 1661
	Net Tours	02 679 4656
	OffRoad Emirates	02 633 3232
	Sunshine Tours	02 444 9914

Dubai	Aerogulf Services Company	04 220 0331
	Arabian Adventures	04 303 4888
	Bateaux Dubai	04 399 4994
	Big Bus Company, The	04 324 4187
	Birdwatching Tours	050 650 3398
	Bounty Charters	04 348 3042
	Creek Cruises	04 393 9860
	Creekside Leisure	04 336 8406
	Danat Dubai Cruises	04 351 1117
	Desert Rangers	04 340 2408
	Dubai Travel & Tourist Services	04 336 7727
	East Adventure Tours	04 335 0950
	El Mundo	04 343 4870
	Fun Sports	04 399 5976
	Gulf Ventures	04 209 5568
	Khasab Travel & Tours	04 266 9950
	Lama Desert Tours	04 334 4330
	Mountain High	04 318 1420
	Net Tours	04 266 8661
	North Star Expeditions LLC	04 332 8702
	Off-Road Adventures	04 343 2288
	Orient Tours	04 282 8238
	Quality Tours	04 297 4000
	Relax Tourism	04 345 0889
	Sunflower Tours	04 334 5554
	Voyagers Xtreme	04 345 4504
	Wonder Bus Tours	04 359 5656
	Yacht Solutions	04 348 6838
Fujairah	Al Madhani Sea Tourist & Diving	050 690 508
Sharjah	Arabianlink Tours	06 572 6666

Further Reading

Flora

- *Checklist of Plants of the UAE* by Marycke Jongbloed
- *Green Guide to the Emirates* by Marycke Jongbloed (Motivate Publishing)
- *Indigenous Trees of the United Arab Emirates* by Dr Reza Khan (Dubai Municipality)

- *Introduction to the Flora of the UAE* by Rob Western (UAE University)*
- *Trees of Oman* by Shahina Ghazanfar (Ministry of Regional Municipalities & Environment)
- *Weeds in the UAE* by Fawzi Karim (UAE University) *

Fauna
- *Arabian Mammals* by Jonathan Kingdon
- *Birdlife in Oman* by Hanne & Jens Eriksen (Al Roya Publishing)
- *Birds of the Middle East and North Africa* by Hollom, Porter, Christensen and Willis (Poyser)
- *Birds of the Southern Gulf* by Dave Robinson and Adrian Chapman (Motivate Publishing)
- *Birds of the UAE* by Colin Richardson (Hobby Publishing)
- *Butterflies of Arabia* by Thorben Larsen
- *Field Guide to the Birds of the Middle East* by RF Porter, S Christensen, P Schiermacker-Hansen (T & AD Poyser)
- *Handbook to Middle East Amphibians and Reptiles* by Leviton, Anderson, Adler, Minton
- *Mammals of Arabia* by D Harrison *
- *Mammals of the Southern Gulf* by Christian Gross (Motivate Publishing)
- *Shell Birdwatching Guide to the UAE* by Colin Richardson & Simon Aspinall (Hobby Publications)
- *Snakes* by Michael Gallagher
- *Status and Conservation of the Breeding Birds of the United Arab Emirates* by Simon Aspinall (Hobby Publications)
- *Wild about Cats* by Marycke Jongbloed (Barkers Trident Publishing)
- *Wild about Reptiles* by Marycke Jongbloed (Barkers Trident Publishing)

General
- *Abu Dhabi Explorer* (Explorer Publishing)
- *Beachcomber's Guide* by Tony Woodward (Motivate Publishing)

- *Coral Seas of Muscat* by Francis Greene & Richard Keech (The Meed Group)
- *Dubai: Tomorrow's City Today* (Explorer Publishing)
- *Dubai Discovered* (Explorer Publishing)
- *Dubai Explorer* (Explorer Publishing)
- *Dubai Street Map* (Explorer Publishing)
- *Ecology of Abu Dhabi*, edited by Patrick Osborne (Pisces Publishing)*
- *Family Explorer* (Explorer Publishing)
- *Fishes of Bahrain* by Wajeeha Sadiq Al-Baharna (Ministry of Commerce & Agriculture)
- *Green Guide to the Emirates* by Marijcke Jongbloed (Motivate Publishing)
- *Gulf Landscapes* by Elizabeth Collas & Andrew Taylor (Motivate Publishing)
- *Images of Abu Dhabi & the UAE* (Explorer Publishing)
- *Images of Dubai & the UAE* (Explorer Publishing)
- *Living Desert* by Marijcke Jongbloed (Motivate Publishing)*
- *Living Seas* by Frances Dipper & Tony Woodward
- *Natural Emirates* edited by Peter Vine (Trident Press)*
- *Seashells of Oman*, by Donald & Eloise Bosch (Longmann Publishing)
- *Sharjah's Architectural Splendour* (Explorer Publishing)
- *Off-Road Explorer - Oman* (Explorer Publishing - Spring, 2006)
- *Oman Explorer* (Explorer Publishing)
- *Trekking Explorer - Oman* (Explorer Publishing - Summer, 2006)
- *Underwater Explorer* by Carole Harris & Tony Schroder (Explorer Publishing)

* These books can only be found in libraries of the Emirates and Dubai Natural History Groups or the Natural History Museum in the Sharjah Desert Park

Useful Websites
4X4 - UAE
www.me4x4.com
Middle East based club for off-roaders across the Gulf.

www.uae4x4.com
Informative site of the Emirates Off-Road Club in Dubai.

www.dubai4x4.com
Dubai based club for off-roaders.

www.autoemirates.com
All kinds of auto-related info and links.

www.ad4x4.com
Off-road club based in Abu-Dhabi

4X4 – General

www.acmetruckparts.com
Shopping site for parts and accessories for Jeep

www.explorer-publishing.com
Off-Road updates

www.lemonaidcars.com
Used car buying guide

www.off-road.com
US site for off-road enthusiasts

www.quadratec.com
Shopping site for Jeep and 4x4 accessories

www.worldoffroad.com
UK's leading online 4x4 publication

Camping & Outdoors

www.campmor.com
Online outdoor equipment shopping

www.coleman.com
Online outdoor equipment shopping

www.mec.ca
Canadian outdoors suppliers

www.rei.com
US outdoors suppliers

www.theoutdoorworld.com
Online outdoor equipment shopping

Climbing

www.backcountry.com
Shopping site for climbing gear

GPS Systems

www.garmin.com
GPS provider

Mountain Biking

www.hot-cog.com
Mountain biking group in Dubai

www.chainreactioncycles.com
Europe's largest online bike store

Basic Arabic

Basic

Yes	na'am
No	la
Please	min fadlak (m) / min fadliki (f)
Thank you	shukran
Please in offering	tafaddal (m) / tafaddali (f)
Praise be to God	al-hamdu l-illah
God willing	in shaa'a l-laah

Greeting

(peace be upon you)	as-salaamu alaykom
Greeting in reply	wa alaykom is-salaam
Good morning	sabah il-khayr
Good morning in reply	sabah in-nuwr
Good evening	masa il-khayr
Good evening in reply	masa in-nuwr
Hello	marhaba
Hello in reply	marhabtayn
How are you?	kayf haalak (m)
	kayf haalik (f)
Fine, thank you	zayn, shukran (m)
	zayna, shukran (f)
Welcome	ahlan wa sahlan
Welcome in reply	ahlan fiyk (m)
	ahlan fiyki (f)
Goodbye	ma is-salaama

Introduction

My name is	ismiy........
What is your name?	shuw ismak (m)
	shuw ismik (f)
Where are you from?	min wayn inta (m)
	min wayn inti (f)
I am from ...	anaa min .....
Britain	braitani
Europe	oropi
India	al hindi
America	ameriki

Route Related

Is this the road to ...	hadaa al tariyq ila
Right	yamiyn
Left	yassar
Straight ahead	siydaa
North	shamaal
South	januwb
East	sharq
West	garb
Turning	mafraq
First	awwal
Second	thaaniy
Road	tariyq
Street	shaaria'
Roundabout	duwwaar
Signals	ishaara
Close to	qarib min
Petrol Station	mahattat betrol
Sea / Beach	il bahar
Mountain/s	jabal / jibaal
Desert	al sahraa
Airport	mataar
Hotel	funduq
Restaurant	mata'am

Accidents

Police	al shurtaa
Permit / licence	rukhsaa
Accident	Haadith
Papers	waraq
Insurance	ta'miyn
Sorry	aasif (m)
	aasifa (f)

Questions

How many/much?	kam?
Where?	wayn?
When?	mata?
Which?	ayy?
How?	kayf?
What?	shuw?
Why?	laysh?
Who?	miyn?
To / for	ila
In / at	fee
From	min
And	wa
Also	kamaan
There isn't	maa fee

Numbers

Zero	sifr
One	waahad
Two	ithnayn
Three	thalatha
Four	araba'a
Five	khamsa
Six	sitta
Seven	saba'a
Eight	thamaanya
Nine	tiss'a
Ten	ashara
Hundred	miya
Thousand	alf

Residents' Guides

All you need to know about living, working and enjoying

Mini Guides

The perfect pocket-sized Visitors' Guides

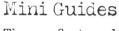

Activity Guides

Drive, trek, dive and swim... Life will never be boring again

Lifestyle Products

The perfect accessories for a buzzing lifestyle

Practical Guides

You've got questions, these books have answers

Maps

Wherever you are, never get lost again

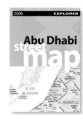  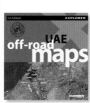 

Calendars

The time, the place, and the date

Photography Books

Beautiful cities caught through the lens

Index

Notes

Please take the time to visit our website (www.Explorer-Publishing.com) and pass along your comments, notes, thoughts and corrections on any aspect (directions, maps, text, photographs, routes) of this book. Your feedback is essential for us to improve our guidebooks.

Happy exploring!

Map Sketch

Explorer Publishing & Distribution • Office 51 B • Zomorrodah Building • PO Box 34275 • Karama • Dubai • UAE
Phone (+971 4) 335 3520 Fax (+971 4) 335 3529 Email info@explorer-publishing.com Web www.explorer-publishing.com

Notes

Please take the time to visit our website (www.Explorer-Publishing.com) and pass along your comments, notes, thoughts and corrections on any aspect (directions, maps, text, photographs, routes) of this book. Your feedback is essential for us to improve our guidebooks.

Happy exploring!

Map Sketch

Explorer Publishing & Distribution • Office 51 B • Zomorrodah Building • PO Box 34275 • Karama • Dubai • UAE
Phone (+971 4) 335 3520 Fax (+971 4) 335 3529 Email info@explorer-publishing.com Web www.explorer-publishing.com

Notes

Please take the time to visit our website (www.Explorer-Publishing.com) and pass along your comments, notes, thoughts and corrections on any aspect (directions, maps, text, photographs, routes) of this book. Your feedback is essential for us to improve our guidebooks.

Happy exploring!

_____

_____

_____

_____

_____

_____

_____

_____

_____

Map Sketch

Explorer Publishing & Distribution • Office 51 B • Zomorrodah Building • PO Box 34275 • Karama • Dubai • UAE
Phone (+971 4) 335 3520 Fax (+971 4) 335 3529 Email info@explorer-publishing.com Web www.explorer-publishing.com

Notes

Please take the time to visit our website (www.Explorer-Publishing.com) and pass along your comments, notes, thoughts and corrections on any aspect (directions, maps, text, photographs, routes) of this book. Your feedback is essential for us to improve our guidebooks.

Happy exploring!

Map Sketch

Notes

Please take the time to visit our website (www.Explorer-Publishing.com) and pass along your comments, notes, thoughts and corrections on any aspect (directions, maps, text, photographs, routes) of this book. Your feedback is essential for us to improve our guidebooks.

Happy exploring!

Map Sketch

Explorer Publishing & Distribution • Office 51 B • Zomorrodah Building • PO Box 34275 • Karama • Dubai • UAE
Phone (+971 4) 335 3520 Fax (+971 4) 335 3529 Email info@explorer-publishing.com Web www.explorer-publishing.com

Rescue Tips

With the increasing numbers of off-roaders in the emirates, there has been a corresponding rise in calls to the rescue services. To make their job easier, you can do a number of things:

1. Don't get stuck - if you are going into the desert, always drive with two cars minimum, have the appropriate gear with you (tow ropes, shovels, jacks) and know how to use it. The majority of calls are for people who are alone or couldn't get themselves out of a very easy situation.

2. Don't get lost - make sure you know how to read a map, and if possible use a GPS to keep you on the exact track.

3. Don't leave your vehicle - it's always easier to spot a vehicle than lone people wandering through the desert, and it's always best to stick together and not split from your group.

If you do need to call for rescue (999), make sure you:

a. know how to give the exact co-ordinates of your location (or rough location if you are lost), either from your GPS or by working it out from the grid on the maps.

b. give local names of wadis, mountains or landmarks nearby rather than commonly used alternatives - this will help the pilots as they use maps showing local Arabic names (eg. Jebel Maleihah not Fossil Rock).

c. make large signs on the ground to be visible from above (only of use during daylight), either by using the contents of the car, digging in the sand or by using rocks.

Standard international signals which can be used are:

V	Require assistance
X	Require medical assistance
→	Proceeding this way/vehicle this way
Y	Yes
N	No

d. light a fire, even a small one, and create lots of smoke (with something damp) - this can help pinpoint your position. Also use a car mirror to reflect sunlight in the direction of possible rescuers.

e. use a torch to show your whereabouts, but avoid shining the light directly at the helicopter and blinding the pilots! It is best to use the beam in a sweeping movement away from you in the direction of a suitable landing area. Lighting a fire or flashing the car lights are also useful ways of showing your location. Sounding the horn will probably not be heard.

UAE Distances Chart

	Umm Al Quwain	Sharjah	Ras Al Khaimah	Masafi	Madam	Liwa	Khor Fakkan	Khasab	Kalba	Jebel Ali	Hatta	Fujairah	Dubai	Dibba	Dhaid	Al Ain	Ajman	Abu Dhabi
Abu Dhabi																		
Ajman																		155
Al Ain																	160	125
Dhaid																108	71	219
Dibba															86	194	157	302
Dubai														159	73	130	30	125
Fujairah													137	71	64	192	135	297
Hatta												49	123	119	72	121	138	226
Jebel Ali											105	174	30	184	98	86	60	95
Kalba										175	41	8	145	68	72	184	143	289
Khasab									206	232	280	198	202	168	208	332	172	264
Khor Fakkan								205	31	190	72	23	160	37	87	215	158	324
Liwa							550	476	519	289	443	533	319	572	486	322	367	212
Madam						411	126	255	95	80	54	77	69	133	47	89	118	179
Masafi					78	517	56	165	41	129	81	33	104	38	31	139	102	250
Ras Al Khaimah				76	166	432	116	89	117	143	191	109	113	79	119	243	83	175
Sharjah			97	88	85	353	144	186	112	46	129	121	16	153	57	146	14	145
Umm Al Quwain		34	63	87	103	387	143	152	128	60	128	120	50	134	56	180	20	180

Head for the Border!

With 26 incredible routes featuring foolproof directions and crystal-clear maps, the **Oman Off-Road Explorer** will help you tame the wilderness and live a life of adventure. So forget hitting the kerb in the supermarket carpark, get out there and tackle the mountains and wadis this weekend, and remind yourself why you bought a 4WD.

When your instincts lead, follow them.

NEVER STOP EXPLORING

The *UAE Off-Road* Team

Principal Author Tim Binks
Editors David Quinn, Jane Roberts
Concept Designer Pete Maloney
Lead Designer Zainudheen Madathil
Designers Jayde Fernandes, Noushad Madathil, Rafi Pullat, **Sunita Lakhiani**
Editorial Assistants Enrico Maullon, Helga Becker, **Mimi Stankova**

Publisher Alistair MacKenzie

Editorial

Managing Editor Claire England
Editors David Quinn, Jane Roberts, Matt Farquharson, Sean Kearns, Tim Binks
Deputy Editors Becky Lucas, Katie Drynan
Subeditor Jo Holden-MacDonald
Editorial Assistants Helga Becker, Mimi Stankova

Design

Creative Director Pete Maloney
Art Director Ieyad Charaf
Senior Designer Alex Jeffries
Layout Manager Jayde Fernandes
Designers Rafi Pullat, Sunita Lakhiani
Cartography Manager Zainudheen Madathil
Cartographer Noushad Madathil
Designlab Admin Manager Shyrell Tamayo

Photography

Photography Manager Pamela Grist

Sales and Marketing

Media & Corporate Sales Manager Giovanni Angiolini
GCC Media Sales Manager Laura Zuffa
Retail Sales Manager Ivan Rodrigues
Retail Sales Coordinator Kiran Melwani
Merchandisers Abdul Gafoor, Ahmed Mainodin, Firos Khan, Mannie Lugtu
Warehouse Assistant Mohammed Kunjaymo
Driver Shabsir Madathil

Finance and Administration

Administration Manager Andrea Fust
Accounts Assistant Cherry Enriquez
Administrators Enrico Maullon, Maricar Ong
Driver Rafi Jamal

IT

IT Administrator Ajay Krishnan R.
Software Engineers Roshni Ahuja, Tissy Varghese

Contact Us

Reader Response
If you have any comments and suggestions, fill out our online reader response form and you could win prizes.
Log on to www.Explorer-Publishing.com

General Enquiries
We'd love to hear your thoughts and answer any questions you have about this book or any other Explorer product.
Contact us at **Info@Explorer-Publishing.com**

Careers
If you fancy yourself as an Explorer, send your CV (stating the position you're interested in) to **Jobs@Explorer-Publishing.com**

Designlab and Contract Publishing
For enquiries about Explorer's Contract Publishing arm and design services, contact **Designlab@Explorer-Publishing.com**

Maps
For cartography enquries, including orders and comments, contact **Maps@Explorer-Publishing.com**

Corporate Sales
For bulk sales and customisation options, for this book or any Explorer product, contact **Sales@Explorer-Publishing.com**

Explorer Publishing & Distribution
Office 51B, Zomorrodah Building, Za'abeel Road,
PO Box 34275, Dubai, United Arab Emirates
Phone: +971 (0) 4 335 3520
Fax: +971 (0) 4 335 3529
Info@Explorer-Publishing.com
www.Explorer-Publishing.com

Extra Info

Explorer Team

Map Legend

Not all features are depicted on the maps. Only important features are indicated, if they help with navigation.

Important

6. Take a right at this T-junction.	Route directions - numbered 1, 2, 3, etc
This dam forms a natural catchment area for the mountains around it.	Diversion directions
	Points of interest - see corresponding text in route highlights
← P58 ↗ P58	Continuation map page
GPS UTM 490,353E 2,624,700N GEO 23°43'59"N 56°54'19"E	Coordinates of strategic points (UTM - WGS84)
	UTM grid & coordinates (UTM - WGS84)

Orientation

↑ LIWA 25KM P12	Nearest main city/town/village - direction, distance, & page number
MUSSANDAM ► P25	Other route name covered & direction

Urban Areas

DUBAI HAYL	City, town, village
HOSPITAL FORT	Landmarks
	Village, house/hut
	Historical landmark, mosque

Roads/Tracks

E 11 S 116	Road numbers
	Highway, roundabout, flyover/interchange, highway under construction
	Main road, bridge, distance markers
	Other road, steep slope, road with dead end
	Graded track, wadi track, hiking trail

Symbols

🚦	Traffic signals	Ⓝ	U-turn
⛽	Petrol station	Bus	Bus stop
GSM tower	GSM tower		Water tower
	Best viewing direction (Map)		Farm/oasis/ forest/trees
📷	Viewpoint		Pools (puddles)
---	Wadi	•-•	Border fence
⚠	Caution/note	P	Stopping/ parking point
	Helipad		Country border
⋏	Campsite	•·•	Power lines